I0824649

the wilder way

the wilder way

A MEMOIR OF ADVENTURE, FREEDOM, AND AN UNCHARTED LIFE

EVA ZU BECK

G
GALLERY BOOKS
NEW YORK AMSTERDAM/ANTWERP LONDON
TORONTO SYDNEY/MELBOURNE NEW DELHI

Gallery Books
An Imprint of Simon & Schuster, LLC
1230 Avenue of the Americas
New York, NY 10020

First Gallery Books hardcover edition June 2026

GALLERY BOOKS and colophon are registered trademarks of Simon & Schuster, LLC

Interior design by Erika R. Genova

Manufactured in the United States of America

10 9 8 7 6 5 4 3 2 1

Library of Congress Control Number: 2026933608

ISBN 978-1-6682-2367-3
ISBN 978-1-6682-2369-7 (ebook)

For my grandfather, who inspired the journey.

For the people I met along the way, who inspired the tale.

contents

author's note

When I first put together the proposal for this memoir, I expected to fill the pages with tales of adventure: some failed, some epic, some foolhardy. But as I sat down to write and the words started flowing, I realized that I wasn't writing a book about travel. I was, in fact, writing a book about freedom.

To write this memoir, I mostly relied on the journals I've kept since I was a teenager, and which I continue to scribble in today. In addition to my notebooks, I have a habit of leaving myself long, rambling voice notes on my phone, which I transcribed in preparation for the writing of this book. My library of over two hundred YouTube films that I've published since creating my channel also helped to bring some of those distant memories and landscapes to the forefront of my mind. However, I never intended for this book to simply repeat what's already been captured on video. The tales that follow offer a fresh perspective on my journeys over the past eight years—as well as many stories that remain untold on YouTube.

I have changed the names and other identifying characteristics of certain individuals.

prologue

There is not a soul around for many miles in every direction. My satellite messenger has stopped working. For the first time in twenty-eight years, I am truly and deeply alone.

"I shouldn't be here," I mutter to myself in a moment of supreme honesty. For the past hour, I have been crouching on the ground, bent over a broken saddle, my dirty fingernails picking at the leather strings that once held the cheap wooden seat together. Earlier this day, one of my horses decided to leap and perform a rather majestic—and destructive—buck while we were passing by a particularly suspicious-looking rock. The result was a train-wreck: all the things I needed to survive alone in the Mongolian wilderness got spilled on the ground within a thirty-foot radius, and the packsaddle broke.

I'm struggling to fix it. The knots are tight and impossible to undo. I need to retie the strings in a way that will hold up for another week of solo riding. In my growing despair, I groan and give the saddle a solid kick, then watch as it rolls a few feet down the hill. Both horses momentarily stop grazing, pick up their heads, and stare directly at me.

"Don't judge me!" I shout. "I wasn't the one that broke the saddle!" With apparent disdain, they drop their heads back into the meadow, and all I can hear is the soft crunching of summer grass between their teeth. They know I am in over my head. They agree that I shouldn't be here.

But I have only them to complain to. The three of us are camped up on the side of a hill somewhere in the vast, rugged expanse of the least densely populated country on earth.

When I decided to set off on a solo horse trek in the Mongolian wilderness, I anticipated running into some challenges. Men, wolves, and bears were at the top of my list. But I didn't expect other things to go quite this wrong. My body aches from long days in the saddle, followed by long evenings tending to my two steeds, setting up camp, and cooking my meals. A new bruise colors my hip purple, the result of the packhorse biting into my side as I tightened his cinch this morning. My head is buzzing with all the things I need to be thinking about that I never really had to consider before: Are my horses watered and well-fed? Am I riding in the right direction? Are those dark clouds in the sky alerting me to an impending storm? Am I being followed by someone? Will I be able to find a safe spot to camp tonight?

There is a lot out here that I wasn't ready for. But I am here, in my self-imposed freedom, and I need to find a way to navigate it. As I pick up the saddle from the spot where it rolled off and get to work fixing it again, I am calm and determined. I chose to be alone out here for a reason.

And deep down I know that bravery isn't something you find by the side of the road. It's something you forge with the entire might of your daring, out of the depths of fear, doubt, and despair.

chapter one

the day i left it all behind

"So, what are you going to do once you get to India?" my mom asked, as if I were just popping across London to see a friend.

"I'll hang out with some friends I made on the internet," I responded, trying to sound as casual as possible. I would first be flying to India on a short layover between London and Nepal, and I was hoping that having an online friend in a faraway country would be better than having no friends there at all.

A short pause followed as her eyes flicked sideways toward me.

"Do you know them in person?" Mom's tone implied she didn't want to know the answer.

"No." I paused. "But they don't look like serial killers." Admittedly, I was setting the bar pretty low.

She nodded, adjusted the speed of the windshield wipers to keep up with the rain, and seemed to take all this strange new information in stride. A lot of what I had been doing recently was strange and new—not only to her, but to all my family and friends. It was all strange and new to me, too.

My mom's lipstick-red station wagon barreled down the wet road, through the downpour of an early March afternoon. We were on our way to Heathrow Airport.

In the back of the car was a massive purple backpack I had spent a small fortune on. Inside it were all the things I would need for an indefinite period of nonstop travel. *I'll give myself a year. Maybe a year and a half*, I'd thought as I crammed in the few essentials I was willing to carry on my own back. My vast hand-picked designer wardrobe had to go to charity, and whatever I didn't have the heart to part with wound up in my mom's closets. My wedding dress was one of those things.

"Okay, so what's your plan for the next few weeks, then?" my mom probed.

"Let's see. I'll be in Nepal for about a month. We're going to fly into the world's most dangerous airport and then spend two weeks hiking in the Himalayas to the Everest Base Camp. And after that, I'm going to fly to Pakistan for a bit."

My mom cleared her throat, which communicated all she did not say.

"It'll be fine, I'll be safe," I blurted out before she had a chance to say anything I didn't want to hear. *Project confidence! Fake it till you make it!* The predictable self-help advice I'd been ingesting for the past few years sounded hollow to me now. In truth, I had no idea whether it would be fine, or whether I would be safe.

At the age of twenty-six, I was about to cross the threshold into a completely new life. There was no way for me to know what waited on the other side. All I knew was that I had never hiked before, let alone on the tallest mountains in the world; that I would be traveling to countries designated as "dangerous" on travel advisory websites; and that this was my Hail Mary attempt to change my life in order not to lose it. I was still shocked that it had come to this.

"Well, this is it," said my mom, stopping in front of Heathrow's Terminal 3.

I looked out of the car window at a steady stream of people disappearing up the escalator here in London, to be tossed out somewhere on the other side of the world. I wavered.

A business traveler dressed in a dark suit pushed along an expensive silver wheeled suitcase. A family rushed toward the escalator, the mom with a baby on her arm and a little girl trying to keep up as she pulled her own pink toy carry-on. A loved-up couple, holding hands, looked like they were heading off on their honeymoon.

What travel cliché did I represent? For the first time, I felt out of place arriving at an airport. Maybe I just needed to accept that I *was* a total cliché: a recovering perfectionistic people-pleaser who'd descended into a quarter-life crisis upon realizing she had been living a lie, and who—instead of going to therapy—was buying a one-way plane ticket and embarking on a journey to find herself. All of a sudden, it all sounded hackneyed and contrived as I stood in front of the airport. Where was all of this taking me?

"Take care of yourself," my mom said as she hugged me. "Be careful out there."

"It'll all be good," I replied. "I just need to get some space. I might come back in a year—who knows?" My stomach sank a little at the thought of having to return, but I didn't mention that.

"Remember, you can always come back and live with me if you need to," she said.

As grateful as I was for her offer, I would do everything in my power not to come back to a city haunted by the ghosts of all my mistakes.

"Okay, thanks, Mom. I appreciate it."

She helped me put on the giant purple backpack. I faltered a little under the weight. Somehow, I was going to have to manage putting it on by myself from now on.

"Mom, can you take a snap of me?"

She took a video as I stood there in my blue jeans, white Converse sneakers that wouldn't stay white very long, and a light gray canvas shirt, hovering somewhere between backpacker-core and Steve Irwin chic. By all appearances, I was ready to head out in search of something that was as yet unknown to me.

I waved goodbye to my mom and headed toward the escalator. *How can you ever find yourself if you don't know what you're even looking for?* I wondered, suddenly envious of the businessman, the family, the couple. At least they knew what their final destination was. They knew the reason for their travels. All I knew was that I had a ticket to Nepal and a window seat, that all the travel websites told me I could get food poisoning in Kathmandu, that the local delicacy to try was dumplings called "momos," and that I was desperate to escape the pain that dogged my every step in London.

chapter two

ewa

Leo and I had met when I was twenty-one years old. He was eight years my senior and incredibly impressive. He had a PhD in law from one of the world's top universities, could carry on a conversation in any of several different languages, and, to my eyes, was the very picture of a Prince Charming: handsome, intelligent, confident. I assumed everyone who met him fell in love with him. *I* certainly did. I was about to graduate with a degree in languages and literature from Oxford University, and with our fancy diplomas and bright futures, I felt like the two of us could take on the world.

After graduating, I moved from Oxford to Brussels, where Leo was climbing the corporate ladder as an up-and-coming lawyer. Soon enough, I found a job in London and started to commute between the two cities, spending my weekdays in London and my weekends in Brussels.

I had been hired as the first full-time employee of a young travel media start-up, working as its editorial director. As the company grew, my role in it expanded. Within a couple of years, I found myself managing a team. Investors became interested in our product and started pouring money into it as we grew. Investment rounds were followed by recruitment rounds. A New York City office was opened. New teams were hired. Old teams were scrapped. The motto of the start-up world seemed to be "Move fast, fail fast, learn fast." Whenever I wasn't working on some new project, I was devouring books with titles like *The Lean Startup* and *Good to Great*. I had fully bought in. *So this is what success looks like*, I thought as I watched the visitor count for our website grow and grow.

Success after success meant more time spent typing emails, drafting documents, and putting together presentations. Nothing unusual: just another young person out to prove herself in the corporate world, spending every waking hour at her desk and fighting corporate fires on her phone en route to and from that very desk. I was duly rewarded with a steadily growing paycheck and, perhaps more importantly, an image of myself as a *successful person*.

Leo and I rented a beautiful two-bedroom apartment in one of Brussels's more affluent neighborhoods, with high ceilings and a view of the city's many gray and terra-cotta roofs. In London, I rented a room in a houseshare. Leo bought a sports car. We traveled across Europe often. On the weekends we didn't spend traveling, we ate out in nice restaurants and partied in cocktail bars. Aspirational. This was how I saw our life. We had money, we had stability, we had great jobs, we had it all figured out. It was the exact opposite of how I grew up. And the further I could get from how I grew up, I thought, the better.

It was unexpected news when my mom got pregnant at twenty-one, and she would joke that I had been "an accident"—the by-product of a youthful love affair that nobody expected would have such life-altering consequences. But she became more generous with her assessment in time. "It's not that we didn't want you," she reassured me. "It's just that you were a surprise." But in 1990s Poland, surprises were taken seriously, and a wedding was swiftly arranged to retain the good name of both families. At the wedding, everyone politely ignored my mom's protruding belly.

Neither of my parents were willing to put their lives on hold and dedicate themselves to child-rearing. After a couple of years, the burdens of a young marriage proved to be too much for them. Eventually, unable to reconcile their differences, they parted ways. After their divorce, my father moved abroad, to the United States, in search of his American dream. In those pre-WhatsApp, pre-smartphone times, keeping in touch was a logistical challenge, and one that wasn't easily remedied when my parents held grudges against each other. My mom was unwilling to create opportunities for communication; my father was busy with his new life halfway across the world. Instead of DMing, I wrote letters to my father in the unrefined handwriting of a seven-year-old, letters I never sent to him as he made his way from the United States to Australia, places that sounded like they might as well have been on a different planet. While he was busy working low-paying immigrant jobs on a tourist visa that specifically prohibited him from gaining employment (and sometimes getting into trouble for this), my mom started a job as a traveling saleswoman in Poland. She was young and ambitious and, given my father's near-total absence, was forced to take over the sole responsibility of supporting us. She moved us from one city to another, following the opportunities given to her. By the time I was twelve, I had already gone to six different schools.

It looked like things would settle down when she remarried and we moved to Warsaw, the Polish capital. But after a year in one place, just as I was beginning to get used to my new home, our lives were uprooted once more. We were moving again, this time to join my mom's new husband in the United Kingdom. I knew very little English and had no idea how to navigate living in a different country. The culture shock was stark.

English schools have a certain reputation, and not always for the right reasons. It was hard to decide what felt more foreign: this new country, or the idea of an all-girls school where uniforms were mandatory. In Poland, I could speak the language, make friends, and wear whatever I liked. But my new school was ruled by a clique of angsty teenage girls, and the greatest sin you could commit was to button your white shirt all the way up or forget to wash your hair in the morning.

English was new to me, and I stumbled over my words, burning with shame every time I had to ask someone to repeat something. This is the sort of thing that makes it hard to blend in and make friends, and the only group I slotted into was a mixed bag of immigrants from other countries. Our misfit group included a very tall Slovak girl called Barbora, Chen from China, and Kiranjit and Mandeep, a couple of second-generationers from India. We all had "weird" names with "weird" spellings that the other British pupils couldn't wrap their heads around. Mine was Ewa. A simple, common name by all the Polish standards I had been used to, pronounced with a *v* sound in the middle, as per the Polish alphabet. Just three letters: nothing to trip you up. *Eh-va*.

"We have a new pupil joining us this year," our head teacher in my new English school said, as she keenly introduced me to the rest of the class. "She's from Poland. Um . . ." She furrowed her brow, leaning into the roll call as if she were trying to decipher some enigma that had been inscribed on it. Finally, with a self-assured air, she continued:

"*You-wa*. Welcome! Welcome, *You-wa*!"

That's not my name.

I wondered how, at twelve years old, I would be able to find my place in this strange new world.

There was some respite from these feelings of dislocation, and that came when I was in places that were unfamiliar to me, where I was under no pressure to conform or fit in, where I could stand as an outsider. Twice a year, during the school holidays, my mom put me on a plane and shipped me off to see my dad, who had since moved to Asia. Around the time I moved to the United Kingdom, my father and I resumed contact. As the internet became more commonplace and apps like Skype allowed us to speak more freely, we began to get to know each other once again. He invited me to visit him in Hong Kong and, at age fourteen, I flew all alone, parents on either end of the journey fretting about my safety.

Over the coming years, I would find myself on an airplane twice a year, up in the clouds, high above everything I dreaded, escaping. On these first trips, my father and I rebuilt our relationship from scratch. Once we had, he felt like my closest confidant, and our adventures together became my windows of inspiration in the otherwise spiritless tedium of my days. We traveled together to countries such as Myanmar, Cambodia, and Vietnam. Because I had spent my entire life in Europe until this point, tasting the aromatic barbecue chicken at Thai street food markets, feeling the humidity of Hong Kong embrace me like a heavy cloak, and speeding past city lights on a moped in Ho Chi Minh City felt like a waking dream.

But at home, back in England, things were only becoming more difficult. As I entered my teenage years, I became more vocal, more opinionated, more my own person. My mother's husband and I began to lock horns over every little thing.

"This is my house, not yours, and you will do as I say." He laid down the law. Although he was technically correct, it certainly didn't help make me feel more at home. The place where I was supposed to find a sense of safety and stability became the place I felt most insecure. Every interaction had the potential to turn into an earthquake that shook the entire household. I refused to do the chores; he refused to let me out of the house. I refused to smile; he refused to acknowledge me. The more tense things became at home, the more I fantasized about moving out and building my own life.

I was a misfit at home and at school. No place felt safe. By the time I was sixteen, I was regularly self-harming, carving lines across my wrists with whatever tools were easiest to grab: kitchen knives, razor blades, scissors. I watched the cuts grow wider and bigger with a sense of satisfaction. It was the one thing I could control in my life. All my self-harming was a cry for help, but my mom had no idea how to handle something like that and swung between debating whether to send me to live with my dad in Asia and wanting to sweep everything under the rug. In the end, all the help I got was a single appointment with a therapist who diagnosed me with "mild depression, possible bipolar disorder" and, having concluded the diagnosis, never saw me again. I continued to cut lines across my body and counted down the days to when I would be allowed to move out of the house.

Despite my home life suffering, my English was improving. Within a couple of years, I became a straight-A student, which permitted my teachers to look past my more rebellious tendencies. I got piercings where I shouldn't have; I wore too much makeup and too much jewelry (on account of the piercings) and skipped school whenever I got a chance. I was put in detention several times for breaking what I felt were regressive, conservative school rules. But the teachers couldn't stay cross with me: my exam results came back as the best in the school's history. When the local newspaper covered this groundbreaking piece of news, my mom proudly showed off the clipping to her friends. It was little consolation to me.

Many years earlier, before he passed away, my paternal grandfather had talked to me about Oxford University. One day, we were driving past a billboard with a giant outdoor pool printed on it. It was decorated with beautiful blue mosaic tiles and appeared to have been photographed in the middle of a perfectly green lawn. I was six years old, but even to a child's eyes, it looked like the definition of success. I stared at it in awe.

"Grandpa, how can I buy a pool like that?" I asked.

He looked at me with a smile and decided to take my question seriously.

"Well, if you study at Oxford University and become a lawyer, you might just be able to afford it," he said, and I nodded, thinking even at that young age that I would do whatever it took to get to Oxford University.

Twelve years after my grandpa had said those words to me, and eleven years after he passed away, I got into Oxford University. It was a proud moment for my whole family. But for me, it was bittersweet, because the person who had inspired it all was no longer around to see it.

As I was busy building my own life as a young adult, on some level, I wanted to prove to my parents that I could negotiate life better than they had done—despite them. I wanted security and guarantees. I wanted normalcy; I wanted to have it all figured out. I could right their wrongs by building a life that followed a predictable trajectory, in which I would never have to worry about money, or getting uprooted, or having to start over, and over, and over. Leo, with his PhD and his stable career, seemed like just the person to create this life with. With our careers both taking off, suddenly all that security was within arm's reach. *Marriage, mortgage, lineage*. We would likely get married, then purchase our own place, and then . . . what then? "Never mind, we have time to think about all of that." I brushed off the difficult questions. "Just think about the here and now."

The here and now was a fairy tale. We traveled, ate well, partied hard, worked harder, and shopped indiscriminately. Our first big purchase together was a ridiculous dining room table that stood on two paper-thin glass legs. It was the kind of table you could not place heavy objects on for fear that the foundation would give way and the glass would shatter. I tucked my legs under the chair every time we ate, worried about accidentally kicking the glass and disturbing the table's precarious balance.

One weekend, Leo and I traveled to Oslo, where we'd booked a five-star hotel suite overlooking the lapping waters of the harbor. We danced around our room in bathrobes, gorged on food from restaurants that had pictures of their famous guests on the walls, and strolled around art galleries, doing our utmost to make sense of contemporary art. On one of those gallery walks, Leo got down on one knee, looked me in the eye, and, from his pocket, brought out a little box the color of a robin's egg.

"Will you marry me?"

Marriage, mortgage, lineage. It was all coming true.

"Yes," I heard myself say. The ring slid onto my manicured finger with ease. A big, blinding diamond on top of a simple white gold band.

I wanted a wedding. We both wanted one. "This needs to be the best wedding any of our friends will ever attend," we resolved. And although today I couldn't tell you what makes a wedding "better" or "best," we were hell-bent on making the vision come true. A custom dress from a South African designer. A custom suit from a Savile Row tailor. A palace in the mountains of Poland for the venue. The most expensive menu available. An avant-garde photographer. An authentic Viking wooden stave church where we would seal the deal. All our energy went into planning the party of our lifetimes, a manifestation of our being young, beautiful, and successful.

But in the midst of planning the wedding, we lost track of the marriage. The images of the party, the dress, the flowers, became so consuming that they blinded me to whatever would happen *after* the wedding—a whole, entire married future that was to follow. I had never asked myself whether I wanted to be a wife. I had kept myself so distracted with all the flashy accoutrements that I had never given myself the opportunity to ask: *Is this really what I want?* Was marriage a promise I was truly able to make at twenty-four? I didn't pause and consider the biggest decision of my life with honesty and introspection. The dissonance did not end with the wedding vows.

"I want to be a young dad," Leo said, as he imagined our future together. Given our eight-year age difference, this meant I would have to be a young mom.

Can I be a mom? I asked myself in silence, a heavy weight settling in my stomach. Motherhood had never been a fantasy of mine. The very idea of watching my body journey through pregnancy felt strange and a little off-putting. The furthest I could stretch my mind was to come up with baby names: that just seemed like a game, something you didn't have to commit to, a purely theoretical endeavor. Everything beyond this—holding my own child, playing with it, picking it up from school—felt so abstract that my mind struggled to visualize it, let alone conjure up any feelings about it. But everyone—every single person I talked to—reassured me that I would change my mind. After all, everyone had children. This was the status quo. Surely, everyone *wanted* children—it was part of human nature, wasn't it? I pushed the nagging thoughts out of my head, convincing myself, as Leo was convinced, that I would grow into it, change my mind, feel the maternal instincts kicking in soon enough. For now, we still had time.

But the wedding date was drawing nearer.

Week by week in the year running up to the wedding, the

waters rose. Long days at the office paired with an intense travel schedule left me exhausted at the end of every day. Leo and I were spending less and less time together as the demands of our jobs intensified. I was spending an increasing amount of time in London, and Leo was pulling long days at the legal practice. We were drifting apart, and there was an undercurrent dragging me away from everything I thought I knew, even myself. The closer we got to the wedding day, the more acutely I felt the panic rising: How were we supposed to make this work in the long term if I ended up never wanting children? The love I had originally felt for Leo began to transform from something that felt steady and secure to a feeling of uncertainty and shame. I could not reconcile our visions for the future. It began to dawn on me that maybe, just maybe, I had accepted other people's dreams as my own and run into marriage like it was just another item to be ticked off the bucket list.

But it was only when we ordered the wedding invitations that the full force of my questioning hit me. I began to have recurring nightmares that I had forgotten to send out the invitations and nobody turned up at the wedding, and I was terrified of telling Leo I hadn't sent them because I thought he would be disappointed, that he would think less of me, that I would have ruined his perfect wedding. But in those dreams, I was never once sad that we couldn't get married.

In reality, I stalled on sending the wedding invitations for as long as I reasonably could. There was something that felt so final about sending them out into the world, having the guests pencil the date into their calendars and book their travel arrangements. There was something so irreversible about it. I desperately wanted to be happy, but the more final the wedding preparations became, the more I wanted to run.

I had this lingering sense that something within me, something fundamental, was out of sync. In the hope of finding out what that "something" might be, I relocated my lifelong journaling habit to the corners of London's bars. Fueled by red wine, I spent the nights clawing at the darkest recesses of my soul and, in my search, I tore through everything I thought I knew about myself.

I unearthed secret dreams, writing, "I want to live in faraway places, I want to write books, I want to go on grand adventures. I want to experiment with my life." But as a lawyer, Leo was tied to one location and one area of expertise. The more carefully I looked at my life—as an aspiring corporate boss bitch living in the big city—the more I realized how miserable it was making me. As I examined my relationship with Leo, I gradually came to a realization that winded me. I had latched on to Leo because he represented everything I did not have yet craved as a child. These were difficult realizations that I had kept hidden even from myself, gleaned over the course of a year.

"I am about to get married despite having a drastically different vision of what I want my future to look like to my soon-to-be husband. I am about to commit to living a lifestyle of comfort, cash, and corporate parties," I wrote. I was tying myself to a life that would be tantamount to a lie.

Having the realization, difficult as it was, was one thing. But actually doing something about it was another thing entirely. I kept willing myself to stay in a life that wasn't mine—dress fittings, menu choices, seating plans—hoping beyond hope that everything I had been thinking and feeling over the past year was just prenuptial cold feet. I tried to convince myself that all the doubt would simply vanish once I stood at the altar.

As surely as the days come, the day of the wedding did, too. My father had asked if he could have the honor of walking me down the aisle. I didn't want to let him down. I didn't want to let *anyone* down. He held my arm as we made our way along the creaky wooden floor of the church toward my soon-to-be husband, standing at the altar, smiling. My wedding dress felt itchy on my skin, and the makeup on my face thick like a mask. In my head, I replayed movie scenes of runaway brides. But we were not in a Hollywood rom-com, and running away was not an option.

Tears started flowing down my cheeks, gently streaking the makeup. I looked around the church. Everyone else was weeping, too—presumably with tears of joy for the beautiful young couple crossing the threshold into their new life together. Only I knew that by walking down that aisle, I was making the biggest mistake of my life. But the current pulled me along, and through the tears, we became husband and wife.

All I had wanted was to reclaim the happy life I'd lost and longed for as a child, and I'd thought I was going to get there by doing the thing that all successful people appeared to do: *marriage, mortgage, lineage*. *If we have a beautiful wedding, I'll be happy*, I had thought. *If I get to fly to the next meeting in business class, I'll look so successful. These shoes make me look like a badass bitch. Yes, the ring* is *from Tiffany.*

I had reveled in the status. I had been sold on the fantasy—until I realized the fantasy was never mine.

chapter three

notes to a future self

When Leo and I finally sat down to talk after a year of married life, I was expecting an explosion of anger, a massive fight. I was expecting harsh words to fly across the room. Maybe a plate smashing into a wall. Surely there would be fury, there would be shouting.

I had betrayed him. I had cheated on him.

As much as I regretted the hurt I had brought about through my actions, which I still regret to this day, I could not turn back time. Looking back, I see very clearly that my betrayal of Leo was pure self-sabotage. Instead of facing, in an honest conversation, the hard truth of my not being ready for marriage, I drove a train of irreversible destruction right into the heart of the relationship. I was young, naive, and had made a colossal mistake.

Perhaps, in some way, I thought that a barrage of insults would cleanse me of the guilt. I wanted the anger because it would prove that he wasn't perfect either, that he was capable of hurting me, too. I needed some kind of explosion. But there was little more than a whimper.

A quiet conversation with few words exchanged. No insults. No plates hurled across the room. Not even "How could you do this to me?"

Both of us were heartbroken, but there was no excuse for what I had done. I had made the kind of mistake that binds to you and stays with you for the rest of your life. I knew that eventually he would heal and find a better match, and have the children he'd been dreaming of. I was certain that things would work out for him, and although I couldn't have known this would happen at the time, a few years later he did start a beautiful family of his own. It in no way absolved me. I felt like I deserved to be punished.

But in that moment, silence hung between us. It felt so heavy with the burden of feelings that couldn't be spoken that it sucked all the air out of the room. I looked around the apartment, decorated with the designer accessories we had collected, books we had both read, furniture we had spent so much time picking out. My eyes pausing on the dining room table, I willed its glass legs to shatter just to break the silence. They didn't budge. Leo and I sat quietly facing each other, each of us contemplating what versions of our respective futures had just been lost.

I knew I was the one who needed to go. That he would keep the life in Brussels, keep the apartment, keep the kettle and the table and chairs and sofa we'd bought together. I have no memory anymore of our final goodbye. As I left Leo, the taxi driver shoved my two suitcases and a cardboard box containing my possessions into the trunk and drove me to the train station. When I arrived in London that evening, I pictured tossing all of it into the Thames. The undercurrent had torn me from all that had anchored me, and I was now stranded without a way to get my bearings, without a port in a storm. Out there in the darkness, I didn't know where I was anymore.

Over the next few months, guilt spread like vitriol into every crevice of my being. I wanted to turn back time, to go back and change what had happened: the wedding, the betrayal, the separation, all of it. I wanted to erase that entire episode from my life, wanted to make it disappear along with all the pain I had caused. Whenever I thought about it, and I thought about it every single hour of every single day, my face prickled with shame, and my stomach cramped. I couldn't control the dry-heaving. But there was no way to go back, and it felt like there was no way forward. There was only down.

What started out as a couple of glasses of wine every evening soon became a bottle a day. *Alcoholics don't drink fancy wine*, I rationalized to myself while strolling the wine aisle in one of London's most expensive grocery stores. My eyes landed on a French Syrah that no street drunk could ever afford. *A connoisseur of wines, an oenophile*, I thought, picturing a future version of myself who, in my mind, *collected* wines. It was a sophisticated, dignified hobby. "Oenophile" definitely has a more tasteful ring to it than "a twenty-six-year-old woman on the verge of an alcohol addiction."

Whenever I hung out with the few friends I had in London, I granted myself permission to drink more. If I was stumbling around on my way back home, that wasn't something to be avoided. That was *good*. That meant I would fall asleep quickly and wouldn't have to lie in the dark, torturing myself with the what-ifs of the perfectly safe, nice life I had just shredded to pieces. I could simply close my eyes and fall into temporary oblivion.

One evening, a friend scattered some white powder on his living room table.

"You want some? It'll probably do you a lot of good," he said, winking at me. I didn't even have to think about it. My eyes lit up. I ran to it. I took a hit. It stung my nostril. A bitterness caught the back of my throat and my mouth felt numb.

Within the blink of an eye—though I wouldn't know, because I wasn't blinking—I went from zero to one hundred. Life was good. Life was good. Life was good. I laughed and danced and I smiled so much that my cheeks ached. It felt so perfect; *I* suddenly felt so perfect I couldn't refuse when more was offered. All I wanted was to be in that elated state, on top of the world again, invincible. That was the fun me. The happy me. The me who felt alive, who saw life as a beautiful adventure, who had something to live for. There she was.

It was a dangerous illusion to be dancing with. The next morning I called in sick, citing a high fever.

Unworthy, destructive, undeserving. Each step hammering a new word into my brain. Every morning on my way to the office, I played this game with myself: for every step I took, I came up with one word that I thought best described me. Step, *ugly*. Step, *unthinking*. Step, *careless*. Step, *pointless*. They had to be nasty words, words that stabbed like daggers. Twisted affirmations. I had hurt the only person in the world who truly cared about me. I'd shattered our dream in the name of something that I couldn't even define. I had ruined everything. *Idiot. Idiot. Idiot.* Black suede Prada heels drummed out the rhythm as they carried me down London's sidewalks.

My journals from that time are filled with poems and verses, some more intelligible than others, all permeated with that same agony and self-loathing, and a longing for *something*. I wrote letters to myself filled with scathing words, the sentences barely strung together, a twisting stream of consciousness being the only form I could sustain:

"FUCK YOU, with all my might, with all the muscles in my tongue, with all the veins that end up in my heart. FUCK YOU. In every direction I turn, every time I open my mouth, the words that flow out are a dirty river of cover-ups, excuses, a farce, a shitload of hypocrisy, but I force it to escape my lips. . . ."

When I reached the river on my way to work on those dim, damp London mornings, I started another game. I would peer over the blue metal barrier of London Bridge and try to estimate the distance between the bridge and the water. How long would it take for a body to fall in? Was it a lethal distance? Would the fall kill you, or just crush your legs? If I jumped in right now, would anyone see it, or would I be able to drown in peace?

Every double-decker bus that approached me with the usual London haste was an opportunity to daydream. I wondered whether the driver would stop in time if I threw myself in front of it. I played the fantasy in my head on repeat: find a spot far from traffic lights, where the bus would be moving at its top speed, and then jump. And just like that, I wouldn't have to *be* here anymore.

I thought about jumping when I stood in the dank halls of the London Underground and watched the lights from the tunnel approach the platform. I thought about jumping when I waited for the train at the London Waterloo station. I could almost feel my teeth hitting the metal railing, my soft body yielding to the million-pound beast on top of me.

Over time, these thoughts became so much a part of my interior world that whenever I saw a large truck, bus, or train anywhere—on a lunch break, while standing outside a pub with friends—I pictured it tearing up my body into a million pieces. The idea of it felt vindictive. Liberating. Picturing myself committing suicide had a way of making me feel hopeless and insignificant. But picturing myself getting obliterated, with all the gory physical details, over and over again, had some twisted charge to it. In the name of atoning, I, the perpetrator, was now also I, the judge.

Why are you still here?

As if to test whether I was really there, I picked up a pair of nail scissors and traced a line on my skin. Falling back on my teenage distress calls, sometimes I used a light touch, just barely enough pressure to leave a faint white line. Other times,

I picked up a razor blade, pushing it deeper, to the point where blood flowed. Every time I cut my skin, I did it in places where nobody could easily see it. My inner thigh. The inner side of my upper arm. The back of my calf, where I could easily claim it was a scrape I'd gotten on a walk, if anyone cared to ask. The thrill I experienced when I harmed myself made me feel *something* other than a constant, numbing self-loathing. Of course, no one heard my call, and I don't know if I wanted them to.

For months that dragged like decades over the autumn and winter of 2017, my mind was like a pendulum, swinging ceaselessly between wanting to obliterate myself and misguided attempts to feel, in some way, alive. Most of the time, I was high, drunk, or hungover. And when I wasn't, I wished I were. But nobody could know. Nobody could know that everything was falling apart.

I managed to keep most of what I was experiencing a secret. My friends knew about the divorce. Whether it was the optimism of our youth or something about the relationship that everyone but me had known all along, nobody seemed all that disappointed by the news. To them, it was just another breakup.

Nobody knew just how dark my thoughts had become. There was no shrink, no best friend to confide in, no family member whose shoulder I could rest my head on. I doubted that anyone would ever understand the depths of self-loathing I had pushed myself to. And in any case, there was no need to burden anyone with my despair, for I had caused enough pain already. I needed to atone for ruining everything. It was my fault, and I did not deserve help.

As the wrecker of my own home, I felt guilty. As a human living in an unjust world, I felt guilty for having what I saw as the privilege to even feel depressed. And all that guilt came packaged in shame, and shame propelled me even deeper into the conviction that I was, in fact, unworthy.

My newfound love for generous servings of red wine—which I, an "aspiring oenophile," continued to explain as something sophisticated—led me to a magazine article about Portugal's famous wine bars. On a whim, I booked a cheap flight to Lisbon to see if a bit of sun could find me down there in the abyss. The night I arrived in Lisbon, I wandered through the historic Alfama neighborhood. The air was still warm from a sunny November day, and the salty smell of the nearby Atlantic Ocean wafted in on the light breeze. Without a map, I meandered through the city's cobblestoned alleyways, in between ancient, tile-roofed town houses. The narrow streets were hushed save for the occasional click-clacking of heels against the stones. They didn't seem to be echoing the drumbeat of *idiot, idiot, idiot*. They were fast and light. I imagined a woman rushing to her beloved, spurred on by sweet anticipation. Yellow streetlamps illuminated the surrounding walls with light as soft as that of candles. When Portuguese privateers had set off to pillage, colonize, and destroy distant lands, this was where they left from. In my disorientated mind, it might as well have been five hundred years ago.

Imagining a gust of wind sending these old, cursed ships to their fate, I followed my feet to the nearest bar in one of Lisbon's historic neighborhoods, a cramped and dark venue where time stood still. Low ceilings, a slightly dank smell, a few weak lights barely illuminating the patrons and the stories their faces might reveal, leaving everything else untold.

I sat in one of the darker corners and picked a glass of the cheap local red wine I had traveled all the way here for. I was about to put pen to paper when a woman's voice cut through the room. I looked up from my journal. Wearing a long, black dress, her eyes closed, the woman started singing. Her resounding, wistful voice was accompanied by a single acoustic guitar. I had found myself at a fado concert—the traditional Portuguese music of heartbreak. She was singing from the depths of her soul, but it was as if she was speaking directly from mine. She could have been singing about her long-lost lover, or a life that had passed by too quickly. I didn't need to understand the words to know that she sang a lament: a world of grief and longing was contained in that refrain.

Throughout her performance I let tears stream down my face. I wanted these tears to wash the story of pain, shame, and guilt from my skin.

The next day, something small and barely tangible had shifted. It felt like a shy ray of light coming through a crack between two blackout curtains. "I don't know if it'll last," I wrote in my journal. But for the first time in months, I felt something lift me, almost imperceptibly, from the waters in which I had been drowning. I tilted my face toward the sun and closed my eyes, letting the violent burst of light fill my mind with whiteness.

Maybe this was what I needed. A change of scene.

When I returned to London a couple of days later, I was forced to accept that my time in Lisbon had not instantly transformed my life or eliminated the unhealthy coping mechanisms I had developed to navigate it. As I would later come to learn, travel is not a magical healing potion. But the getaway had offered my soul a seed to nurture. It had opened my mind to the possibility of leaving London. I had never seriously considered a life outside of the city. Since graduating with my Oxford degree, I had always been told that all the best career opportunities were in London, New York City, Paris—the urban sprawls that are home to executive suites and important decisions. I assumed that this was the only world for me—the only world you could be "successful" in.

But if this was what success felt like, I wasn't sure if I wanted it anymore. I had split from Leo because I had wanted a different life, but instead of building that new life, I had fallen into a tailspin. Now, the idea that I didn't have to stay in London—or tie myself to any big city, or any company, or any job title—began to germinate. It felt like the seed of something that I had never previously considered. Something new, exciting, and terrifying.

This idea, however, came with a whole host of issues I began to consider. Where would I even go? And what would I do? If I wanted to travel for a while, how would I be able to afford it? Presumably, I would need to put an end to my wine habit, if I didn't want to blow through my savings in the first month. I considered my options: I could try to find a job in a different country, a desk in a slightly sunnier office. Or . . .

The thought sent a shiver down my spine. A small contraction squeezed my stomach. *Or I could take some time off to travel.* I opened up the calculator on my phone and crunched some hasty, ill-informed numbers: the cost of a cheap breakfast, lunch, and dinner, and bus fare, and some pocket money, and a bed in a hostel. I had to google the last one, since I had never stayed in a hostel in my life, and to this day I'm not sure what gave me the idea. Multiply by . . . eighteen months. One and a half years. Press "enter."

No way. I reran the calculation to make sure I had gotten it right. The number that popped out matched the number I could see in my savings account. This was money I had saved up over the course of the past five years. Money that I had originally set aside to put down a deposit on an apartment one day in the future. But, according to my calculation, it was also just enough to support a year and a half of budget travel.

Hold on. I tried to pace myself. *Even if I have the money, what about my career?* Eventually, when I came back to London, would a gap on my résumé raise eyebrows? The idea of tearing myself from the only remaining safety in my life—career, money, status—felt unnerving. But it was safety without happiness, and my mind wasn't safe in this life.

In my head at the time, there was no such thing as a one-way ticket. I assumed I would travel for a while, reach some sort of personal nirvana on a mountaintop, and then come back to my old life, ready to spew out pretentious dinner-party stories. I knew that if I wanted to seriously consider this travel idea, I would need to be much more careful with money. I made a promise to myself to return the things I'd bought during my latest shopping binge—another unhealthy coping mechanism I had developed for want of something to have control over, if only my appearance. The worse things got on the inside, the better I had tried to make myself look on the outside. A glittery dress for $600, a pair of leather boots for $1,000, a cashmere sweater for $400. The refund for this particular shopping binge would give me an extra $2,000 to travel the world, which suddenly felt like a fortune.

I convinced myself that I could find—would need to find—ways to explain my impromptu year off work to any prospective employers. Maybe I could even make it sound like a good thing. If an HR rep ever asked me, "How do we know you won't disappear to travel the world again?" I could probably come up with something like, "Well, you see, all the travels made me realize that the London corporate ladder is the only mountain I want to climb after all."

But who in their right mind left their dream job? Over the past five years, I had helped this company grow from nothing to a massive platform with tens of millions of dollars in financial backing. Leaving it would mean forfeiting the shares I had in the business and the promise of future wealth. But what shook me much more deeply was the idea that I might never find a job like it again. It was something I had helped develop from scratch, my "baby." But it did not make me happy. No matter how much I told myself I cared about this job, I had to confront the fact that life in London was rotting me to the core, and that even in a seeming "dream job," I was, in reality, working to build someone else's dream. The business would happily go on without me. But my own life wouldn't. I knew that, to find my spark again, I had to strike a different flint.

I stalled and stalled, fearing what might become of me if I disrupted the precarious remainder of normalcy in my life. On New Year's Eve, I booked a cheap last-minute flight and escaped to Marrakech, Morocco. As the year ended, no power could hold me in London. On that symbolic night, I wanted to find myself in some kind of no-man's-land: a place that held no intimate memories, far from familiar faces, a clean slate. Nourished by the sweetness of Moroccan mint tea, I spent most of the day within those sandstone walls journaling about what life could be like if I left London. I dispatched my mind to faraway places and distant scenarios. I pictured myself riding horses across the landscape, the distant horizon pulling me on a wild journey with no obvious finish line. Hooves against the ground, dust rising behind me, the horse and I becoming a singular presence, faster than the racing clouds. I imagined living with few possessions, with campfires instead of drinking binges, and bare feet in wet grass instead of shoes drumming out intrusive thoughts. This version of me got to travel to remote places in search of a life far from the one I had been living. For the first time in months, I felt a spark.

And this spark gave me hope. I had not *wanted* to do anything in a long time. All of a sudden, a desire began to awaken within me. This "travel thing" sounded like a convenient escape. And who knew? Maybe if I ran *away* from this, I might eventually find something worth running *toward*. Perhaps there was a place, somewhere in the world, where I might feel alive again.

I watched the old medina of Marrakech teem with movement as hawkers showed off their colorful wares: embroidered carpets and gleaming bronze vases, desert-inspired paintings and spices that promised virility and eternal health. Here, life was pulsating, the beating heart of the medina set in motion by the countless tourists and locals who navigated its maze of tangled alleyways every single day. Amid it all, I felt small, insignificant. But, for the first time, it was the kind of insignificance that made me feel reassured. Looking at the crowd wandering around these red medieval walls, I realized something that I had never thought of before:

"Whatever happens," I wrote in my journal, "changing my life will not be the end of the world. Life will go on, in all its rich tapestry and constant motion. It will change, because it always does, like a river flowing, ever-expanding, ever-transforming."

There, surrounded by contrast in all its humming magnificence, I finally saw that, to find my own path, I had to be willing to flow with the river, taste the waters of its different tributaries, and sometimes even swim upstream. To change my life and find a path that was uniquely mine, I had to be willing to lose everything I'd ever known. I would watch it sink away. Everything I'd accumulated, everything I'd believed to be mine, everything I'd seen as true up until now. But eventually, if I sought the light, it would come, and I would begin to rebuild. The sun set over the bustling ocher medina, and in the last of that year's light, I made my decision: *I will leave it all behind and start from scratch. I will rebuild.*

"I'm so happy for you . . . and a little bit jealous." This was not the reaction I'd been expecting to hear. "I just know you're going to find yourself."

My roommate Ness was gushing over my decision. I had expected her to give me a reality check, to set me straight. "You're going to ruin your life!" was the response I had been betting on as I told her about my tentative plan, my tail already tucked between my legs.

"Do you really think that?" My body immediately relaxed, more in surprise than in relief. "It honestly feels like a total wild card."

"It *is* a wild card, but sometimes that's the card you need to play." Her gaze met mine, calm and reassuring. "We all have chi, this innate life force, inside of us. It's universal, and it's always there, but sometimes we can feel like our chi fades away. If you sense that something is missing, then you need to go and find your chi again."

Chi was something that Ness deeply believed in—according to Chinese philosophy, every living being has a spiritual energy that drives them and carries them forward. This chi is innate, and must be nourished. My own spiritual landscape felt barren from months of self-abuse, so, hearing her speak, I latched on to Ness's beliefs like they were my own.

I was shaking with fear, but I knew that if I continued my life in London, I would arrive at a point of complete self-annihilation.

After one of our last conversations in London, Ness sent me a message that read, "You're stepping into your true self. Enjoy the ride."

Enjoy the ride. All throughout that dark night of the soul, I had a hunch that life was not just for existing. Humans were not made to merely survive. We were made to thrive. With our vast emotional palettes; our ability to experience awe, to bounce from the deepest lows to the highest highs; and our epiphanies and revelations and capacity for great creativity, we were not made to live a life of mind-numbing sadness and regret. We were not made to sit in front of a desk for forty-five years of our lives, repeating the same soul-crushing set of tasks day in, day out, while we grew indifferent to our miraculous, one and only life.

No. We were made to feel, to experiment, to laugh, to cry, to fail miserably, to triumph gloriously, to explore and discover and learn and fill our minds with wonder. That was what we were made for.

I am going to leave London and I will not come back.

The next morning, on the first of January 2018, I quit my job, gave my one month's notice in my houseshare, and called my family to say I was moving out of London.

"But what about your job?" "You're going all alone?" "What if something happens to you?" "Can't you fix things with Leo?" When I called my maternal grandparents, they launched their questions at me like long-range missiles. There was nothing I could say to reassure them because I myself did not know any of the answers they were seeking.

"I don't know. I'm still trying to figure it all out. I just wanted to let you know." The silence on the other end of the line lasted for a moment too long.

I did not call my father. He had taken Leo's side in the divorce—all the more baffling and painful, given that no one was asked to pick sides. He was the person I most wanted to share the news with—ironic, since he himself had run away to distant lands when he was younger. He should have understood my decision more than anyone. But something told me that with the tables now turned, and him firmly on Leo's side, I couldn't count on him.

My mother sighed. "I know why you're doing this, but I hope you stay safe."

"We will miss you," said my housemates from London.

Later that day, I wrote:

Notes to my Future Self:
Ignore whatever stands between dream and reality
Walk the roads you don't know
Deprive yourself of the luxury of fear.

As Heathrow Airport disappeared behind me, the rumble of the engines grew louder. Like an elephant slowly rising from a long slumber, the jet began to move laboriously forward. The lights inside the cabin flickered and switched off. My hand gripped the elbow rest as it gradually picked up speed. From one second to another, the plane kept accelerating and I could feel, with every bone in my body, just how badly this heavy beast yearned to get off the ground, to finally leave the tarmac behind and do what it had been created to do.

Suddenly, with a light upward jolt, we were in the air. Now the jet seemed less like an elephant and more like an eagle soaring through the sky, headed east.

I relaxed my fingers and looked out the window. There it was: London, with its million lights, shining on the horizon like a galaxy of stars. The constellation of the Thames emerged below me, clearly outlined like an artery across the city. It took a short moment for the glow to disappear far behind us.

I closed my eyes, let my head fall back on the headrest, and took a deep breath.

Well, I thought. *Enjoy the ride.*

chapter four

finding yourself in a land that isn't yours

"Come on, you can do it!" My friend Maxime, who had already been traveling for a year, urged me to join him when he heard that I had just left London. "You can definitely make it. It's really not as hard as they say."

Maxime had been planning to complete the infamous Everest Base Camp trek and wanted me to join him. Known as the EBC in the hiking community, it follows a high-altitude trail in the Himalayas that leads to the base camp of the tallest mountain in the world, Mount Everest—or Sagarmatha, as she's known locally. Over the course of two weeks, you ascend to an altitude of seventeen thousand feet, where the oxygen level drops to half of what it is at sea level. A grueling and remote trek, it requires you to physically adapt to the harsh conditions while maintaining a brisk pace over the course of many back-to-back hiking days, all the while carrying a heavy pack. The trail is frequented by the indigenous Sherpas, whose bodies have genetically adapted to these extreme conditions over generations of high-altitude living, and by Herculean Everest climbers hoping to summit the world's tallest mountain.

And, apparently, I would join them.

My plan to attempt the infamous Everest Base Camp trek was, to put it simply, a ludicrous idea. Never mind the fact that I was still adjusting to a life without all the guardrails of who I had been. I still had no reference point, no clear goal, no clarity. Most importantly, though, I had never hiked more than a day in my life.

I had always looked at the outdoors from a safe distance; my family, despite all our travels, was not the "outdoorsy" kind. The grand feats of endurance I sometimes heard about seemed like news from some parallel world inhabited by human-shaped, ultra-fit aliens: someone summited Everest without supplemental oxygen, or skied a thousand miles across Antarctica solo, or free-climbed a vertical wall in some remote part of the world. These achievements might as well have been rocket science to me.

I had no experience of being at high altitude save for a few gondola rides on skiing holidays. I had never hauled a heavy backpack up a mountain or experienced back-to-back hiking days. The longest distance I had ever run was an accidental eight miles after getting lost on a jog in London. My very recent first-ever visit to an outdoor shop had rendered me mute with incomprehension as the shop assistant attempted to explain the difference between a soft-shell jacket and a hard-shell one. Then there was the punishing routine I had been putting my body through recently, spending months getting high or drunk every night with no regard for my physical well-being.

On paper, these were hardly ideal conditions in which to be undertaking a feat like this. To most amateur hikers, the EBC is a dream hike: tough but achievable. To me—unfit, out of shape, my self-belief in tatters—it was about to become the most challenging journey I'd made to date. But I needed something to revive me. The past year of my life had left me feeling like I had lost my place in the world and, along with that, my identity, my self-esteem, my sense of meaning. I knew that in order to reclaim all that I had lost, I needed to put myself on an entirely new path. I needed radical change.

Maxime had made the Everest Base Camp trek sound very achievable, and in my head, it was the perfect challenge. I had read so many stories of people finding themselves in the mountains, and I hoped the vital part of me that I'd lost along the way was out there, waiting for me, too. What I didn't consider was the fact that Maxime was much fitter than me, with much more outdoors experience, and had already spent time in the Himalayas. But sometimes you just have to take a leap of faith.

As I made my way out of Kathmandu Airport, I caught the scent of Leo's aftershave, carried on the air from someone else's body. Shortly afterward, at the hotel, a notification had popped up on social media, and his photo along with it. The world continued to remind me of his presence, and every time it did, I felt a wave of remorse. I still missed his steady gaze and all the guarantees I had forfeited by choosing not to be with him. Most of all, I regretted how I had left things. How suddenly I'd left him, as if I'd been scared that pausing to think would cause me to change my mind and backtrack. Perhaps it would have.

Leo had eventually found out about my plans to travel the world through the grapevine, though we had not spoken in any meaningful way since I had moved out of Brussels. Before leaving, I had wondered whether I should tell him about my plans—whether I owed it to him, whether he would care, whether it would make things better or worse for him. A part of me was ashamed to admit to him that I was leaving, because that part of me knew he would think I was just running away from everything. It wasn't wholly incorrect. I felt sure he would have preferred that I stayed and fought.

It didn't help that a divine connection still lingered between us. In the suddenness of everything that had happened between us, we hadn't gotten around to dissolving the church marriage that bonded us together. Though these vows were not legally binding in the eyes of the law, and we were therefore not legally required to dissolve them to officially separate, they did carry a spiritual significance. And, despite my trying to rationalize my way out of the feeling, it still weighed heavily on my heart.

But for now, I needed to relax my grip on my *old life* to give this new one a fighting chance.

The musky smell of temple incense filled my nostrils. Kathmandu is a spiritual city, and you can't take more than a few steps without running into some place of worship, a shrine or a temple, however small it might be. But its proximity to the world's highest playground gives it an edge: there is giddiness and excitement in the air, a sense of possibility and new beginnings, and I immediately felt myself, let myself, get wrapped up in this magic.

Macaque monkeys perched on shop tiles and wandered the pavement, picking at each other while observing passersby with their wide, mischievous eyes. Small shrines lined the streets. Brightly decorated rickshaws raced by. Pigeons wheeled above the rooftops. Mopeds swerved around dazed tourists. Street food sizzled in deep pans, filling the air with spices, filling my mind with memories of the days spent exploring Asia with my dad. The relationship that my father and I had so carefully rebuilt in the years following his move to Asia had suffered in the aftermath of my and Leo's breakup. We were still not speaking. Perhaps my failure to succeed in a happy marriage reminded him of his own shortfalls. I may never know, and he may never explain, claiming as he did that he was "not good with these things." In putting all my effort into *not* being like my parents, I had made a similar mistake. Perhaps the lesson was to stop trying to be, or not be, like anyone else. Perhaps the lesson was to stop living in reaction to others and start living in alignment with myself.

The streets of Kathmandu embraced me, and I missed my father's company and the long, rambling city walks we used to take together. I wanted him to urge me on, to root for me. If there was anyone who could understand my choice, it should be him, I thought. But he didn't.

The city swept me up in its chaos and, suddenly, I didn't have the time or the inclination to dwell on things I couldn't change. I allowed the familiar excitement of faraway travel to whisk me away. I lapped it all up, greedily inhaling as deeply as I could to absorb all the smells of the world around me.

The ancient city was a labyrinth of narrow alleyways teeming with life. I walked through these streets as the long afternoon settled into dusk, illuminating the capital in a dusty rose glow. In the backpacker neighborhood of Thamel, outdoor shops selling counterfeit North Face gear competed with souvenir stores chock-full of plastic prayer wheels, hole-in-the-wall restaurants, and all kinds of tourist traps. Small Hindu and Buddhist monasteries and stupas—dome-shaped shrines—were decorated with flowers and colorful figurines and bathed in the smoke of smoldering incense sticks. Trekkers in their technical gear perused souvenirs, crossing paths with stoic Buddhist monks wearing robes the color of a rising sun to represent the sacred realm and the divinity of nature. Above the chaos, forming a ceiling over the maze of narrow streets, myriad prayer flags representing the five elements fluttered in the wind.

I found it liberating to be a passerby in a foreign land. Here, I was just part of the tourist throng and didn't have to define myself by my job, my relationship status, or the size of my wallet. It didn't matter who I was, where I was from. I just *was*. Like the other travelers from all corners of the globe who had descended upon Kathmandu sporting their bum bags and elephant pants, I, too, was a holidaymaker, a vagabond, and a seeker, part of their contingent. All of us were here on our own personal quests (occasionally interrupted as we got scammed out of our food by the local monkeys). I felt a sense of kinship with them, this anonymous lot of foreign travelers, that I had not experienced for a very long time. "This is the trip we've been dreaming of for years!" I overheard an American tourist exclaim, overcome with enthusiasm for this place. I felt his life force—his chi—aflame. None of us belonged there, and yet we all hoped that we would find something of our own in this land that wasn't ours.

A rickshaw driver with two tourists in the back of his rig jolted me out of my reverie as he whizzed past me, missing me by an inch. The humming and honking of Kathmandu's traffic reminded me to be more mindful of my surroundings. I would need to start soon, because our departure for the mountains was fast approaching.

Our plane into the most dangerous airport in the world was a tiny propeller jet that rocked and swayed in every breeze and thermal it traveled through. As we flew from the historic city over highland pastures, the little plane steadily climbed into the air. Soon we were soaring up, up above the green mountains, lush with fir and juniper.

The journey to Lukla—the gateway to the Himalayas— takes only half an hour in favorable conditions, and before we even reached cruising altitude, we were already descending toward the mountain town—fast approaching the most perilous stage of the journey. All the passengers began to shift around nervously and lean toward the squint windows, looking down. In the seat behind me, Maxime was pointing his camera at the window, the shutter snapping away furiously to capture the landscape. The average runway for a plane is roughly five thousand to eight thousand feet, but we were about to land on a sixteen-hundred-foot-long strip of pavement carved into a remote Himalayan town at an altitude of nearly ten thousand feet above sea level. Due to the high altitude and the extremely short runway, both of which affect how easily a plane can land safely, only the smallest aircraft and the most experienced pilots could operate here. This flight route might also explain the popularity of the portable plastic prayer wheels.

Knowing that several deadly crashes had taken place at this airport, I was not thrilled about the idea of having to land here. I had set out on this new path in life, and I was keen to give living another shot—at least for a little while. But the alternative was a twenty-hour drive from Kathmandu, followed by a five-hour trek. All things considered, a twenty-seven-minute, sensibly priced scenic flight seemed like a reasonable option. Besides, it was worth the investment for a video I could make about the flight for my brand-new YouTube channel that I'd just launched to document my travels and give them—me—a sense of purpose.

Flying below tall, jagged peaks and the sheer rock face that rose all around and above us felt like passing between the ever-tightening walls of a giant Himalayan tunnel. As the plane continued to descend and with no airport in sight, it seemed like we were about to fly into the side of the mountain. But finally, I saw it. The airstrip came into view, hardly longer than a running track. I knew what I had to do now, whether I was ready or not.

I picked up my camera, pointed it at my face, and pressed the record button. For a moment, I stared down the lens, trying to think of something to say.

"Um, so . . ." My mind went blank, as did my face.

I pressed the button again to stop recording.

What do I say? I asked myself. *Anything*, was the answer that came back. *Just say anything. We're about to land.*

I pressed the button again.

"So we're . . . landing! I think . . . we're about to land at the world's most dangerous airport here in Nepal. Wow!"

Stop recording. I shook my head. God, that was awful. Definitely not YouTube-worthy. *Who would ever want to listen to this boring nonesense?*

Come on, I coaxed myself, *you're in one of the craziest places in the world! Say something interesting!*

The plane continued to dive toward the tarmac, and this was truly my last chance to make a statement if I wanted to capture my reaction to the landing.

"This is the world's most dangerous airport! Aaargh!" I blurted out, immediately disappointed with myself, and then pointed the camera away from me, with intense relief, and toward the window of the plane.

Looking out as a scattering of dwellings around the summit of a mountain came into view, along with the tiny runway we were about to make contact with, I wondered whether this vlogging thing would ever get any easier. This was the third video I had ever filmed for my YouTube channel, and it wasn't exactly going as smoothly as I'd hoped. My less-than-eloquent reaction to the landing did not make the final cut. In fact, when I sat down to edit the vlog a couple of weeks later, I cut most of my speaking parts, leaving only the most essential sentences to keep the narrative semi-intelligible over the shaky, overexposed B-roll that I inexplicably chose to pair with stock electronic music.

At that point, in early 2018, YouTube was already well established as a platform, with various creators publishing travel and adventure content from across the globe. As my personal life fell apart, I consumed their videos hungrily, escaping to my own fantasies of traveling the world while telling interesting stories and visiting beautiful places. Incredibly, some people had managed to turn this into a full-time job. As I watched and wondered whether this was something I could ever do, I noticed one very significant gap in the travel content offered on YouTube: there were very few women adventurers creating regular content about their solo travels. I struggled to find anyone who did the kind of travel that I was intrigued by: travel that took you beyond the postcard views, off the beaten track, to hidden corners of the world and cultures you'd generally only read about in *National Geographic*. These were the magazines I had grown up with, the yellow border drawing me in like a portal to a distant land every time I opened a new issue. My paternal grandfather was passionate about travel and had amassed a huge collection. They had arrived by mail every month straight from *Nat Geo*'s headquarters in the United States to his home in small-town Poland.

Everyone has a role model, and my grandfather was mine. He was born a traveler. When he was an infant in 1944, in the last year of the Second World War, his parents were exiled from their eastern home by the Soviets and had to escape on foot. As they made the arduous trek west, they carried a little baby wrapped in blankets, sometimes traveling by horse cart, sometimes walking, constantly on the move toward safety. They slept in barns and ate whatever bread they were given by villagers en route. After hundreds of miles, they finally reached a city in western Poland where they were allowed to settle. These were my grandfather's first lived experiences. A nomad in the cradle. In my mind, he was born to move. Given how my life had unfolded from an early age, perhaps I was, too. Perhaps it was in our blood.

As was apparently his destiny, my grandfather started to travel in his adulthood. A man hungry to escape the gray of Soviet Poland, he'd had more barriers to overcome than most world travelers at that time: back then, Polish citizens were forbidden from keeping their passports at home (the government "took care of them" at the local police station), and the Polish currency proved as valuable as old newspapers abroad. But, if anything, those obstacles only steeled his determination to go farther afield and expand his previously limited worldview. Much to the chagrin of the authorities and at a great personal cost, he organized trips for himself and his friends to places such as Mexico, China, Indonesia, and Japan.

Just before I had left for Nepal, I had traveled to my hometown in Poland. My grandfather might have been long gone, but he left much behind. One afternoon, when visiting my grandma, I snuck into his old study and scanned the bindings of the books lining the shelves. Finally, I found what I was looking for. The cover of the big leather-bound book embossed with gold read, "Kenya, Uganda, Tanzania—1995." This was but one of many of my grandfather Leszek's travel chronicles: books he had typewritten that told the tales of his journeys in hair-splitting detail, his signature style. The book's spine creaked as I opened it. I wondered how long it had sat there on my grandma's shelf in Poland. Perhaps I was the last person to turn its pages, many years ago. This was the first time I had opened this book since I was a teenager.

Every page was filled with worlds of wonder and color, charged with adventures that had the capacity to teach me something. I let the book fall open to a page at random. It opened to his time in Tanzania. Glued onto the light blue paper were photos of street sellers beside mounds of vivid oranges—hundreds upon hundreds of the fruits, like a vein of gold on the potholed road. On the opposite page was a small group of men rowing a wooden boat, crossing a river to the shore my grandfather stood on with his camera. Behind them was a settlement crowded with palm trees under a warm sky whose humidity I could almost feel sticking to my skin despite the cool Polish air around me.

I breathed deeply, absorbing the dust and his words, typed up from scribbles made while he was sitting on a minibus as it rocked its way down a rough road in the Tanzanian savannah. I could picture him there, looking out the window, circles under his eyes, his face slowly turning green with motion sickness. But, still seeing the beauty around him, he wrote, "I've noticed something changing in me: I've lost all my haste. The miles no longer impress me. Whether there are one hundred, two hundred, or six hundred of them, they leave me indifferent, because I must cross that distance anyway.

"So I'm not afraid of distances anymore. And the same goes for time. Whether I'm on the road for five hours or seventeen—what's the difference? Either way, I must reach my destination. I don't get anxious about the slow, snail-like pace. I simply get into my vehicle and I drive so far and for so long, in absolute peace, until I finally reach the destination that I have set for myself. I also don't let the discomforts bother me, be it a hard seat, heat, dust, or the lack of water. All of this, in its own way, is beautiful and wonderful.

"Whoever cannot adapt to this kind of life . . . in fact, whoever cannot come to love this kind of life, cannot be a true traveler. To be a true traveler requires strength of character."

With his travel writings to keep me company through many lonely days growing up, he had given me sufficient proof that travel and storytelling could transcend all boundaries of time and life and death. His own death had come suddenly, the result of a drunk driver causing a head-on collision. He died in the helicopter on his way to the hospital. Though he was gone, he continued to tell me stories I could retreat into. I carefully plucked photos from the pages of his chronicles and moved them into my own journals, wishing to preserve the things that his eyes had seen, and keep his vision close. Aware that I was committing low-key theft, I never told anyone about these transgressions. But I couldn't help it. His travel books were my nest of comfort in an otherwise unpredictable, dangerous world. And in moments of doubt, I tried to remind myself that I could always return to them, to him.

With his willingness to dive into the unknown at the forefront of my mind, I took the things I knew—I knew I wanted to travel the world, I wanted to learn about the world beyond what the guidebooks could teach me, I wanted to tell stories about it all much like my grandpa—and decided to take a risk. I would try to break the mold. I was embarking on a new life, and I needed to make it count. I wanted to do something that would truly alter the course of my existence and help me find my own sense of purpose. If I could tell stories of my travels, stories of my own, in my own voice and my own style, I had a feeling that I could once again find that sense of belonging I'd always felt when snuggled up with my grandfather's travel writings. But this time, the sense of belonging would be of my own creation: it would be mine, tattooed onto my very being.

If I could pull this off, perhaps the greatest win would be to prove tradition wrong. I had grown up watching travel shows in which the hosts were overwhelmingly male. And while I loved these shows and watched them with my mouth wide with awe, they always felt like the exclusive domain of men. Even today, if you browse the programming offered by the biggest travel channels, like National Geographic or the Discovery Channel, you struggle to find a show hosted by a woman.

Boys could pick from a whole roster of male role models; they had David Attenborough and Steve Irwin, Anthony Bourdain and

Rick Steves, Michael Palin and Simon Reeves, Bear Grylls and Levison Wood and Ben Fogle, and the list goes on: a whole spectrum of great travel hosts to look up to. Not so for girls. It's hard to picture yourself doing something if you've never seen anyone like you doing it. In order to be it, you first have to be able to see it.

I wondered whether there was some intrinsic quality of women that explained this: Were people simply not interested in watching a female adventurer? Even to my untrained eye, this sounded far-fetched. It suddenly felt like the chi that Ness had told me about was waking up. I wondered if I could blaze the trail for other female adventurers on YouTube and turn this new venture into a sustainable lifestyle. This was potentially my one-way ticket out of the London grind.

It sounded like a great plan: a mission I was passionate about, doing something that filled me with excitement, creating something that nobody had done before. There was only one problem. I had never made a video. Not a single one. I had not gone to film school or taken any courses in filmmaking. I had no clue how to capture good footage, how to edit, or how to tell a story in video format. I didn't even have a camera capable of capturing video—all things I needed to quickly rectify.

A month prior to leaving for Nepal, I invested a couple of hundred pounds in a secondhand Canon camera, a "vlogging lens" as recommended by a YouTuber, and a basic microphone that looked more like a dead rodent than a real piece of kit. I had a very basic understanding of camera settings but found them too intimidating to play around with, so I simply set the camera to "automatic," pointed it at things, pressed "record," and hoped for the best.

But if my shooting skills were, at best, minimal, then my editing abilities were . . . Where were my editing abilities? With no budget for a professional editor, I had no option but to learn. So

I spent the weeks in the run-up to Nepal down a rabbit hole of YouTube tutorials dedicated to video editing. For any query you might have about video editing, there is an instructional video on YouTube courtesy of a faceless guy, quite possibly living in his parents' basement, explaining how to do the thing you're trying to learn about in a level of detail worthy of an encyclopedia.

With these burgeoning filmmaking "skills" and two hundred subscribers, most of whom happened to be family members or Facebook friends, I was a very long way from creating the kind of adventurous, trailblazing content that I dreamed of. But it was a start.

The end of the Lukla runway was now directly in front of us, and it ran straight into a mountain. My little secondhand camera kept rolling. The aircraft's wheels hit the ground, and with a few gentle bumps, the pilot expertly taxied us along the tiny airstrip.

We appeared to be alive, and were hurried out of the plane, our luggage thrust into our arms on the tarmac. We were shown our way out of the airport through a small metal gate, and then we were in the Himalayas. But in the rush of the short transit out of the plane, I lost an important part of my microphone, which meant that whatever sound I recorded on my videos for the next two weeks would suffer. *Great start*, I thought as our local guide, Kumar, greeted us with a shy smile.

"Hey, guys, how are you? Are you ready?" he asked.

He was a short and sturdy man with a handsome face and happy, playful eyes. Kumar had spent his entire life in this region and, as a local guide, he knew every twist and turn of the trail we were about to embark on. I could only imagine how strong he was judging by his backpack, which looked heavier than all our luggage put together.

"Yes, but we're starving," I said, glancing at Maxime, hoping

Kumar wouldn't make us climb Everest without first having a quick lunch. We headed into one of the small local restaurants in Lukla. And as we devoured our portions of dal bhat (lentils) and rice, we took in our first glimpse of a true Himalayan town.

Lukla is the gateway to Everest, which means that everyone hoping to see the world's tallest mountain from the Nepali side must pass through it. Low stone buildings lined the narrow pathways where hikers and their guides crossed paths with local Sherpas, while great hillocks of yaks hiked alongside mules and donkeys. Everywhere you looked were the signs of a tourist economy: hand-painted boards advertising trekking agencies and currency exchanges, hole-in-the-wall stores selling basic mountain gear for those who needed last-minute supplies, and restaurants with menus in a number of different languages. It was a literal world apart from the high-end shopwindows and cocktail bars of London. A flashback reminded me of the wine, white powder, and guilt I'd left behind there. I was glad to be so far away.

But the thing that stood out to me the most about Lukla was its quiet: unlike in chaotic Kathmandu, here there was no sound of traffic. Aside from the whirring of the occasional plane or helicopter, there were no engines or horns. It was this silence, more than anything else, that signaled to me that we were about to embark on a real adventure. This was the farthest I had ever been from a car, or a taxi, or a paved road. I wondered what the way to the nearest hospital looked like. Could you even get an Amazon package delivered here? All the unknowns filled me with a nervous, tingling excitement.

"Okay, guys, let's go. It's time to head out." Kumar urged us out of the plastic restaurant chairs we had slumped into. "We have a long hike today." The three of us walked up the stone streets toward the gates of the Sagarmatha National Park, a UNESCO World Heritage Site and the home of rare species such as the snow leopard, the red panda, and the musk deer. We passed an old whitewashed Buddhist temple with an ornate entrance carved in wood and painted in myriad colors. Inside, it was all shadow, but I caught a glimpse of something shiny. Drawn toward it, I discovered that it was a huge, gold-plated prayer wheel standing at the heart of the temple.

Local Buddhists believed that if you walked alongside a prayer wheel and spun it in the clockwise direction, it could bring you good karma. I placed my right hand on the prayer wheel and, gently spinning it, made my round of the temple. I was about to trek to Everest Base Camp having not hiked a day in my life, and if this temple was handing out free karma, I was going to grab as much as I could carry.

Our planned route would lead us on a steady ascent toward the revered Everest Base Camp and a mountain pass just beyond it. The higher we walked—ascending to the village of Phakding with its bright turquoise roofs at about nine thousand feet, then Namche Bazaar at eleven thousand feet, and on to Dingboche at fourteen thousand feet, and beyond—the smaller the settlements became. All of them were completely cut off from Nepal's road network, hospitals, and schooling infrastructure. This was truly life on the edge.

Unlike our porter, whom we would hardly see the whole trip as he raced comfortably ahead of us at his own pace while carrying a portion of our luggage, we would take it slow, Kumar reassured us. Ascending at a gradual pace to allow our bodies to acclimatize would minimize the risk of altitude sickness—the symptoms of which range from headaches, dizziness, and nausea to fluid on the lungs, coma, and death. I could already see that the slow going was leaving Maxime feeling restless, and I knew that both he and Kumar could have left me in the dust. But this was my first-ever long-distance trek, and I secretly thanked Kumar for taking it slow. I imagine he had guided enough people up this mountain to be able to see through my bravado.

The sandy loam trail ascended steadily up the side of a mountain. The higher we climbed, the more the vegetation receded, transforming the topography from lush forests in the foothills to a landscape of steely alpine shrubs and bare rock at the higher elevations. I had only ever seen landscapes like these in photographs. Now they rose all around me, the magnitude of the cliff faces and the depths of the valleys on a scale I had never experienced before. With every step, the world appeared to be expanding far beyond the skyscrapers I had been used to. I was just hoping these valleys would let our flesh and bones pass through them, despite being very capable of swallowing us whole.

This being the first mountain I'd ever climbed, my legs weren't used to constant upward movement. Predictably, within a few hours, all my muscles were aching and stiff with effort, my thighs and glutes burning. I had not properly broken in my heavy trekking boots, either, and they started rubbing, leaving my feet raw with blisters. My shoulders ached as my backpack weighed on them. We were only just getting started, and already my limbs were refusing to cooperate. I wasn't used to committing my body to something so extreme, and all these sensations felt alien and new. How much discomfort was too much discomfort? But I couldn't spend much time wallowing. The trail was bustling and I was constantly having to ensure that I didn't crash into anyone else.

"Whoa!" shrieked a surprised female trekker as a cargo mule brushed up against her, nearly sending her falling down a cliff. "Holy shit, these things don't watch where they're going!"

Kumar snickered and gave a knowing look to another Sherpa.

There were the trekkers themselves, sometimes in large groups, and sometimes in small teams of two or three. They were almost always guided by locals. But there were also all the locals providing food, supplies, and gear to settlements at high elevations. Some of these loads were stacked impossibly high, and the person carrying them often disappeared underneath full-size mattresses that took up most of the space on the trail, entire wardrobes, and towers of unidentified necessities bundled up with plastic sheets. These moving heaps of stuff with legs still managed to overtake us.

The people carrying this cargo with the sun beating down on them as they ascended to the highest altitudes on the planet were the world-famous Sherpas, many of whom worked in the Himalayas as guides and porters. Although the word *Sherpa* is commonly used to describe all the Nepali support staff on treks and climbs, it specifically refers to an ethnic group indigenous to the Eastern Himalayas. With their own unique language and culture, they have historically inhabited high altitudes across Tibet and Nepal. Known to them as "Chomolungma," Mount Everest holds a special place in their culture. She is regarded as the protector goddess, "Mother of the World." They pray to her as someone might pray to a deity, or to the angels. This is a sacred land, home to spirits and supernatural beings with a deep significance in the local version of Buddhism.

In contrast to the tourists, who struggle to adapt to the high altitude, the Sherpas have acclimatized over centuries of Himalayan living, their bodies using oxygen more efficiently when they exert themselves. With guiding and portering being some of the best-paid gigs in the region—frequently offering what amount to life-changing sums in Nepal—and pay allotted per pound, the incentive to load up is high.

But even with these mammoth loads, the Sherpas aren't the largest trekkers along the Everest Base Camp trail. *Those* are the yaks. These giant animals have horns that could easily gore a human. With their long, matted strands of hair covering their entire bodies, they might be mistaken for the legendary Himalayan yeti, were it not for the share of bags and boxes they carry on their backs, and the ringing of the bells on their necks.

As I watched yet another Sherpa carrying a load twice his size pass us on the way up the mountain, I asked Kumar, "Why don't the yaks carry all the supplies, instead of humans?"

Kumar chuckled as his gaze followed the Sherpa porter. "A good Sherpa can carry much more than a yak," he replied. "If you put too much weight on a yak, he will refuse to budge."

Even if the Sherpa porters were the real superheroes of the mountain, the enormous yaks still commanded priority on the trail, and I quickly learned to jump off to the side as they passed, and get as far away from their horns as possible. We looked down from our new vantage points as we climbed; the trail we had already covered wound back below us, and ahead was a forest of white, cloud-capped peaks. I breathed it all in—the atmosphere one of light and ice—and continued trekking up toward the endless blue of the sky.

Bent double in a village whose name I did not catch, I was resting my hands on my knees, trying to regain my breath while Maxime high-fived Kumar and exclaimed, "That was amazing!" Slowly, and with an excruciating amount of effort, I raised my arm to join in their enthusiasm. "Yeah," I added, "and hard."

It had been a tough first day, but we'd finally arrived. Exhausted and sore, I was apprehensive about the increased physical and mental effort that would be required for the coming days. But I could also sense, as clear as the air, a feeling of accomplishment brewing within me—something I hadn't felt for a very long time.

With my hands clasped firmly around a mug, hoping to absorb any warmth it was willing to offer, I slowly sipped on my hot tea. Every sip warmed my cold, aching body and tasted like the nectar of the gods. It was late afternoon, and we had just settled into our teahouse, one of the many guesthouses dotted along the trail. Simple but functional, it had a few small rooms furnished with single beds and padlocks on the doors. There was no central heating, the walls were paper-thin, and the single-pane windows did little to insulate us from the elements. With temperatures sometimes dropping to 14 degrees Fahrenheit at night or lower, you'd best have a very warm sleeping bag if you planned on getting any sleep.

I took a stroll around the teahouse and stopped in mild shock when I saw the toilets. No en suites here. All the washrooms were communal, and most were of the hole-in-the-floor variety. Like many people living in the convenient embrace of Western civilization, I had never spent the night away from a source of running water, or a wall socket to plug my electronics into. I walked up to a large plastic bucket that hung from the wall in the hallway. Twisting the tap, I placed my finger under the trickling stream. Out of habit, I expected it to be warm. It wasn't. Without much of a choice, I splashed my face with ice-cold Himalayan water. It hit my skin with such intensity it was as if that splash contained the energy of the world's tallest mountains, the energy that made planets. I felt myself smile at the novelty of it all and, separated from the elements only by a thin corrugated-iron roof, went to bed exhausted.

Until now, in London, I had been used to going to bed drunk, crashing on my pillow, then lying awake for hours, harassed by too many thoughts before finally drifting into a shallow and unsatisfying sleep. But this was a kind of tiredness I was wholly unfamiliar with. It was the kind of tiredness that enveloped you after a day of breathing in fresh, cold air, smiling into the shining sun, putting one foot in front of the other until your thighs burned. It was the kind of tiredness that came from knowing that you'd lived the day to its fullest physical potential. A visceral tiredness that lulled you gently into a deep and restful sleep. *This is what tiredness should always feel like*, I thought as I drifted off, wrapped inside my warm sleeping bag.

chapter five

"i don't have it in me"

Onward we trekked, and as we climbed, we were tasked with crossing three-hundred-foot-long swaying bridges that rolled between two distant mountainsides, their constant swinging made more intense by all the humans and animals making their way across them all at the same time. Below us were sheer drops plunging hundreds of feet into the depths of distant valleys, chasms carved over eons by ancient rivers. Each of these nerve-wracking bridges offered a shortcut that saved us hours, if not days, of walking the roundabout way. Treading carefully, one hand on the railing and one hand holding my camera, I continued filming the trip, gradually becoming accustomed to talking to the camera and capturing the rhythm of the day.

Some of the sections we hiked were incredibly steep. My legs started to cramp and there was nothing I could do to keep up. I fell behind Maxime and Kumar and was overtaken by porters carrying heavy loads on their backs. Every now and then, as I struggled with the grueling physicality of it all, I just broke down in tears. But I kept walking.

The physical challenge was doing something strange to my mind.

In London, busy trying to hustle and survive each day, I had been operating in a state of stress and panic. With a constant onslaught of work and personal commitments, I always needed to be somewhere at a specific time, I always had urgent emails to tackle, and my thoughts had to constantly flip from the latest HR crisis to a social gathering I'd promised to help out with to a fast-approaching project deadline. Doomscrolling social media and news to unwind, I had been constantly feeding my brain new input without allowing it to rest. Juggling all of this felt imperative to my survival there, and dropping the ball felt too risky. Without anything to compare it to, I'd assumed that this constant tension was a normal way to live life—and, unfortunately, to so many people living in the world today, it is.

But out here, putting one foot in front of the other, I began to experience something novel. I noticed that once I got into the rhythm of each day's hike, my thoughts gradually evened out and calmed down. No more *Oh, I forgot to respond to that email* or *Let me just check what's new on Instagram*. I thought more deeply and with more clarity than I ever had. My mind finally had the time to begin processing everything that had been happening with me of late. I thought about the alternative, of being with Leo for the rest of my life, and it felt like I would have been willingly walking into a gilded cage, locking the door myself, and swallowing the key. I knew I had been lucky to find a man so wholesome, but in that moment, I also knew that this uncontainable desire for freedom I'd been experiencing had been beyond my control. When I thought back to the wedding and imagined what our future might have been if I hadn't left, I saw weekends that revolved around finding matching cherry red KitchenAid appliances, and I saw a white picket fence and conversations about starting a family. Perhaps I had made a lucky escape. I exhaled a sigh of relief and, watching that visible sigh hang in the dazzling mountain air, I marched right through it.

For me, walking up that trail felt like the thing that made the most sense in the world. I didn't have to question whether my email hit the right tone, or whether an interview candidate was right for the job. The simple act of walking was real and fundamental. It challenged me, but it also came so naturally, it was as if I had been put on this earth to walk.

White flares in a deep sea of rock, the snow-covered peaks dominated the horizon and illuminated the distance as we ascended higher and higher. Some of the mountains looked soft and rounded. Others seemed intent on piercing the blue ceiling with their jagged silhouettes, and I wondered how anyone could climb these near-vertical walls and make it out alive. Many of their peaks were partially obscured from view, hiding behind other mountains. In fact, there are so many tall peaks in the Himalayas that the locals don't even bother naming those under nineteen thousand feet. But some of the tallest hold a spiritual significance in Sherpa culture.

As we turned a corner, we saw a white stone stupa emerge around the bend, and behind this Buddhist place of worship was a view that nearly brought me to my knees. Across a long valley from us, a tall mountain stood in all its glory, completely unobstructed. Flanked by long, wing-like ridges on either side, it rose dramatically skyward like a phoenix of the rocks. This mountain was so immense it felt like it had a gravitational pull of its own: the air around it vibrating, whispering in the language of the infinite.

I felt urged to call this peak a "she." My instincts were right: *she* was Ama Dablam. The name translates to "mother's necklace," owing to her wide, embracing arms and her pendant of a glacier. I stared at her in awe. We were only a few days into this trek, but she was already the most beautiful thing I had ever seen in my life. A presence so immense, she made everything around her feel transient. In her eyes, we passed as quickly as the cool Himalayan breeze.

Standing face-to-face with this enormous, mystical mass of rocks, I had a radical, timid thought: *How generous of the universe to offer me this short, intense human life.* I had spent so much of my time on earth fretting about my status, what I owned, or where I fit in. But in that moment, it started to dawn on me that the universe I existed in didn't care whether I became a successful manager, or a doting mother, or a vagabond wandering the world. So why was I afraid of following my own path? Looking up at Ama Dablam, I began to suspect that taking my life into my own hands and molding it into a unique shape was the only thing I could feasibly do with my limited time here.

Like so many of us, I enjoyed the immense privileges of a passport that allowed me to travel freely, a higher education, a sound mind, and a capable body. That was a foundation you could build an empire on. I had taken my own life for granted for too long, and it felt almost like a betrayal *not* to take advantage of those privileges. I had the responsibility to recognize them, make use of them, and build a life that truly belonged to me.

"Are you okay?" Maxime noticed my pale countenance and my pace visibly slowing down. It was the fifth day of the trek. The elevation had become brutal and the ascents steep—every step felt as if someone had tied dumbbells to my ankles. I was physically exhausted and reeling from the effects of the altitude. But the shortness of breath, burning throat, dizziness, and constant headaches were to be expected for a rookie in the Himalayas.

"I think so. Honestly, though, I don't really know what should feel okay at this point," I admitted. "My legs are killing me."

Maxime laughed. "Yeah, it's supposed to be hard! I'm pretty tired, too."

I suspected that while we were walking the same trail, we were on very different journeys. I didn't want to hold the others back.

"You guys go ahead; I'll just take a quick break," I said, taking a seat on a rock by the trail. Kumar and Maxime examined me, wary, wondering whether they should leave me alone. "Seriously, guys, go!" I implored them, not wanting to be a burden.

"Okay, the teahouse is just up this hill and around the corner. You can make it there in half an hour," said Kumar, struggling to resist the opportunity to race Maxime up the hill.

"Great. I'll be right there," I promised, and watched them jog up the trail, their bodies light and strong.

I collapsed by the side of the path as mules and porters hurried past, and I broke down in tears. I couldn't do it. The sheer, ruthless physicality of it all was starting to overwhelm me.

After I'd spent so many months in London feeling worthless, this trek was supposed to be a way for me to prove to myself that I was worthy. But as I sat there, my head in my arms, unable to go on, I felt like maybe I was defective after all. Maybe this new life of mine had all just been a reckless mistake; maybe

I had simply made a shortsighted attempt at running away from my problems. I had been delusional to think this would change me, save me. I couldn't even walk up this mountain, so how could I expect myself to film it and tell an inspiring story, too? Before I'd left London, a well-meaning friend had suggested that I might just need to take an extended vacation, some time and space to think and recalibrate before coming back. Sitting there on a Himalayan mountainside, far from everything I knew, collapsed into myself on the trail, I suspected she might have been right. Why had I decided to throw everything away when I could have simply taken a short hiatus? I didn't have it in me to become the adventurous YouTuber, the brave storyteller, that I had thought had been dwelling inside me. Had I gotten it all wrong?

I tortured myself with every scene that had made me doubt myself over the past few weeks. A couple traveling together, holding hands. Someone's post on Instagram of one of my old haunts that had triggered an anxiety attack. The smell of Leo's aftershave in the airport making me wonder whether I'd really had to break everything off so dramatically. Maybe there was something about me that was broken, I thought, and I was like a compass with a faulty magnet that was simply incapable of pointing north, so instead quivered frantically, spinning from one direction to the next.

Still crying, I slowly lifted my head and looked around. Maxime and Kumar were probably already relaxing in the teahouse. Sherpas and their animals still climbed the mountain, passing me by, barely noticing. They must have seen their fair share of inexperienced trekkers in crisis. The wind was still blowing, the sun shining. The universe's indifference to my plight forced me to accept that if I didn't move from this spot, then I would simply stay there. It was my choice, and my choice only, to stay or to keep going.

My feet still fettered by invisible weights, tears still in my eyes, I got up and started walking again. One foot in front of the other. And with each step, as my mind shifted back into the rhythm of hiking, it slowly left behind the heavy train of thought that had followed me here from London. As I walked, in my head, I pictured myself leaving behind those doubts and fears, on that very spot on the trail high in the Himalayas.

Nine days into our trek, we finally approached Everest Base Camp at about eighteen thousand feet above sea level. At this elevation, the oxygen had almost halved compared to that at sea level. My breathing had become slow and heavy, and walking had become a mammoth effort. But we were so nearly there now.

Turning a corner, we spotted the Everest Base Camp boulder. As if in celebration of our arrival, the mantle of colorful prayer flags the boulder was covered in fluttered in the wind. So this was it. What we had come all this way for.

Beyond the boulder, toward the base of Mount Everest, stretched the Khumbu Glacier: a giant, extreme "campsite" for those who attempted to climb the world's tallest mountain. Every year, hundreds of hopefuls spent a couple of months here, acclimatizing, training, and preparing for their summit bid. We had arrived before the start of the climbing season, but there were already little yellow dots scattered across the glacier: high-altitude storm-resistant tents set up in preparation for the arrival of the climbers. But the summit of Everest itself was not visible from this spot. I wondered what it would be like to keep going from here: up, all the way up, to the uppermost limits of where a pair of human feet could carry you.

Meanwhile, at the boulder, Maxime, Kumar, and I took a few snaps, and then it was time to leave. We ventured to a nearby teahouse and celebrated our achievement with a shot of local cognac, which burned as it flowed down our throats and sent us into a fit of giggles with the exhilaration of having achieved what we had set out to do. This was my kind of high.

I will admit that the short moment we spent at the Everest Base Camp boulder, without so much as a glimpse of Mount Everest, after a nine-day trek was, in some respects, a little anticlimactic. Yet I felt a sense of accomplishment, excitement, giddiness even, as well as relief at having finally made it. After reaching base camp, I had checked it off my list of things to do, and in a new life where I was keen to embrace what little structure I had imposed on myself, this was an important milestone. But there was no major epiphany to accompany the green tick. It wasn't the same soul-ripping elation that I had experienced while gazing at Ama Dablam. It wasn't the same state of flow that had taken over my mind and body after several hours of simply shuffling my feet.

Still, the destination had been necessary to justify the long trip and to give us something to keep moving toward: an arbitrary spot on a map that would pull us toward it like a small gravitational field. But the true goal all along was simply to experience the journey, to repeat that well-worn cliché that my grandfather had come to appreciate so keenly. The real triumph was in feeling the stinging blisters on your feet and to keep going. The greatest achievement was to feel the sunshine and the freezing wind on your cheeks and to keep smiling.

Several days later, sitting in a café back in Kathmandu's backpacker district, I was putting together the first video from the trek for my YouTube channel. As I moved the files around on my laptop screen, arranging them into a chronological sequence, my mind wandered back to the moment I'd experienced while gazing at Ama Dablam.

I was free to live. I promised myself to make the most of the limited time I had on this earth. This adventure had challenged me in the most unexpected ways, and I knew that there was still so much more to learn, so long as I continued beyond the realm of comfort and familiarity.

chapter six

adopted by a pakistani family

The white two-wheel-drive sedan bumbled along the remote mountain road, narrowly avoiding the gaping potholes that occupied a large portion of the road surface. Ismail, the driver, jerked the steering wheel to the left, then to the right, with one hand. The other was pressing his tiny phone to his ear as he argued with someone on the other end of the line in Urdu.

Pressed against the backseat, and overcome with severe nausea, I was trying hard to keep my gaze fixed on the unmoving horizon. The problem was that there was no horizon: in front of us were peaks so tall they ended high above the windshield of the car, somewhere near the roof of the world. To make matters worse, to our left, the road suddenly plunged into a ravine and I couldn't stop myself from rubbernecking at the sheer drop.

It was the summer of my first year of travel, a few months after my Himalayan trek. I was heading into the mountains in the north of Pakistan to live with a local family in their home. There were only two ways to get there: by plane, on one of the world's worst-rated airlines, or by car, along a road that was dubbed the most dangerous in the world.

"So, have people died while driving down this road?" I asked, peering down into the abyss.

"Yes, many, many accidents here. But don't worry, I have driven here so many times!" Ismail smiled, moments before picking up his phone again to begin the world's most poorly timed call.

On the one hand, I felt reassured by his casual confidence, as he relied on what appeared to be muscle memory to steer the car. But on the other hand, I could very clearly imagine us both plunging to our deaths in this beat-up sedan. I had survived a flight to the world's most dangerous airport earlier that year, and I prayed, *Please don't let me die on the world's most dangerous road.*

We had now been driving along the Karakoram Highway (KKH) for over twelve hours. The KKH connects the capital, Islamabad, with the isolated north of Pakistan and the country's border with China. It's considered to be the new Silk Route, built upon the old one over twenty painstaking years by twenty-four thousand Pakistani and Chinese workers. It is often dubbed the "Eighth Wonder of the World" and, aside from its breathtaking scenery, it allows for trade and transport between Pakistan and China, countries with a combined population of over 1.6 billion. The road cuts through impossibly treacherous terrain, snaking its way up high-altitude passes, down the sides of giant mountains, and through long, dark tunnels. It cost a fortune to build and continues to eat up huge sums of money to maintain, with rockslides and landslides being commonplace, given its location.

The repetitive beauty of the landscape lulled my busy mind, and it drifted over everything that had been happening since I'd left London four months earlier. Having visited an old school friend in Pakistan earlier that year, I had become enamored with this country, its landscape and its people, and the division between its complex reality and the binary way in which it was too often portrayed in the media. When it had come time to leave after my allotted two weeks here, it had felt too soon. As the border official stamped my passport to formalize my exit from Pakistan, I'd felt like I was leaving something important, unfinished, behind. Even before I'd left, I knew that I needed to come back.

The trek to Everest Base Camp earlier that year had encouraged me to trust that I could rely on my own resources when things got tough, and I felt assured that I could travel farther afield alone. Over the subsequent weeks, I train-hopped across Asia, jumping on an old-school train in Vietnam and heading north. Those few weeks came straight out of a backpacker's tale: I got detained on the Vietnam-China border for not having the correct travel documents, only to be helped by kind border officials. I crossed into China on foot with only my bulky purple backpack for luggage and took local trains across the lush green province of Guangdong, with its karst hills straight out of *Avatar*. Every day brought new places, people, and experiences. And with all that novelty suddenly swooping into my life, I felt like I was managing to tear myself away from everything I'd left behind in London, the memory of a life abandoned still an open wound I was desperate to heal. Every meal I ordered at a street food stall without questioning its provenance felt like another step away from the à la carte dinners in London's Shoreditch. Every turn of the train's wheels on Asian railroads ushered me further from the dreaded daily commute. Every night in a backpacker hostel or aboard a sleeper train was a world away from the warm marital bed I'd once shared with someone. It wasn't so much that I had processed what had happened since leaving London; I'd simply found excellent ways to distract myself from the hurt.

Eventually, I took the Trans-Siberian train from Beijing to Ulaanbaatar in Mongolia, a country that had stolen my heart on a past trip and that I knew I needed to see again. In Mongolia, I spent six weeks volunteering at a horse camp, where I helped a local family with their guided horseback treks and all the admin that surrounded them: bookings, emails, social media. Living with the Mongolians and their horses gave me an idea for a wild expedition, one that I would come back to in the not-so-distant future. But in the meantime, through all my travels across Asia, something kept nagging at me: Pakistan.

Now, a few months later, here I was back in Pakistan, pleading with the universe not to let me die on the world's most dangerous road (but, deep down, happy that I had found enough joie de vivre to wish for another tomorrow). My YouTube channel was finally gaining some traction. The videos I had made across Asia over the past few months had, to my surprise, attracted a decent viewership. A couple of clips had even gone viral, and the subscriber numbers were growing steadily. These were still not the numbers that I needed in order to support myself financially, but they were the first glimmers of hope that I could make this into a sustainable lifestyle one day.

As of very recently, I was based in Islamabad, and I had just started dating someone in the city. A year after leaving Leo, I hadn't wanted to get into another relationship. But Nadir, a successful musician with supernatural levels of charisma, had intrigued me so deeply that I couldn't resist. With his olive skin, piercingly dark eyes, and chiseled features, he swept me into a romance I'd neither expected nor desired—at least, not at first. But there was something about embracing him that made me feel like I belonged, and I couldn't stop myself from latching on to that feeling in the midst of what still felt like a whirling, frantic world. He was much older than me, and with an established career, a beautiful home, and a rock-solid reputation, he brought a sense of stability into my newly nomadic life. I felt myself pulled toward him like a wandering wave that rolls through a vast ocean, devoid of connection, only to crash into a safe island. I was wary of falling into yet another relationship, and I questioned it and myself constantly. But, for now, I'd decided to just let things unfold and go with the flow.

Despite Nadir's having become a presence in my life, I insisted on traveling alone. And that was how I found myself in Ismail's car. By the time we arrived in the remote region of Gilgit-Baltistan, night had bruised the sky, and we made our way beneath the invisible peaks of the Karakoram and above sporadic lights from villages in the valleys below—and we passed them pretty slowly, given that our average speed was that of a tractor. The two-hundred-mile drive took us eighteen long hours, but eventually I made it to my hotel for the night, where I lay awake, overexcited, like a child, to be back in Pakistan's remote countryside. Beyond the epic landscapes and the human kindness, there was something else that drew me back to this country. My first trip had made me question the knowledge on which I had built my entire belief system about the world.

I had previously assumed the country to be an arid desert, devoid of culture and ripped apart by years of war, dangerous and unwelcoming. Nothing could have prepared me for the buckets of chai I was offered, the countless invitations to stay in people's homes, the jaw-dropping beauty of the country's mountainous northern landscapes. If I had been so wrong about Pakistan, I thought, what else might I be wrong about? A nascent curiosity was awakening in my mind, and it quickly began to dissolve some of the most fundamental assumptions I had made about the world and myself. And I was finding it liberating to admit my own ignorance, because admitting it meant that I was free to explore a whole new planet that had been hidden by my limited perception. With every preconception that I proved wrong in my own mind, new possibilities arose. Suddenly, the world had opened up, and I felt like I wanted to question things, to experience it all from within my own skin, to reach my own conclusions. And Pakistan—owing to its bad reputation—had provoked this impulse in me more than any other place.

Over the following week, I was to stay with a Wakhi family and experience life as they lived it. The Wakhi are an Indigenous group who live in a small but majestic corner of the world, currently divided between China, Afghanistan, Tajikistan, and Pakistan. They are mountain people, and for countless generations they have braved the harsh seasons of the Karakoram and Pamir Mountains, living as traditional shepherds and high-altitude farmers. With their own language, culture, and customs, they are one of the many ethnic groups who call Pakistan their home.

Through a chain of Instagram friends, I was connected with someone called Pervaiz Posh, whose family has been calling these mountains home for generations. They had readily invited me to come and spend as long as I wanted living with them in their home. As I hastily repacked my backpack in the hotel hallway, a young man confidently pushed open the reception door. He was slim but strong, his hair short and his face clean-shaven. He was wearing a pair of jeans and a sports jacket—a world away from the traditional *shalwar kameez* (trouser-and-tunic combo) I was used to seeing in Pakistan.

"Hello, are you Eva?" he asked as he approached me. No formal *assalamu alaikum*s, no stiff greetings.

"Yes, you must be Pervaiz!" I wondered whether it would be appropriate for us to shake hands, seeing as how unmarried members of the opposite sex weren't meant to touch in Pakistan, but before I could decide, his hand was already shaking mine. I immediately got a sense that we would get along just fine.

Pervaiz's beat-up white sedan (apparently, the unofficial car of the Pakistani mountains) continued on the very last stretch of the Karakoram Highway. Lining the road were birch, poplar, and apricot trees bursting with hyperreal-looking green leaves. All around us rose massive snowcapped mountains, their serrated peaks practically piercing my lungs and taking the breath from them.

"What are they called?" I asked, looking up and shielding my eyes a little from the glare reflecting off their high white caps.

"These mountains here are the Passu Cones." Icebound at the very tips, the Passu Cones are a juddering range of peaks and crevasses that catch the ever-changing light and seem to shape-shift depending on whether you're looking at them in the morning or in the afternoon. The Cones are also referred to as the Passu Cathedral, owing to their almost Gothic spikes; the peaks create the appearance of vast pointed arches that vault into clear blue sky. This erratic vista before us was the habitat of Himalayan ibex, bears, lynxes, wild sheep, and the elusive snow leopard.

After an hour of following the road as it wound its way through the Hunza Valley, we finally arrived at the small village of Jamalabad. This was one of the last settlements in Pakistan before the Chinese border. The village was perched high above the Karakoram Highway, at about eight thousand feet above sea level, and tucked into one of the many valleys that swung down the side of the main road. It sat on a lush plateau and felt like a cocoon, surrounded on all sides by tall, dry, rocky mountains. I counted about twenty small houses, all made from local stone, all surrounded by their own freshly plowed fields.

"We grow potatoes here. Hunza potatoes are the best in the world!" said Pervaiz, beaming.

It was a warm and sunny late summer day, and women wearing bright *shalwar kameez* in yellow, red, and green were raking their fields using traditional wooden tools. As we drove past them, they lifted their heads. It was clear that despite the natural beauty, or perhaps because of it, it was tough living out here. The women's faces were tanned, with deep wrinkles, but strong and smiling as I smiled back from the open window.

We pulled up in front of a low house constructed from the same large gray rocks that constituted much of the mountain range here. Beside it was a large yard, filled with sunlight and apricot trees, and a small shed for the family cow, who wandered around grazing on whatever leaves she could find. Pervaiz's parents were waiting at the front door like I was some long-lost relative coming home after years away.

Sifat Shah, Pervaiz's father, shook my hand with a warm smile. A distinguished-looking older man, he wore a traditional white *pakol* cap over his silver hair and a long traditional *shalwar kameez*. Goher Nema, Pervaiz's mother and the matriarch of the household, was a short, stout woman in her sixties, her long black hair in a thick braid. She wore a traditional Wakhi cap—an elegant band-like headdress, embroidered with pink and purple flowers. In accordance with local custom, she wrapped a loose dopatta over the top of it, letting it fall on her shoulders. Bright-eyed and smiling, she took my hand in hers, brought it to her lips, and kissed it. I didn't know it yet, but this was the traditional Wakhi greeting exchanged by women: a handshake combined with a hand-peck. I reciprocated the gesture clumsily, and she chuckled.

We left our shoes at the door, and I followed the family inside the house. On entering, I noticed a pair of huge Himalayan ibex horns that hung on the wall, greeting every visitor. Sifat Shah pointed at them, then pointed at himself proudly. "He shot this ibex," Pervaiz explained. "The horns measure forty-five inches. It was a really big animal."

We continued through the reception room, which was arranged on a couple of step-high levels. There was no sofa, no table, and no chairs, but the entire floor was covered with rugs, blankets, and cushions in every imaginable shade of red.

Pervaiz pointed at the floor and asked me to take a seat and make myself comfortable. Assuming a cross-legged position that felt like advanced yoga, I sat down. Over the following years of traveling across Central Asia and the Middle East, I would get used to sitting cross-legged on the floor. But at the time, it was an unfamiliar stretch, and I can't say it felt comfortable.

A tall, slim woman with big eyes and thick black hair covered nonchalantly with a dopatta entered the room bearing a tray of glass cups filled to the brim with steaming caramel-colored chai. "*Assalamu alaikum*," I said, impressed that she hadn't let a single drop of chai escape the cups.

Pervaiz introduced her. "She is Sayeda, my sister-in-law."

We exchanged smiles. With a cup of chai in my hands, I took a closer look at the room around me. It was decorated in the traditional Wakhi style, with wooden columns hand-carved with intricate, wavelike details rising toward an entirely wooden ceiling. In the center of the ceiling, a skylight was buried in a nest of overlapping wooden beams, and through it the bright mountain light poured down into the room.

The house was immaculately designed—there was even a bathroom with a concrete floor and a white porcelain squatting toilet. Given that there was no running water, the bathroom was devoid of a shower or a sink. Instead, there was a large pail in the corner and ample space to give oneself a bucket wash. In this region, many people still used outhouses, so just to have an indoor bathroom was a sign of wealth.

The warm milk in the chai we were drinking had come from the family cow I'd seen just outside. I would soon find out that chai was of central importance to life here and that its making was a ritual performed throughout the day. As soon as everyone woke up, someone would start brewing the chai on the cast-iron *bukhari* stove, and whoever happened to be sitting in front of the pan would take charge of stirring the pot. The loose-leaf black tea turned the milk a light caramel color. It remained a mystery to me as to how to decipher exactly when the chai was ready. But at some point, mid-stir, one of the women of the household inevitably decided that it was done and poured the chai into thick glass cups. This process was repeated several times a day, the whole family gathering every time, sometimes chattering away about the day's events, laughing and talking over each other, and sometimes in a comfortable and easy silence.

As the chai slowly disappeared, Pervaiz diligently translated from Wakhi into English, and back again. "We are all from this area," explained Sifat Shah. "We have spent our entire lives here, in these mountains. We know every single village and every single person here. But our sons prefer to live in the city." Two of the Posh sons, Akram and Syed, had gone off to study and work in Islamabad, where jobs were plentiful and the living easier.

"Everything here is changing," Sifat Shah continued. "Life is much better and much easier now than it was when we were growing up. Back then, we didn't have shoes or cars. In the winter, we survived on the potatoes we'd harvested on our own fields in the summer, because there were no shops where you could buy other things."

I showed the family photos of my maternal grandparents on my phone, explaining that they lived in a small town in Poland and that they, too, had experienced many potato-fueled winters as children, back when the country was a Soviet state. As I said this, I suddenly felt very far from home.

"I miss them, but I try not to think about it too much," I said. Goher Nema squeezed my hand in hers.

"We can be your family here," she said. "Your Wakhi family in Jamalabad. You can come back here anytime."

Later that evening, we gathered back in the family room for our evening meal, and I really did feel like a part of their family; how could I not? We ate with our hands, dipping our fingers—only our right ones, as they were deemed halal, or clean, in Islam—into one communal bowl placed on the floor. All the traditional recipes were dishes meant to be shared, not individually plated. And with running water a scarcity in these parts, the idea of washing ten separate plates and bowls was preposterous, and wasteful.

I was already starting to put together a pocket Wakhi dictionary in an attempt to learn some of the language. Wakhi is more closely related to Dari—sometimes known as "Afghan Persian"—than to Pakistan's official language, Urdu, but it exists in a linguistic group of its own, having originated alongside a variety of related dialects in the mountains and plains of the Pamir.

My Wakhi lessons involved pointing at various items inside the house and asking Goher Nema what they were called. I pointed at a pot of milk.

"*Žharž*," said Goher Nema slowly, enunciating every sound.

"Zh . . . ar . . . sh . . ." I noted the spelling phonetically in my notebook. "*Žharž*. Milk."

Wakhi was filled with harsh, sharp sounds that flowed into soft syllables. This intermingling of hard and soft mimicked the landscape in which the language had evolved: canine peaks that swept into vast plateaus and fragrant meadows before plunging into deep ravines and river valleys. These sounds tickled my mind with echoes of Polish, my mother tongue, which I barely ever spoke these days. Family phone calls were few and far between. My grandparents and my father were baffled by my sudden departure. When I'd left, all they'd asked was: "When will you come back? Have you spoken to Leo? Will he join you?" I could not bear to explain, perhaps because I myself wasn't completely sure what I was doing. Temporary silence, like a ceasefire, seemed like the most convenient option. To practice my Wakhi with its *sh* and *zh* sounds and its hard *h*'s was to utter sounds that felt familiar, like a home I had once had, thousands of miles away.

Next up, I pointed at the fire in the *bukhari*.

"*Raxniy. Rax-niy*," she said patiently.

"*Raxniy. Shobosh.*" Fire. Thank you.

Goher Nema nodded with a smile, seemingly satisfied with my progress.

The first words I was taught in Wakhi, the most essential and commonly used vocabulary, were those relating to the home and to the weather. Fire, stove, wood, milk—it's raining, it's sunny, it's cloudy. It felt very different from learning how to say "What's your job?" and "I would like the check, please" on Duolingo. Over time, my dictionary expanded to include longer phrases, and I wrote them down as I heard them: *Chai goma?* Want more tea? *Zakh pev!* Take more! With every interaction that followed during my stay in the village, I tried to say a couple of things in Wakhi. Aside from being a sign of respect and intention, learning another person's language brings you a little closer to understanding their culture and roots. You start to see the world through their eyes.

Once we'd finished eating and chatting for the evening, Pervaiz showed me where I would be sleeping. It was the decorated reception room, where a pile of blankets was waiting in the corner. In traditional Wakhi households, guests get to stay in this spot, considered to be the "best" in the house. I buried myself under the soft blankets, piling a few on in order to stay warm, and lay back and listened to how still it was. There was no traffic or street noise. My phone wasn't picking up any signal. Lying on a thin mattress in this dark room, I looked through the large window in the ceiling. Stars twinkled outside, their cool brilliance uninterrupted by light pollution. *Raxniy, shobosh, žharž*. Softly, my mind played the Wakhi record on repeat.

One of my greatest fears at the outset of my traveling alone out here was that I would end up feeling lonely, isolated from human interaction and missing my family and friends. And although I did miss them—particularly my father, the silence between us growing deeper—as it turned out, solo travel was quickly becoming a blessing. I was on my own, with no familiar topics of conversation or inside jokes to fall back on. There was no choice but to immerse myself fully in every interaction with my new hosts, dedicating all my attention to them. It was becoming clear that when I traveled alone with an open heart and an open mind, I would never really be alone.

chapter seven

an old lady in the mountains

Everything was changing, and fast. In the past year, I had chosen to let go of the reins, and for the first time in my life, I didn't have much of a plan. Drifting between a burgeoning new relationship and an exciting, free life as a wandering filmmaker, I had started to realize that plans had a tendency to be fickle, to change. Growing up in Europe, I had always subscribed to the idea that a planned life was a good life. Having it all figured out sounded like the sweetest idea just a few years back, *master plans and guarantees* ringing like a chorus in my head alongside *marriage, mortgage, lineage*. But it was precisely a *lack* of planning that had brought me to Pakistan in the first place, on a friend's last-minute invitation. It was precisely a *lack* of planning that had allowed me to see the country with fresh eyes. As I surrendered to the natural course of things, the path ahead of me seemed to take shape on its own.

I could feel a fire inside, a burning excitement in a place where there had only been ashes. I felt alive when I traveled, and the delight of discovering new places and cultures filled me with a keen sense of optimism. I was coming around to the notion of embracing the unknown, with all its twists, turns, and serendipities. If living an adventurous life meant navigating uncertainty and even embracing it, then I was finally allowing myself to start living adventurously.

On a cloudy morning a few days into my stay, Pervaiz offered to show me a nearby valley that very few outsiders ventured to. Avgarch Valley was once connected to the Karakoram Highway by a dirt track, but violent floods had obliterated the road a few years earlier, and the valley was now cut off. During the summer months, only about twenty people lived there part-time. The only way to reach it now was on foot. If you asked locals how long it took to get there, they were likely to say, "Two hours for me, four for you."

We followed a smooth pathway along a calm canal swathed in greenery. Soon, we descended close to the riverbed and navigated our way around its rocks and boulders, only to find ourselves on slippery paths in the debris of landslides. Pervaiz hopped from rock to rock like a mountain goat, while I crawled on my hands and knees like a harbor seal on her first mountain trip, conscious that we were a four-hour drive from the nearest medical facility and an entire flight away from the nearest hospital. Suddenly, he stopped in his tracks and pointed at the mountainside rising above us on the other side of the river.

"Can you see them?" he asked.

I followed his finger and squinted to see the distance between us and the mountain he pointed at. Initially, I could see nothing but snow and rocks. And then, as my eyes continued scanning the mountain, I spotted a few shapes moving across the dusty, rocky mountainside.

"Wow, are these ibex?" I asked Pervaiz.

"No, they are markhor," he explained.

The markhor is the national animal of Pakistan, and the ancient regional myth is that they kill and eat snakes. The tale is believed to have been inspired by their winding, snakelike horns. These markhor stood perched on some precarious rocks. Majestic and tall, they observed us with equal interest, their thick horns twisting high over their heads.

I remembered the large pairs of horns hung in prominent spots across Pervaiz's family home. "So, do you hunt these?" I asked.

"I don't hunt, but my father is a hunter guide. He has been guiding people to find these animals for many years. He is the best," Pervaiz replied.

I had mixed feelings about trophy hunting, especially the drive to kill one of these majestic creatures just to have their horns become a mere decoration for a mantelpiece. But Pervaiz explained that whatever meat was harvested from a slaughtered animal was distributed among the family. Somewhat ironically, a portion of the high fees paid by foreign hunters went toward a local wildlife fund and supported the local community. Pervaiz's father was able to build his house as a result of getting paid well as a guide for these hunts, which were performed as sustainably as possible. I wrestled with my initial judgment, appreciating that the people here were just making a life out of what was available to them.

We reached the lush Avgarch Valley in just over two hours, having taken less than the predicted four hours. I was feeling pretty self-satisfied with my effort. As I launched my drone—a must-have gadget for every filmmaker on YouTube, and one that I decided to invest in early on—into the air, its bird's-eye view revealed that the narrow valley went on for miles, and in its heart was a ravine with a raging river, dark waters of pure glacial runoff, foaming and churning as they barreled down the land. On all sides, tall, unnamed peaks rose toward the clouds, all dust and rock without any visible vegetation, capped with a white dusting of snow.

We stood in an oasis. Leveled, modestly sized fields in which a green sea of barley grew were overlooked by barely visible stone houses that mimicked the surrounding boulders. Some of these dwellings dated back to the sixteenth century, and a few of them were decorated with ornamental wooden carvings, cut out by hand by the skilled craftspeople who had once lived here. Yaks and cows grazed purposefully as the clouds above us began to thicken into a dense gray curtain that sent the first warning drops of rain from the sky. The wind picked up, and the drone was now struggling to stay upright high in the air, so I brought it down as Pervaiz turned to press on. "Follow me," he said. "Quickly!"

Trying to get ahead of the freezing downpour, we ran toward the ancient village, where he led us to what looked like an old pile of rocks. The only way you could tell it was a dwelling was by the low wooden doorframe, which only reached my chest. I wasn't entirely sure what was happening or whose house this was, but Pervaiz knocked on the door and we waited in suspense.

The door creaked open, and behind it stood a tiny, wizened woman wearing a tattered yellow dress, a long woolen cardigan, and a traditional embroidered Wakhi cap. Long gray hair hung down her shoulders. She could have been anywhere between sixty and eighty years old: the deep wrinkles on her face told the story of a lifetime spent outside, in the fields, with the animals.

Her hands were small, but her handshake was firm and confident. "Bibi Nigor," she introduced herself. "*Weze, weze*." She urged us to come inside quickly. We had to bend double to fit through the door, which was for the best: in local lore, this bowing upon entry was believed to be a sign of respect from the guest to the host. As I took a long step down, the heavy smell of old, sour smoke hit me, and we found ourselves in a dark, windowless room partially buried underground. The layout was almost exactly the same as at the Posh home, with a couple of levels to sit on, a *bukhari* in the middle, and decorative wooden beams arranged in a square. The difference was that smoke over countless years had darkened the walls here and turned the beams almost black. In the wooden ceiling above us, a skylight let in the only light, which was shrouded as the smoke hurried up there in visible white clouds.

Bibi Nigor urged us to sit down next to the fire as she busied herself in one of the dark corners of the room. She scuttled back carrying a large metal pan filled with milk, which she placed on top of the fire. Out of a small plastic bag, she grabbed fragrant black loose-leaf tea and sprinkled it into the pot of milk. Holding a ladle in her right hand, she stirred the chai, lifting the ladle high and letting the liquid pour back down into the pot. Outside, the rain was beating against the rocks like an enraged drummer, reminding us of how lucky we were to have found shelter.

"Bibi Nigor is my aunt," Pervaiz explained. "She lives down in the village, but she has come up here on her own to graze her cows."

"*Baf.*" I looked at Bibi Nigor and smiled. *Good.*

"*Shobosh, shobosh.*" She laughed.

"She probably doesn't get many visitors here, does she?" I asked Pervaiz.

"You know, she doesn't have any children, and her husband usually stays behind in Jamalabad when she comes up here," he said. "But we are always visiting her. She has a big heart."

As she chatted away with Pervaiz in Wakhi, she barely looked at the pot or the ladle in her hand, her movements quick and fluid. There was something in her slightly scruffy and lonesome but warm presence, out here in a distant valley all by herself, that made me think ahead to my journey, my own future. I realized I had so many questions for Bibi Nigor. Did she regret not having children? Did she ever feel lonely being out here? Were we intruding, or did she welcome our brief visit? As I sat there, observing her with a cup of chai in my hand, I wondered where this new life of mine would lead me and whether I was making the right decisions for my future self.

Over the past few months, as I had made my way across Asia, blowing through my savings and pretending I knew what it meant to be a "YouTuber," engagement and baby announcements from friends back home had seemed to flood my social media accounts. A close friend from childhood was expecting her first child. Another friend from university had invited me to his upcoming wedding and I'd had to decline, knowing I simply couldn't afford to fly back. My former housemate had shown off a diamond-studded engagement ring in an Instagram post with a caption that read, predictably, "I said YES!" So did I, in another life.

I sighed and took a sip of my chai. It was sweet, almost syrupy. A world away from everything I had known before, I pictured Bibi Nigor making her way across the valley, into Avgarch village, wearing a heavy backpack laden with tea leaves and sugar and flour, to return home to an empty house. If one day I stopped traveling long enough to have a home, I wondered how I would feel coming back to an empty house of my own, with no husband or children to return to.

In marrying Leo, I'd never really thought past the wedding, past the white dress and the flowers. I had avoided thinking that far because I had always known that I didn't want to have children. Motherhood was never something I had any interest in. I could list a hundred reasons why I didn't want to have children, but most of them boiled down to the fact that I simply didn't want to assume the role of a mother. There was no part of me that wanted to spend my limited time in this world raising children, no part of me willing to deal with the ups and downs of bringing up a human being, no part of me ready to direct all my creative energy and emotional attention toward a child. I'd always known that motherhood did not feel right for me.

I wanted to ask Bibi Nigor what that had been like for her: Was it a choice, or was she unable to have children? Women without children could be ostracized from the community, and even in instances of medical infertility, the blame always fell on the women. This could make life exceedingly hard. But Bibi Nigor exuded so much warmth. She glanced at me with a mischievous glint in her eyes. Her smile didn't leave her face. And although these thoughts, doubts, and questions of mine remained internal, it was as if we were having a silent dialogue with each other. In that space, something started shifting within me.

I thought ahead to fifty years from now, and I could see myself being like her. Living on my own in a mountain hut, with my animals, near a small community of trusted neighbors. Like Bibi Nigor, I would always make time to welcome them for tea and regale them with the stories of my past travels.

In that dark stone house with Pervaiz and Bibi Nigor, warming my hands over the fire, I felt a sense of gratitude wash over me. As I sipped on Bibi Nigor's chai, the sweet liquid sending waves of warmth through my entire body, for the first time I knew, without doubt, that I had made the right decision. I might not know what lay ahead, but I knew in that moment I would continue following my bliss through Pakistan.

chapter eight

what happens when you go viral

On a foggy Sunday morning in Islamabad, I woke up in Nadir's bed. Beneath the high ceilings of the bedroom, the room was dark. The only sound was the ceaseless thrum of the air conditioner, which played like an anthem in the homes of well-to-do Pakistanis. Every few seconds, the machine expelled a burst of ice-cold air right into my face. In retaliation, I screwed up my lips and blew warm air from my mouth up to my freezing nose.

I looked over at Nadir, who was still sound asleep with the sheets covering only half of his warm body. He was like a heater, and was used to sleeping in these arctic conditions. Cursing this thermal difference between us, I shivered.

Some mornings, when I woke up and saw this man next to me, I would feel a familiar sharp pang of guilt course through my body. This wasn't Leo's back, and this man wasn't Leo, to whom I had promised a lifetime of love and loyalty in our wedding vows. Although we had separated a year before, waking up next to another man still felt like a new betrayal. I was plagued by doubts. Was it too soon to jump into another relationship? Had I repented of my sins enough to even deserve another shot at love? Would I ever? But logic and reason didn't stand a chance against Nadir's pull on me, so strong he might as well have been a planet.

The AC unit exhaled another burst of freezing air into my face. I grabbed my phone from the bedside table and slipped the duvet over my head, burying myself under the thick blanket.

Illuminated by the backlight of my phone, a fluorescent blue stream ran through a green meadow, with a flourish of tall mountain peaks on the horizon. This new "wallpaper" was a photo I had taken on the recent trip Nadir and I had made to Swat, a lush valley in a formerly terrorist-infested region of Pakistan. When Nadir and I were together, I felt like I was in love, completely smitten with his easy, casual charm and the ferocious intensity of his gaze. But whenever I traveled without him, which was with increasing frequency, we argued over the phone, his jealousy clashing with my newfound—and fiercely guarded—desire to be my own person, living on my own terms, and to not make the same mistakes in this new life. I was hoping that this was just a period of adjustment before we found our rhythm, because when we were together, things were easy, exciting, romantic, and then it was hard to imagine things were ever any different. In Swat, we'd spent a few days happily hiking down little-trod mountain trails, chasing hidden waterfalls, and making love oh-so-very-quietly in our guesthouse so as not to attract more scrutiny than we already were in the ultraconservative area we'd traveled to.

Though our relationship thrived whenever we were together, our limited travels as a couple were proving to be tricky—compared to what I was used to back in Europe, anyway. A Pakistani man and a white foreign woman looking to rent a double room as an unmarried couple in one of the most conservative areas of one of the most conservative countries in the world was not a common sight at most hotels there. As we made our way toward Swat, we passed through several military checkpoints and, for the sake of convenience, Nadir told the armed guards manning them that we were married in the hope that they wouldn't ask too many questions. It worked.

We had found a family-run guesthouse that allowed us to stay in the same room. As we didn't talk about our relationship status, and our hosts didn't ask, everyone was free to arrive at whatever conclusion best suited them. This should have made for an easy time for us on that trip, but, if anything, this unstable ground only exacerbated concerns I was trying to ignore in a relationship where the reality was constantly in flux.

Some days, Nadir played me love songs on his guitar, and we dreamed of what life would be like together twenty years from now. Other days, the fragility of our romantic affairs wasn't helped by my frequent absences as I pursued my dream of turning YouTube into a full-time travel filmmaking career, and we would be at each other's throats because I had forgotten to call him while on a trip to some new and exciting location with people he didn't know. We had been dating for only a couple of intense months, but the roller coaster we were on was already taking a toll on both of us. It didn't help that I still hadn't given myself time and space to fully reconcile with my past.

"It's easy to fall in love with you," Leo had once told me, "but very difficult to love you." Every time Nadir said "I love you," Leo's words echoed back. I had become fixated on those words and the idea that Nadir's love for me—*anyone's* love for me—could never be true and deep. It was merely infatuation, hollow and brittle, ready to disintegrate at any moment. So I lived on the edge of this new love with Nadir, halfway between fear and devotion, never allowing myself to fall into that all-encompassing, trusting embrace because I could never fully trust that someone would catch me.

As I replayed the darker episodes of my old life, I felt unworthy of receiving love. Self-reproach and shame plagued my nightmares, and I sometimes jolted awake, covered in sweat. Nadir joked about how much I talked in my sleep. Though I had no idea what I was saying, I desperately hoped that my subconscious rambling wasn't something that would become another bone of contention between us.

With my YouTube channel taking off, I was torn between an easy desire to nest within the safety of a relationship and the harder calling to strike out alone, into the big world, in search of something that was my own. Because I'd spent most of my adult life in relationships, the shaky footing I found myself on with Nadir still felt more comfortable—safer—than the idea of "ending up alone," somehow. I didn't really know what it meant to be single for an extended period of time, and despite my best intentions to try it when I set off for Nepal, I had been swept onto the familiar train of a relationship, with all its momentum and tumult.

In Swat, things with Nadir had felt good and natural again. But aside from the time we spent between the sheets, I was keen to see as much of the region as possible and capture it for my social media pages. "You are the first foreign visitor we've had here in a year," Mr. Khalid, the owner of a Swiss-inspired, almost Alpine guesthouse in the valley town of Kalam, told me. He was an older, distinguished-looking gentleman and spoke perfect, slightly accented English. "People are scared to visit because they think the Taliban is still here. But that's old news now. They're long gone."

Everywhere I went, hoteliers, tour guides, and anyone who had anything to gain from tourism bemoaned Pakistan's bad PR. Their gripe was understandable: the country was stunningly beautiful. From deserts cascading into the Arabian Sea in the south to snow-capped peaks and green valleys in the north, I had been captivated by the natural bounty that Pakistan had been blessed with. When people lamented all the missed opportunities for the local economies and communities, I felt all I could do was agree and empathize.

On that foggy Sunday morning in Islamabad, sheltering from the AC, I checked my notifications. Thousands of them had accumulated over the short few hours I had been asleep. I scrolled down to one of my photos from Swat. In the picture, I was in front of a mountain panorama, mid-twirl, wearing a purple embroidered dress, a garment that women in the region traditionally wore before the Taliban radicalized the area and forced most women into uniform dark robes. This was a garment I had been lent by a generous shopkeeper. He would not hear of payment, no matter how many times I insisted. On the way back from the shop to the hotel, the taxi driver had said to me, "You see, our name has been tarnished, but we are good people."

I had written about this moment of generosity with the shopkeeper, the dress, and the taxi driver in a caption about the day on Instagram. The post had garnered thousands of likes overnight, and the comments section was teeming with activity. "I think you are inspiring many to visit Pakistan and showing us all of its beauty!" and "Thanks for coming to Pakistan and representing the beauty of Pakistan," wrote people whose usernames I did not recognize. Hundreds more shared words of gratitude and respect.

Over the past few weeks, my videos and photos from Pakistan had started attracting a lot of attention. I had switched off Instagram notifications a few weeks earlier when a barrage of loud pings assaulted my phone at night following a particularly popular post and woke me up. It was becoming a regular occurrence, and I watched the comments pour in, feeling at once horrified and mesmerized.

Because of the popularity of these posts, I was becoming a minor sensation in the world of Pakistani travel media: a young *gori* ("white girl") traveling across Pakistan and telling the world about the human kindness and natural beauty she encountered along the way. For me, it felt like I was letting people around the world in on a precious secret, and for the Pakistani media it was the perfect story to help with the mission of redeeming the country's tarnished image. Inadvertently, through my adventures and evident love for the country I had created the perfect PR tool to show people everywhere that Pakistan was ready to welcome tourists. Without realizing it, I had come to Pakistan at just the right moment.

I scanned the comments beneath the photo of the purple dress, liking and responding to as many as I could in quick succession, until a notification popped up: "This action is blocked: Instagram has detected spam activity on your profile. Try again later." I had successfully spammed my own page with thank-you notes. This outpouring of love and gratitude felt so good. It validated me on a level that had hitherto been hidden from me; I had never experienced this feeling before.

Invitations to come on live talk shows and radio programs started pouring in, and I lapped them up, drawn in by the special treatment and the intense sensation of being wanted and needed. "Thank you so much for loving our country and promoting our country to tourists online," a much-loved TV anchor said to me on a morning show that aired across the country. "*Shukria*, thank you." I smiled in response, thanking him in Urdu, my face plastered with a thick layer of over-the-top makeup that the show producers insisted I wear for the cameras. With the knowledge that this was going out to millions of people, I was so nervous that I was trembling. All I could do was hope that the cake-like foundation would mask my red and anxious cheeks and keep smiling until it was over.

Riding on the high of this burgeoning internet fame, I had good, if slightly naive, intentions, and I was utterly captivated by the country. But what I wasn't yet ready to admit to myself was that the positive response I had been getting was stroking my ego. My social media popularity was making me feel like I was needed, and for my shaken sense of self, this proved to be the greatest compliment I could have wished for. But other people's approval was a shifting foundation to prop your self-esteem on, and where you built towers one day, on another day you would find nothing but quicksand.

"Good morning," murmured Nadir as he turned around to spoon me, his voice still hoarse from a long sleep. "What are you up to?"

I shut off my phone and turned toward him. "Oh, just another post going crazy. I think I gained, like, five thousand followers since last night."

"Mmm, that's great, baby. I'm happy for you."

The warmth of his body felt like home. I buried my face in his neck and closed my eyes again. Nadir was no stranger to fame. Here I was, a minor internet celebrity, sharing a bed with a *real* superstar. His musical career had taken him to all corners of the world, performing on massive stages in front of tens of thousands of people. And although I loved listening to his wild rock 'n' roll stories, one of them had struck a particular chord with me. "When you're on the stage, performing for all these people who love you and your music, and they're all singing along to the songs you wrote . . . it's just the greatest high. There is nothing like it," he'd told me once, his dark eyes lit with excitement. "But then the concert comes to an end, the music dies, and you go back to a silent hotel room, completely alone."

Whether you were a rock star or a social media sensation, one truth remained constant: fame was a fickle mistress.

"Eva," Ali, a new friend, exclaimed on the phone in his typically loud, assertive tone. "The prime minister wants to meet you."

"Huh? What are you talking about?" I blurted out. "Do you mean *the* prime minister? Imran Khan?" I was baffled. Why would the prime minister of Pakistan want to meet me?

"Yes, Imran Khan, who else! Give me a few days to confirm everything, but . . . you're in, right?"

I had met Ali during my travels across Pakistan. He was deeply involved in the endless and difficult work of making Pakistan seem like a friendly tourist destination, though it remained unclear to me whether he was doing this to profit his own businesses or as some kind of tourism tsar working on behalf of the government. Naturally, the content I was creating for social media slotted nicely into his strategic plans, and he approached me now and then with various esoteric ideas. I always took his grand visions with a grain of salt.

"I mean . . . yeah, I guess I'm in." I hesitated. "But why would Imran Khan want to meet some YouTuber?"

"The prime minister is very excited about travel vloggers coming to Pakistan. He really believes you guys can bring tourism to the country. He wants to hear you out."

After hanging up, I got on with my day. But a few days later, the phone rang again.

"The meeting is scheduled!" Ali said. "I'll send you all the details. It's gonna be great!"

The next thing I knew, I was sitting in a large, wood-paneled hall in one of Islamabad's government buildings, alongside a few other travel vloggers who had been putting Pakistan on the tourist map. I'm sure we were all wondering how on earth we'd ended up getting a formal audience with the prime minister of Pakistan.

When Imran Khan finally walked into the room, we all stood at attention like schoolkids eager to please a notoriously strict teacher. A few stiff greetings followed. We sat down again and listened to the prime minister give a short, unconvincing diatribe about the importance of travel media in bolstering tourism in Pakistan. I wondered whether he cared about what he was saying and whether any of the bold plans he raved about would ever come to fruition. Each of us travel vloggers gave a short, complimentary summary of our experiences in Pakistan, the prime minister nodded in approval, and that was that. When the meeting ended, I felt deflated and underwhelmed, like I had been turned into an unwitting puppet for the sole gratification of a corrupt politician.

As far as I was concerned, tourism in Pakistan blossomed not thanks to government officials but in spite of them. It was all due to the hard work and genuine intentions of ordinary people—like Pervaiz Posh and his family, and the shopkeeper who'd lent me the purple dress—that tourists felt welcome in this country. Meanwhile, government officials took bribes that allowed rich businesspeople to build unsustainable hotel infrastructure and shy away from the many responsibilities they should have undertaken to protect local culture. But I knew it was not my place to say those things as a mere passerby. As our little group posed for a photograph with the prime minister, I felt more than ever that I was unintentionally playing the role of a PR mascot, and I wasn't so sure I liked it.

Although the meeting itself had made very little impact on me, the photograph we took with Imran Khan would make an impact—whether I liked it or not. A few of us uploaded the picture to Instagram, and the people of social media quickly took up arms and divided into camps.

One camp was convinced that the prime minister had put himself in harm's way because we were all foreign spies, waiting for an opportunity to get our hands on sensitive government information. Another camp accused us all of being on the payroll of the Pakistani government and, therefore, being the puppets of whatever corrupt officials were steering our narrative. Some of the allegations were more outrageous than others, but it became clear that many took offense at the country's precious resources, in the form of the prime minister's time, being wasted on a group of foreign vloggers. "These people should get a real job!" I read over and over again. I suppose, in a way, they had a point. Some went as far as to suspect me of being on the Pakistani government's payroll, or pushing a political agenda. Although it was unpleasant to be on the receiving end of criticism, I managed to rationalize myself into ignoring most of the comments.

However, there was one strand of the social media debate that did end up gnawing at me. "Why are all these vloggers foreigners?" some voices on social media asked. "Shouldn't the Pakistani government be making an effort to recognize Pakistani vloggers? This is white privilege at its worst!" This perspective quickly multiplied and soon had a viral moment of its own, as local bloggers, including my friends, shared it across social media. It was true: none of the guests invited to Imran Khan's office were locals. For all of us, Pakistan was simply one of many stops on our journeys. And though some of our pit stops were longer than others, none of us were Pakistani, and none of us had any real stake in the country's future.

My knee-jerk reaction was to defend myself. The idea that I had been invited to an official meeting just because I happened to be a white travel vlogger stung my pride. The part of me that relished all the social media praise and attention refused to believe that my success had anything to do with my background or privilege or how I looked. It was all down to my own effort, a little bit of luck, and the kindness of the people around me. I began to justify it all to myself because I had been working so hard to create content that few other people made. I had put myself out there to travel the country, to capture some of its stories, to share those stories with the world. *What* privilege?

But no matter how much I tried to distance myself from these newly forming critiques, I couldn't deny that they had awoken another, deeper voice inside me, a voice that cast doubt on my justifications. The social media bubble that I existed within had started to leak. It would burst soon enough, and my views on what it meant to be a traveler in today's world would shift forever.

chapter nine

kalashnikov street

The October nights were drawing on, and on our journey to the remote land of the Pashtuns the darkness we drove through was absolute. Only the occasional headlights of passing cars and the sudden ascents that made my ears pop helped me to discern that we were in the hills. We were driving into the now-former Federally Administered Tribal Areas (FATA), the area in which Malala Yousafzai, the Pakistani educational activist, was born and ultimately shot for wanting to continue her schooling.

The FATA is a subsection of the Khyber Pakhtunkhwa (KPK), a region of Pakistan bordering Afghanistan that for seventy years was a semiautonomous region with its own set of laws. It is widely considered to be one of the most dangerous regions in the world, with frequent clashes between the Pakistan Army and the Taliban, and various other terrorist groups. There are only a few pockets of KPK that have been deemed "cleared" of terrorist activity by the Pakistan Army and that tourists are allowed to travel to, and they are stunningly beautiful.

Most areas, however, like the one we were traveling through the night to, were still off-limits to foreigners, except for the rare journalist traveling in a military convoy similar to mine. Even among Pakistanis, it's a place that most people would shake their heads at with fear. On my travels there, I would find that I was the first foreigner whom many of the younger generations had ever seen in real life.

The meeting with Imran Khan, and the backlash it had provoked, had offered a new, uncomfortable perspective on my travels, and despite many of the comments striking me as unnecessarily spiteful, it was something I was doing my best to understand and appreciate. This wasn't particularly easy to do, as I hadn't yet seen where that perspective originated with my own eyes. All the while, my YouTube channel had continued to gain traction, and I'd been invited to host a small-scale travel show. I had no experience presenting in any formal capacity and was still trying to wrap my head around talking to my own camera, let alone a camera with an entire crew behind it.

Our brief was to travel to the four borders of Pakistan—Iranian, Chinese, Indian, and, finally, Afghani—and explore the more remote pockets of Pakistan along the way. I knew this documentary would be an opportunity like no other to see more of the country and to gain access to places that were typically out of bounds. My crew was Pakistani, which meant I would be able to sneak into these areas on their permits. Though I was worried I might not have the eloquence and insight of a seasoned travel presenter, I sincerely hoped I would be able to learn along the way. As an aspiring travel filmmaker, I needed all the experience I could get. And despite the fee being underwhelming, given the intense time commitment required, not to mention the danger involved, it was something. My channel wasn't bringing in any money yet, and any cash was much needed if I wanted to continue my travels. So there I was, driving through the night in lawless tribal areas and wondering whether accepting the offer to host the show might not have been the wisest decision after all.

Pashtuns, the people who traditionally inhabit this region of KPK, are the second-largest ethnic group in Pakistan and one of the largest ethnic groups in Afghanistan. Also known as Pakhtuns or Pathans, they speak a branch of Indo-Iranian known as Pashto (as well as Dari in Afghanistan and Urdu in Pakistan). They live in a very traditional, conservative way and abide by the traditional code of conduct called the Pashtunwali, a code of honor that defines most areas of their lives. As I ventured deeper and deeper into their territory, it felt necessary to remind myself that almost all Taliban were Pashtuns, but not all Pashtuns were Taliban.

One of the most important tenets of the Pashtunwali is hospitality, known locally as *melmastia*, and there is an anecdote that's often told by Pashtuns: even if your mortal enemy knocks on your door, a good Pashtun will welcome him, feed him, and make him feel like the most important guest he's ever had. Dangerous as this area might be, I felt secure in my hopes for a good meal.

I spotted a road sign indicating that Kabul was only 150 miles away. Our proximity to Afghanistan, a country that had long captivated me, raised every hair on my body like a magnetic force. I turned on the radio in the hope of catching an Afghani station, but the finder only rushed through the frequencies without stopping, over and over again. There was nothing here. No phone reception, no radio, no lights. We were in no-man's-land.

My status as a white woman in no-man's-land had ensured that we would have a military escort at all times. The makeup of the escort had already changed three times on our journey. In the city of Peshawar, there were three army SUVs with us. When we left the city, two SUVs filled to the brim with levies accompanied us. Now that we were deep in FATA, there was just a single sedan ahead of us, a civilian car. You'd imagine the intensity of our escort would have been the other way around, but a civilian car wouldn't attract as much attention as a military convoy and, perhaps counterintuitively, actually made our passage safer.

Our destination was a remote outpost not far from the Afghan border where the local assistant commissioner, Mr. Imran, had agreed to be our host for the next couple of days. We arrived at his house to find it was a gated compound secured by a number of guards. After having our documents checked, we drove through an imposing gate comprising a huge stone wall that stood about twenty feet tall and a reinforced metal barrier with sharp, foot-long metal spikes at the top.

Imran was new here, having started only the week before. I tried to imagine who, if anyone, had been here before him because when we entered the once-palatial mansion, it was immediately evident that it had fallen into disrepair after years of neglect. The house was filled with framed photos of important dignitaries and celebrities from the past, all of whom had visited the mansion in safer times—including, I was told, Princess Diana. We were taken into a huge, hall-like space, where male servers offered us sweet grapes imported from Afghanistan, now only about ten miles away. Because KPK was so conservative, no woman would be allowed to work in someone else's house.

Imran was originally from Swat, the pine- and cedar-filled valley that I had just visited with Nadir. He had a sudden, forceful laugh that he erupted into every once in a while. He was easily amused, but as we chatted, I grew to feel that he had the countenance and mannerisms of someone who was very uncompromising and accustomed to being feared. I noticed a ring on his wedding finger, but we never saw his wife.

As we waited for dinner, I looked around the vast room, noticing more framed photos of VIPs. On the surface, things looked rather grand, but on closer inspection, there were more signs that this place had seen better days: peeling paint in the corners, dust on top of shelves and frames, and a couple of buzzing, flickering lights.

Trying not to let the lights' death rattle distract me from the feast we were being served, I fixed my eyes firmly on the table. In accordance with the local culture, important guests were welcomed with a variety of dishes, and, true to form, we were served beef, chicken, and Afghani pilau rice. While we ate, Imran and I talked through the notion of a jirga, which was a Pashtun tribal council that made decisions and settled disputes by consensus and according to Pashtunwali, the Pashtun social code. I was scheduled to be attending a jirga—traditionally an all-male assembly—the next day. As if sensing my trepidation about partaking in such a traditional, conservative ceremony, while dessert was being served, Imran suggested he get a headscarf for me. I recoiled a little bit, suddenly feeling culturally out of my depth, but got the message and said, "I will bring my own, thank you." *Note to self: put on a longer shirt tomorrow to cover up your jean-clad European bum, button it all the way up, and do not forget the dopatta headscarf.*

I sat chewing dry sponge cake for a few minutes, waiting for the kahwa, a traditional green tea with sugar, to be served. "After kahwa you are free to retire to your quarters, if you like," Imran said.

I decided to seize this opportunity immediately and asked for the kahwa to be delivered straight there. Thanking my host, I left the dining hall and went straight to my room, which looked like it hadn't been swept in decades. The toilet didn't work, and the water inside it was as black as the night outside. There was dirt and hair on the soap and all over the sink. There was also half the body of a gecko sticking out of the only wall socket—electrocuted as it tried to climb inside. I decided my best course of action was not to touch anything.

There was a knock on the door.

"Hi, Eva," Zayer, the documentary's director, said quietly as he came in. "Just remember, don't post anything from here, okay? We don't want to attract any unwanted attention. This place is still really volatile, and you never know who's watching."

Earlier that day, I had excitedly posted an Instagram Story from our long drive. I teased my audience, sharing just a few snippets of what I assumed were unidentifiable stretches of land. "Guess where I am!" I'd written. "No tourists ever come here . . . But we have VIP access." My excitement at being here was emboldened by our military escort.

"No, of course not. I won't say anything," I assured him, adding, "Those Stories I posted, I don't think anyone will guess their location. It could be anywhere."

"Well, you'd be surprised. Just . . . don't show anything else, please."

Zayer was concerned for our safety and had expressly forbidden me from live-posting our locations. I felt like he was going overboard with all the safety precautions. I had never experienced any hairy situations in Pakistan, and since we had security, what else was there to worry about? I was convinced that the world was a good place and, having crisscrossed Pakistan over many months now, I had started to feel a sense of naive invincibility in my travels.

Frustrated with Zayer and what I perceived to be his attempt at controlling me, I huffed into my sleeping bag and called Nadir, hoping he would reassure me. But his voice on the other end of the line sounded stilted and indifferent, as it often did when I was away.

"I was worried sick, you didn't send me a single text today," he admonished me. "I had no idea if you were safe."

To have someone worry about me should have been comforting, but Nadir's tone was cold, accusatory. I hadn't had access to a cell signal for most of the day, and with such an intense filming schedule, I hadn't had time to ask anyone to use their local phone. No matter how many times I would explain this over the many weeks I was out filming, our conversations always ended up falling into the same pattern: Nadir felt left out and forgotten, and I felt guilty and torn between wanting to be a good partner and satisfying my newfound love of the road. As a result, we had already broken up several times, our perspectives clashing so hard that they often felt impossible to reconcile. But we kept getting back together. The same fire that pushed us apart engulfed us whenever we saw each other again.

After we hung up, I was left feeling more demoralized than before I'd made the call. I lay there staring at the fan on the ceiling, wondering if Nadir was going to end things with me the minute I went back to Islamabad and just didn't want to do it over the phone. It had been getting complicated between us: I was traveling more frequently, and with this new hosting gig, I would be away even more. I could understand his jealousy and frustration at being, in a sense, left behind. But I still hadn't fully healed after the breakup with Leo, and the visceral hunger I had to keep traveling had only increased. As I curled up in my sleeping bag, I couldn't help but wonder whether our relationship was doomed. I couldn't shake the image of the gecko somewhere in the dark corner of the room, electrocuted as it attempted to cross a new boundary. Cooped up, I spent the rest of the night dreading what was starting to feel inevitable between Nadir and me.

The next morning, I woke up and shook our conversation from the night before out of my mind. I wanted to focus on where I was, reminding myself that I was here to work, and that this was likely to be a once-in-a-lifetime opportunity.

After breakfast, my crew and I were taken to film in the local market of Landi Kotal, a sheltered mountain town, the last Pakistani town before the Afghan border six miles away. The streets there were lined with cars, pickups, vans, vendors, and men milling about in the traditional dress of *shalwar kameez* and *pakol* caps. Telephone wires were slung low between the concrete buildings, which often sported colorful balconies and windows, with the occasional fruit seller calling from below.

From the main street it appeared as if there was only a single row of buildings there, but our security pointed us toward a tiny staircase going down into what looked like a darker, almost subterranean section of town. I descended and found myself in a bustling market full of sellers and their wares—from dangling animal carcasses and the odd goat's head to a rainbow of spices and imported goods—all tucked in between buildings and hidden from sight. Like the compound we were staying in, the grounds on which the jirga would later take place and almost every home we passed—everything in this region, seemingly—was hidden behind walls. Pashtuns wanted to protect the modesty of their women in their homes and, conveniently for any Taliban members, tall walls were also a way for people to potentially hide away and not be seen within gated compounds.

We filmed in the labyrinthine streets, often followed by a large and curious audience. While I salivated over some of the street food, I received an invitation to try a shinwari tikka (goat liver cooked in tomatoes) in a local shop. Idrees, the handsome man who invited me in, was young, maybe thirty years old, and wearing a white shawl and a white *pakol* cap. He spoke good English and was keen to talk to me about Landi Kotal, the region, and the traditional food we were eating. He was hoping to set up his own business and supply solar electricity to the market.

The cameras started rolling as we sat down for a chat.

"I haven't seen any foreigners in Landi Kotal since maybe 2005," he told me as he offered me kahwa, in a typical small, flat white cup.

"When I saw you at the market, I needed to invite you in," he continued. "I thought, 'She has to come and eat.' You will tell people around the world that we are good people. It's a good message for us. I feel very happy."

We left, offering payment that was vehemently refused, and continued into what felt like the heart of the bazaar's maze. Turning into a street where all the shops had glass windows, I quickly realized that all of their displays were of ammunition belts, gun cases, and, of course, shelves stacked high with guns and bullets, too. Many of the weapons in the windows were either Russian or American in origin, stolen by or perhaps sold through the armies warring in the region. And, as it turned out, we were on what was colloquially known as "Kalashnikov Street."

To see so much weaponry lying around so casually in shopwindows, and even more slung across people's chests as they walked past, was unsettling. These guns in front of me had the potential to annihilate an entire population, and they were so easily accessible—any passing shopper could go in and buy a machine gun on a whim, provided they had the capital. My eyes took in the weapons on display, their sharp edges and glistening finishes, and I felt a shudder run through my body. I had a hunch that nobody would ask for your ID or do a background check if you went in hoping to buy a bazooka (which, by the way, were also for sale).

Inside these shops, we encountered old men with long beards sitting and sipping kahwa while they chatted with one another. This was the very picture of the so-called Kalashnikov culture, as the local prevalence of AK-47s and other armaments was termed, as well as the role these weapons played in the continued breakdown of civil order in the region. The Kalashnikov culture was a direct result of the ongoing wars across this region, and of many people's desire to defend themselves and their families. For context, there was infinitely more choice with regard to guns than there was with regard to food at the market.

As our tour of the market came to an end, we were guided to a rooftop where a charcoal-filled grill was burning, filling the air with the thick, familiar scent of barbecue. I stood looking out at the town, its streets illuminated in bright sunshine. I watched a young boy pushing a wooden cart full of watermelons. Local traffic, people walking around the streets buying and selling wares—there was nothing out of the ordinary about this picture if you zoomed out. When you looked closer, you saw that many people had machine guns slung casually over their shoulders. And there was not a single woman anywhere to be seen.

That I was being given access to all of these traditionally male spaces felt like a huge honor, but I was also starting to appreciate that this was indicative of the kind of privileges that only a *foreign* woman would receive in these parts. As I stood there, I couldn't help but wonder whether I would have received the same royal treatment if I had been a local. The answer was, "Probably not."

I could have remained there for hours, absorbing the calm pace of the most dangerous place in the world, but we were hurried on to our next appointment, the jirga. As we set off on our way out of Landi Kotal, a man waved happily at me from the street and sent a big smile my way. Then I spotted one woman in the back of a pickup, dressed in flowing black robes, her face completely covered.

chapter ten

selfies with tribal elders

I entered the garden where the jirga would be held: leafy and manicured, it felt like an oasis of peace compared to the streets of Landi Kotal. The camera crew followed me, and a group of men gathered in the garden immediately shuffled away from us to another corner, not wanting to be overheard. The men were the elders of various tribes, their caps adorned with rich fabrics to make up large turbans, which signified tribal associations. These men would constitute the tribal court session I was about to witness.

Imran confided that this would be his first jirga in this particular area, as it was his first week in his new post. “I’ve conducted thousands in other places,” he rushed to add, with the camera and crew as his audience, keen to make a good impression.

He led me toward a large circle of seated men and asked me to sit down to his left. I was now part of the jirga circle. The man on my right pointed at me, speaking in Pashto. I immediately sensed that he had a problem with my being there, and I watched as Imran said something back to the man. Imran then turned to me to translate the interaction. "This man has taken offense at your presence here." We were off to a good start, then. Feeling a crowd of eyes fixated on me, and my cheeks turning crimson, I wanted to shrink, to disappear somewhere beneath the ground I was sitting on. All of a sudden, I felt the heavy weight of being the only woman in a place designed for, and by, men. The air felt suffocating.

"Should I leave? I can leave if it's more appropriate," I whispered to Imran while making gestures at Zayer to alert him to a potential issue.

"No, please. You are my guest. Don't worry about it." Imran turned to the man in question and spoke with him for a moment. Tension hung in the air. As Zayer walked over, Imran explained what had happened.

"Relax, just stay," Zayer urged me. A few seconds later, the jirga began, and I had to work to prevent my gaze from dropping to the ground in discomfort and shame.

The matter being discussed that day was a money dispute. One tribe had detained the member of another tribe, someone's father, because that tribe owed them a large sum of money. The money owed was for a digger, and the claimants argued that this was worth $60,000. However, during the course of the jirga, it transpired that the machine was worth much less, and the lender had added on interest over the years, which was un-Islamic in principle and therefore disallowed by the assembly.

The elders took turns standing and expressing their views over the course of the jirga, which lasted over two hours in this instance, though jirgas could last several days—swift compared to a traditional court system. The elders stood in white, green, cream, and brown *shalwar kameez*, sometimes complemented by exquisite shawls, and gesticulated regarding the matter at hand.

They were all confident and well-spoken, their pace measured. But more eye-catching even than the men's outfits was the row of machine guns that had been placed on the grass in front of the elders. I wasn't sure if they were loaded or just symbolic of the power these men could wield when they wanted to.

"Why are the guns here?" I asked Imran.

"They put their guns down to guarantee that the verdict is consensual," he replied.

I should have been completely out of my depth there. I was the only foreigner, the only non-Muslim, the only person wearing Western clothes, and, of course, the only woman there. But my apprehension started to dissipate as I continued to observe the proceedings. I was watching an ancient ritual in motion, a social practice that had been a part of the Pashtun way of life for centuries. My ears tuned in to the harsh sounds of the Pashto language; my eyes opened wide, taking in the posturing, the energy, the gestures of the elders. Focusing on their body language and tone, I did my best to decipher how the proceedings were progressing. I was witnessing something that was normally out of bounds for travelers, as though I had opened a book of secrets that showed me all the different ways to live life. And with every new page, my little mind was expanding. I was hungry to learn more: from these elders, from other people, from everyone.

Mercifully, there was no cause to find out whether the piled-up machine guns were, in fact, loaded as the jirga came to an end. The verdict was accepted calmly. But then I noticed the elders looking at me, as if trying to make sense of my presence. I smiled in an attempt to mask my concern that I might have inadvertently done something to offend them. I quickly straightened my headscarf and pulled down the hem of my shirt to appear as "modest" as I possibly could, but they continued to look at me with what felt like distrust.

My welcome there had felt precarious from the start and, by all appearances, it seemed to have now expired. I was moving to find my crew and let them know that I should get out of there, when one of the elders came up to me, looking stern.

"Welcome," he said in English. Sizing me up and squinting, he looked like he had something very serious to communicate. I took a deep breath as he opened his mouth again. "Can we take a selfie?" he said.

Relief. Exhale. *Did not expect that.* "Yes, of course." I smiled as more and more elders gathered around me to take photos. It seemed my presence there had been a novelty for us all.

We eventually packed up our camera gear and headed back to Islamabad. En route, we stopped in a small village, our army escort now reduced to a couple of vehicles following lazily behind us. Zayer got out to buy some batteries in a local store. I followed him out of the car to get some fresh air.

As I stood there, head to the sky, a man approached me, wearing traditional Pashtun dress. "*Assalamu alaikum*," he greeted me, and then asked, "What are you people doing here?"

"*U alaikum salam*," I responded, adjusting my headscarf. "We are filming a travel documentary about Pakistan. We were just filming a segment here in Khyber Pakhtunkhwa."

"I see," he replied. "And how was it?"

"Everyone's been so kind and welcoming," I said, smiling. "It's been wonderful."

He looked at me knowingly and then said, "You know, if we went to your country, you would not be so welcoming to us."

I was stunned into silence. How did you respond to something like that? I knew that, unfortunately, this man was right.

"Your armies came here and destroyed this region," he continued. "You took everything away from these poor people. You bombed our houses and our schools. I lost my whole family to your war."

I had never heard anyone in Pakistan speak so candidly before. Everything he was saying was true. There was no way I could deny it, or would want to. "I'm sorry," I replied. "War is senseless. I'm really sorry about your family."

As I heard these hollow phrases come out of my mouth, I knew that there were no words to right any of the many wrongs done to his people. No words could bring any comfort to this man, who had lost everything in the past few decades of conflict.

"Good luck with your documentary," he replied, turning away.

This was the first and last interaction of this kind that I had in Pakistan. I could feel his pain, and I appreciated everything he said. Considering the circumstances, this man had been restrained in his words to me. The wars had ripped this whole region apart, and the aftershocks continued to ravage the local communities to this day.

I turned his words over in my mind—*if we went to your country, you would not be so welcoming to us*—and thought of the many people escaping this conflict, turning to the West, which was largely responsible for it, only to be dismissed at the European borders, often beaten by European border guards and humiliated. And yet here I was, a European woman receiving royal treatment, protected from every possible eventuality, in the very area where people had been fighting for their lives and living in fear.

It began to dawn on me that the social media comments I had previously seen as hateful were, in fact, spot-on. As a foreigner, I *was* being treated differently. The standards that applied to local women did not apply to me—if my dopatta slipped, my life could go on as if nothing had happened. To most of the people living there, I might as well have been from a different planet: free to visit as a guest, to exchange a few sentences, and then to fly off to my home in another galaxy. I could not pretend to understand what it was like to live in Pakistan as a local embroiled, directly or indirectly, in the conflicts and complexities of this region.

I had thought I understood this place so well. I had thought that my infatuation with the country was enough to justify my media success there. But I hadn't thought deeply enough, because when you find yourself in a position of privilege, your mind quickly identifies a million reasons why you deserve to be there: it's thanks to your original ideas, your unique perspective on the world, your wisdom and insight, and all your hard work. All of those things may be true, but they often hinge on the hard-to-swallow reality that the circumstances you were born into will always dictate the barriers, or lack thereof, that life will put in your way.

Of course, I didn't choose to be born with a Western passport. But in the world as it stood at the time, holding this very powerful document in my hand meant that I could cross almost any border, visit practically any country in the world. A strong passport was equivalent to winning the geographical lottery, and most Western travelers took this for granted. This life-changing symbol of entitlement that I could hold in the palm of my hand became a humbling reminder of a world divided by politics but inhabited by ordinary people who wanted nothing more than to have a decent life.

I had been so arrogant as to think myself invincible here, in one of the most volatile regions in the world. Something as simple as an Instagram post revealing our location could have posed a genuine threat to our entire crew. Militants who were active in the region as a direct result of Western political meddling could have easily taken advantage of my being there to make a flashy media statement, or kidnap me in exchange for ransom. And could I have blamed them? Their actions would have been a natural reaction to the chaos that had been unleashed upon their homeland. In my hubris, I could have endangered not only myself but my team and the military escort who had been assigned to protect us.

Reflecting on my time in Pakistan's tribal areas, I was struck by just how much of a privilege it was for me to be there. People had gone out of their way to welcome me into their homes and make me feel like a special guest—all that, in an area so deeply wounded by decades-long conflict. It was humbling to think back on every single act of kindness I'd experienced while traveling across Pakistan, the generosity far beyond anything I had known back home. These were profound lessons in human kindness that left me with the conviction that most people in the world were good people, and that the world was nowhere near as dangerous and threatening as we were sometimes led to believe.

When I'd accepted the invitation to host this TV show in Pakistan, I could never have anticipated how much this trip would inform, change, and mature me. As we approached the end of filming, I imagined returning to Islamabad, to Nadir, and experienced a sense of foreboding. Every single trip I made seemed to put another dent in our relationship, and deep down I knew this one would be no different. I wondered whether I would even have the opportunity to tell him about everything I had learned out there, to share my thoughts and insights; my sadness, wonder, confusion, and hope; my newfound appreciation for this country. Or whether we would simply clash, again, over perceived misdemeanors and petty misunderstandings.

chapter eleven

how to buy horses in mongolia

I recognized the dusty track that wound its way toward the camp and the *gers*—traditional Mongolian dwellings sometimes known as yurts—that lined the hillside. I pulled my belongings from the car and absorbed the view I'd stepped into, the wide, cloudless canopy a manifestation of Mongolia's other name: the Land of the Eternal Blue Sky. The surrounding hills had streaks of green grass but were otherwise barren, with no trees or even shrubs, offering a glimpse of the famous Mongolian steppe that stretched, raw and hostile, for thousands of miles in every direction. A small herd of horses stood grazing, their long tails lifted by an ancestral wind. The air smelled like freedom.

I was back in my soul spot, a place where I'd once felt an inexplicable, profound connection that defied time and space. The moment I arrived there, I felt like I'd come back to a long-lost home, a place in which I would have the time and space—in every possible sense of the word—to recalibrate after the inevitable breakup with Nadir. I had spent a year in Pakistan, traveling, learning, loving, but in the end, when Nadir and I parted ways, I knew it was time to leave.

As soon as I was out of it, I could see that our relationship had been a passionate love affair with all the hallmarks of toxic co-dependency. I had tried to divide my attention between living my dream as a travel filmmaker and navigating a semi-long-distance relationship, but had ultimately found myself controlled by a man who in theory loved what I did, but in practice struggled to cope with the reality of my being gone, traveling solo, so much of the time.

The relationship had been the antithesis of everything I'd had in mind for myself when I'd left London the year before. By the end of our time together, we were seesawing violently between blocking each other on social media one day and falling into each other's arms the next, promising never to leave again. We talked about getting married, then broke up a few hours later. We drove each other to such depths of madness, our fights becoming more and more heated, and the words exchanged cutting deeper every time. In the flames of what felt like passionate hatred toward each other, we said things we did not mean, but those charges branded us forever. We split up but then got back together at least once a month, and, for a long time, we could not untangle ourselves from this rhythm. A part of me didn't want to let go, because letting go would mean giving up. And to give up would mean failure. I would have failed at yet another relationship.

But breaking up had felt inevitable for a reason, and eventually we said goodbye for good. I moved my things out of his place, shipped them to my mom's house an entire continent away, and vowed not to return to Pakistan anytime soon. A month later, here I was, back in Mongolia, hoping to regain a sense of control over my life once again and figure out what could possibly come next. In order to do that, I knew I needed to be alone for a while. As one of the least densely populated countries on earth, this seemed like just the right place for me to find solitude and gather my thoughts in peace. At least, that was what it had offered me when I'd visited the year before, when my relationship with Nadir had still been in its infancy. But this time around, my plans looked a little different. I was in my second year of full-time travel, and I was ready for a bigger challenge.

"So you want to do a solo trek on horseback? Just you and the horses?" asked Mendee, the camp owner, looking at me sideways, as if he wanted to double-check that my decision-making had been sound. We hadn't seen each other since the summer before, when I'd spent a couple of months volunteering at the horse-trekking camp he ran near the capital, Ulaanbaatar. He looked like he was trying to assess whether I might have lost my mind since then.

"Yes," I responded hesitantly, "that's the idea. Just me, two horses, and the wilderness."

"You know, it's a little dangerous."

I nodded in agreement. I'd been imagining various scenarios since deciding to do the trek, and I didn't have to stretch my mind far to come up with an extensive list of what could go wrong for a woman traveling solo on horseback.

There was the distinct possibility of getting lost in the wilderness. Violent storms could block my path, trap me in a bog, hit my camp, or spook my horses. A tree could collapse and crush my tent. Someone could steal my horses. A wild animal could get into my food at night. I could get surrounded by a pack of hungry wolves intent on ripping me and my horses apart. I could run into a territorial mama bear protecting her cubs. I could get attacked by a rabid stray dog. My horses could run off, leaving me stranded. I could get hypothermia, or a parasite from drinking contaminated water. My horse could break a leg. My saddle could snap. I could drown in a river.

The most likely scenarios, however, were not the melodramatic ones. "Eaten by wolves" would make for a captivating headline. I might even settle for "hit by lightning." But the most realistic threats were also the most prosaic. The most likely scenario was falling off my horse and hitting my head on a rock or breaking a bone. A physical injury could debilitate me to the point where I couldn't move and would be trapped. I could lose consciousness in the Mongolian wilderness and possibly nobody would find me for days or weeks.

I was aware of the dangers, as I'd already told Mendee, and the closer I got to my departure date, the more vivid they became in my mind. But Mendee didn't seem satisfied with my answer. "You know about that girl, right?" he asked me.

I shook my head. "What girl?"

"Very bad situation." Mendee sighed.

I pried a little more, but he wouldn't say anything else. I asked around the camp and, eventually, I got my answer. A month prior, another foreign woman, perhaps not unlike myself, had decided to embark on a solo horse trek along the same route I had in mind. Some days into her adventure, as she was camping alone in her tent, she was spotted by a man living nearby. Drunk, he stumbled into her tent. She was unable to protect herself. He raped her.

Mendee's concern for my safety was well-founded. Though tragic, the fate of this woman was not a one-off. Gender-based violence was rampant here, and Mongolian women bore the brunt of it. The country had some of the highest rates of sexual violence against women in all of Asia, with half of all women having suffered violence from an intimate partner, and one in ten girls experiencing sexual abuse before turning fifteen. Many more of these crimes went unreported.

Mongolia is hardly an outlier in this regard. The threat of sexual violence is ingrained in the female psyche everywhere on the planet. Since I started traveling solo, the two questions that people asked me the most were "Are you not scared?" and "Have you ever encountered any dangerous men?" Yes to both. In truth, fear is my loyal companion, but most of the time, it's a background hum—part of the noise I have accepted as accompanying being alive as a woman. But that fear wails like a siren whenever a man I don't know looks at me in a certain way, or whenever I find myself alone with a taxi driver or a hotel receptionist showing me to my room.

While traveling alone, I've found a number of ways to navigate unnerving situations: I've worn fake wedding bands, claimed to be waiting for my boyfriend, pretended I was on the phone with my made-up husband, shared my live location with my mom in particularly tense situations. I've rarely ventured out alone after dark and have never accepted invitations to go to parties with people I don't know, and I don't go on dates. But there's only so much a woman can do to protect herself, anticipate someone else's actions, and mitigate an encounter. In my conversations with women passionate about travel, the fear of sexual violence is always the number one reason they decide against traveling solo. It is my number one fear, too.

After hearing what had happened to this woman, whenever I thought about my trek, a palpable tension crept in, casting a shadow over my excitement. My hierarchy of concerns was revised, and I became less preoccupied with accidents and more concerned with humans. I played out potential scenarios in my mind, trying to come up with an escape plan for every eventuality. The first rule: I knew I should never admit that I was alone. If someone approached me while I was out riding, I would tell them that I was meeting friends nearby. If someone rode up to my camp in the evening, I would say that my boyfriend had just gone out for a walk and would be back shortly. If this, then that.

The theory made sense, the logic added up, and the scenarios always ended well in my head. But in practice, things could go very differently.

What if there was more than one? What if they were drunk?

I considered the different weapons I had at my disposal: two small cans of pepper spray I'd managed to smuggle into Mongolia in my check-in luggage. A five-inch knife. Money for a bribe. A metal pot.

I didn't have much trust in any of these weapons. Pepper spray would be unusable inside a tent. A stronger arm than mine could easily pull the knife out of my hand and use it against me. Money could work, but money was not an antidote to a stranger's sexual arousal. When I went over all the options, a metal pot didn't sound so daft after all.

As I entertained these scenarios, I began to arrive at an uncomfortable truth: It all came down to luck. It came down to good or bad timing and random encounters along the way. In many respects, as I could find myself leaving my safety in the hands of a stranger, I was also leaving my safety in the hands of pure chance. To my surprise, the notion that chance was dictating my safety felt, to some degree, liberating. Beyond being prepared, I would have little control over the worst-case scenario, so I was free to stop obsessing over it. At a certain point, there would be simply nothing I could do. Either it would happen, or it would not. Accepting that there were only certain things I could exert a degree of control over, I just had to trust that luck would be on my side. Some of my anxieties would prove to be justified, though.

In the here and now of the camp, my ever-expanding to-do list was keeping my uneasy mind occupied. I still had to figure out exactly what route I would be taking. I still needed to buy my horses and all my tack and equipment—including a saddle and enough food to last the whole trip. There was transport to organize, and there were basic Mongolian phrases to learn, safety protocols to figure out, and content to shoot. I knew that purchasing my horses would be comparatively easy. Still, I would need to learn how to manage them while alone in the wilderness: from handling their tack to watering and feeding them, securing them for the night, and recognizing signs of sickness, along with how best to communicate with them while riding.

Before flying to Mongolia, I had agreed with Mendee that he would sell me two of his own horses for $1,300 total. One would be my trusty riding steed. The other would be the packhorse, carrying all my gear and following along. Assuming I managed to return both horses to camp in good condition, we had agreed that Mendee would then buy them back from me for half the sum.

A small stack of US dollars later, I became the proud first-time owner of two horses. And not just any two horses. Mongolian horses were some of the hardiest, most resilient animals on earth.

Unlike most domesticated horses in the West, a Mongolian horse with an owner will remain comparatively wild. They live in vast herds and spend their entire lives outdoors. Under Mongolia's high blue sky, they travel immense distances every year as their nomadic owners move them between winter and summer pastures. They don't wear horseshoes or blankets, they don't eat hay or supplements, and they don't stay in heated barns or stables. In the summer, they stand under a blazing sun in temperatures reaching up to 104 degrees Fahrenheit. In the winter, they huddle together to survive ferocious blizzards with temperatures dropping to *minus* 40 degrees Fahrenheit. During particularly harsh winters, when the infamous *zud*—a sudden and disastrous change in weather leading to the animals' being unable to fend for themselves—hits the steppe, mortality can be extremely high. Some years, entire herds numbering thousands of horses are wiped out. Only the strongest survive, and those are the famous sure-footed Mongolian horses: robust and capable of covering long miles across the steppe without rest. After all, these are the very horses that Genghis Khan and his armies rode when they conquered Asia and Europe.

My new companions didn't exactly look like empire-conquering, blizzard-defying champions. They were a ragged pair. My riding horse was a chestnut, calm and stoic, the kind of horse that seldom breaks into a gallop, and only ever with the sole aim of catching up with the herd. The packhorse, however, had a glint in his eye that told me he was not quite as calm and collected as his friend. All black, with a mane that was half flowing locks and half mohawk, this horse had hardly been ridden. He was younger and more feral than the riding horse. *He's my wild card*, I thought as I watched him kick another horse while at camp. But I trusted Mendee to have selected the best horses out of his herd.

"Great! They look perfect," I said. "What are their names?"

"Oh, they don't have names," Mendee replied. "This one is brown. And this one is black. But you can give them names if you like."

Traditionally, Mongolians don't name their horses beyond a description of their color and markings—and there are hundreds of words to describe a horse's appearance. Also, it is said that a horse's soul should not be tethered to the earth by an earthly name. Additionally, the herds here are so large—often numbering in the hundreds or even thousands—that there are simply too many horses to name. I decided not to go against tradition—I wouldn't have wanted to accidentally tether their souls to the earth. So they remained nameless, identified as "the chestnut horse" and "the black horse."

Buyna was a man known to most people in the camp as "the crazy horseman." He was also the man Mendee had assigned to teach me how to tack up the Mongolian way. Despite having worked with foreign tourists for many years, Buyna communicated using little to no English and had seemingly little to no interest in learning any. He was two years younger than me, with a lopsided smile that never left his face, a physicality straight out of a cartoon, and a knack for getting himself into trouble. Buyna might not have been the obvious choice for a teacher, but his experience with horses was unmatched.

When he galloped across the plains, at one with the steed beneath him, it was as if he were flying, rising like a ghost on the wind. As soon as he dismounted, it was evident he had quite literally been molded by a life spent on horseback: his legs formed a neat O, as if he had walked straight out of a Western. On warm days, he rode around shirtless. On cold days, he wore the traditional Mongolian *deel*, a heavy wool tunic with a silk belt wrapped around his waist, paired with a baseball cap on his head.

We began our apprenticeship on a cold, wet August evening with Mongolian bridles, which mostly consist of a few strips of rawhide strung together in the shape of a horse's head. In order to put them on, you have to tie some knots. In order to take them off, you have to know how to untie them. This was to be my first challenge.

We sat near the tack room on that cool summer's night, practicing knots, my fingers stiff from the cold. No matter how many times Buyna showed me the correct way to tie it, I kept getting the knot wrong. "Maybe I just can't do this," I groaned.

"Do it, do it!" he replied, willfully ignoring my building despair.

I tried again and again. But the more I tried to tie his knots and the more I failed, the louder my doubts became. *Why are you even here? This is serious shit. You have no clue. You're not a real adventurer. You can't even tie a knot—what makes you think you can go on a solo horseback trek in the wilderness?*

I knew that voice had a point. I had embarked on this adventure bolstered by a huge dose of optimism. After the breakdown of my relationship with Nadir, the idea of being alone in the wild had pulled me in. I'd felt not only that I wanted to but that I *needed* to experience this level of solitude and independence. But I hadn't thought about the practicalities of how every little thing might come together. I was so enchanted by the idea of it that I didn't question whether my technical skills were on par with the adventure. Until now, I had never camped alone, and I had never ridden alone. A double whammy of solitude I had never experienced before. And in that moment, it all began to feel overwhelming,

Perhaps because he had no idea what I was saying, Buyna continued to ignore my looming nervous breakdown, and I began to find this oddly reassuring. He didn't appear worried about me. If he thought I could do it, perhaps I really could?

We spent a lot of time putting on saddles and taking them off, securing the horses to stakes and poles, practicing watering and tacking and basic horse maintenance. But what I looked forward to the most was the riding.

Twice a day, Buyna and I would head out on rides in the area. Sometimes we were accompanied by other guests or volunteers, sometimes we were alone, but we always started out with a gentle walk that warmed up to a trot, and when Buyna shot me "the look"—his eyes glistening with mischief—it was the sign that we were about to break into a gallop. "*Choo!*" Buyna shouted the universal Mongolian command for horses to pick up their pace. "*Choo*," I echoed. "*Choo, choo*." I heard the others in the group coaxing their steeds to speed up.

The sound of hooves battering the ground engulfed us as a cloud of dust rose up. I felt the wind blow through my helmet-less hair. I loosened my reins, squeezed the saddle with my calves, and rose a few inches above the seat, balancing my body with the movement of the chestnut horse. I was flying. Buyna screamed at the top of his lungs, and his voice echoed far across the steppe. I couldn't stop smiling: this was true freedom. The speed, which sent the wind rushing past my ears. The oneness I experienced with the animal beneath me. The thrill and exhilaration—that fine and electrifying line between feeling deeply alive and knowing that I could fall and perish at any moment. In that instant, my horse and I moved so fast that all my troubles wouldn't be able to catch up with me until we stopped.

This feeling seems to be universal, and the Bedouin have a saying for it: "The wind of heaven is that which blows between a horse's ears." The Mongolian proverb is "A Mongol without a horse is like a bird without wings."

To buy all my tack for the horses, I ventured to Narantuul, in Ulaanbaatar. Also known as the Black Market, it's a sprawling mini-city crammed with thousands of tiny stands with sellers from across Mongolia, Russia, and China. The horse section of the Black Market has everything anyone could possibly need for a horse in Mongolia.

When I was growing up, I could never afford to do horse riding on a regular basis, although I had been obsessed with horses since childhood. In Mongolia, though, horse riding is part of the national identity, and therefore a much more accessible pastime. Instead of leather reins, Mongolian horsemen use rope. Instead of stainless steel for the stirrups, they use copper. Everything is simpler and more rudimentary, but functional. And the world's best horsemen make do with this assortment.

As I carried my haul out of the market, wearing rubber boots, a pair of worn-out jeans, and cutoff gardening gloves, I felt like a real adventurer.

Now I just needed to plan my route. Mongolia occupies more

land than Texas, California, and Montana combined. But while the amalgamation of these three states is home to over seventy million people, in Mongolia there are three and a half million inhabitants—and some five million horses—making it the least densely populated country in the world. There's no end of space in which to roam, and hundreds of different wild trails to choose from. I was drawn to a ride that went all the way to the infamous Black Lake. The Khagiin Khar Nuur is a remote cold-water lake tucked beyond a stretch of dense taiga and treacherous bogs in the Khentii Mountains. It felt like a mystical destination that called to me as soon as I saw it on a map. In good weather conditions, it should take me five or six days to reach it.

The night before my departure, I sat by the faint light of a solar-powered bulb in my *ger* realizing, a little too late, that I had not made the smartest packing decisions. Instead of light freeze-dried hiking meals, I had opted for pasta sauce, which came in heavy glass jars—it was the cheaper choice. I wanted to have some fresh food available, but the packet of cherry tomatoes and a bag of raw potatoes added a huge amount of weight to my setup. The bags were clunky and heavy and their contents easily broken. Had I been an experienced trekker, I would have known to bring lighter, more protein-dense food and switch the packaging.

It was 11 p.m., and, to top it all off, with less than twelve hours before I set off, my lifeline—a satellite messaging device—was giving me trouble. I played around with it for over an hour until, finally, it seemed to work again. It wasn't the last time it would cause me problems.

Am I really doing this? I thought to myself, my eyes filling with tears. I didn't feel ready in any way and wondered if I could, if I should, hold off on the trek. Maybe just one extra day, or three.

Maybe I would feel more prepared if I had just a little more time. But deep down, I knew it wasn't really about the time. It all boiled down to either staying here, in the safety of camp, or heading out into the unknown.

Now, I firmly believe that when you take on big, life-changing challenges, you may never feel fully ready. When faced with something that will truly test your character, skill, and endurance, you should feel a little terrified, a little humbled. This shows that you have a healthy amount of respect for the perilous journey ahead. It may never be the right time. The circumstances may never fully align. You may never feel ready enough. But what matters is your willingness to jump. Your willingness to create the right timing, and to simply go. If you let yourself get bogged down by the weight of the planning and the prep, it can quickly grow to monstrous proportions and overwhelm you with a million small practicalities. But if you commit to a decision, then you've already crossed the threshold. You must only take the next step for everything else to follow.

Before I could change my mind, the driver and Buyna loaded my horses and all my luggage onto the truck bed. I hugged everyone goodbye in haste, barely registered their "good luck" wishes, and hopped inside. The driver started the old truck, it clunked like some medieval machine, and we rolled out of camp down a dusty trail toward the main road.

The reality of what I was getting myself into dawned on me as we left the comfort of the camp behind. Back at camp, the fantasy of going on a solo horse trek had felt like a romantic adventure. I got to role-play the hero learning the ropes, planning her route, and getting ready for a life-changing expedition. But, in fact, I'd been merely cosplaying it in the safety of my own head.

The few days of training with Buyna had afforded me some basic skills, but, truth be told, I had no idea what I would do if I ran into serious problems with my horses or my kit. My route wasn't difficult to navigate on paper, but nobody from the camp had been to Khagiin Khar Nuur that year, so I had very limited information about the conditions out there, the feasibility of crossing the muddy bogs and the dense forest. There was also the looming threat of wild animals and, worse, other humans. Added to all this, I would be camping alone for the first time in my life.

"*Gantsaaraa*?" The truck driver interrupted my spiraling train of thought.

"*Gantsaaraa*," I confirmed. *Alone*. There goes, I had not even started my trek and I'd already broken my first rule of safety: I'd told the first person I met that I was out there on my own. I could almost sense my late grandfather shifting nervously in his chair as he watched me from whatever life he was now in.

"Oh," he responded with a long, pensive sigh, as if searching for the right words to communicate something important to me. "Dangerous," he finally said in English with a heavy Russian-inflected accent.

"No, I think it'll be fine," I said with a smile that felt contorted, "not so dangerous." Perhaps I was trying to reassure myself more than I was him. Or perhaps on some level the breakup with Nadir had left me feeling so worthless that I no longer really cared what might happen to me out there.

"Hmm . . . dangerous men," he responded, and looked at me furtively. Then, using a mix of Russian, English, Mongolian, and sign language, he managed to communicate a message that I believe boiled down to this: "If a drunk man comes to your tent, you should tell him to leave you alone." Unfortunately, this (and my metal pot) was about the extent of my safety protocol.

After three hours of driving, the truck stopped at the end of the road. We were by the bank of the Terelj River, which marked the boundary between the world of roads and cars and the world of mountains and trails. There was no bridge connecting them, as if to ensure that only those with conviction in their hearts crossed between the two realms.

In order to start my trek, I had to traverse the deep, rushing waters to the other side with my horses in tow. The river looked dark and foreboding. I turned to my luggage and the horses. They seemed unfazed by the long drive and the new location. Clinging on to any shred of reassurance, I took this as a sign that all was as it should be. With the horses hitched up to a fence, the truck driver bade me farewell and drove off, leaving behind him a cloud of dust and me, standing alone, watching my last possible escape route disappear down the road.

I looked back at my trusty steeds. "Well, it's just us now, you guys," I sighed. They did not respond as I tried to get them ready for the river crossing. The saddlebags slid around and seemed poorly balanced. I needed to figure out how to prevent them from moving around. A very small part of me saw these initial troubles as portents that I should reconsider this adventure, and the idea of turning back became very tempting. I could still return to camp, citing gear issues. At camp, I would be safe again. I wouldn't have to worry about deep river crossings, or dangerous humans, or being alone. I could go on perfectly good horse rides every day guided by Buyna and spend the nights in the warm, cozy *ger*. Sure, it would be nowhere near the adventure I had set out on, but it would be comfortable. Convenient. Safe. It would be good enough.

Good enough for what? a mischievous little voice whispered in my ear. *Good enough for a perfectly comfortable, convenient little life?*

No. It wasn't good enough. I hadn't come all this way to seek comfort, convenience, and safety. I'd come here because I was seeking something greater than myself. I'd come here because I wanted to challenge myself and reach beyond the horizon of who I had been. I was not here to feel safe. I was here to be alone and to feel afraid, and to prove to myself that I could overcome it all.

I gripped the packhorse's rope in my left hand and hopped onto the chestnut horse. As we stood facing the rushing waters of the river, fed by ice and rain, I looked ahead and said, "*Choo.*"

The chestnut horse walked toward the river, stopping just before the water's edge. "*Choo,*" I repeated, "*choo,*" and swayed my hips slightly forward to encourage him to step in. We had a long way ahead of us: the opposite bank was about sixty feet away. I knew that the river could be crossed on horseback, but there was no way to know how deep it was at this time of the year. I watched as it tore past, rolling around the boulders it had been nudging down the mountains for centuries, the roar of it like a million clapping hands, urging us into the arena.

The chestnut horse took an apprehensive step forward and his front hooves became submerged in the water. Two more steps, and the water reached up to his knees. "*Choo,*" I said softly, encouraging him to go on. I looked down at my stirrups and realized we were about to go belly-deep. I lifted my feet. The swift blue-black water was already caressing the chestnut horse's belly. With every step, the river tightened its embrace on us, gathering more strength the deeper we went. The black horse followed behind, watching his companion intently for any sign of trouble. But the chestnut horse just kept going. With an air of self-assured bravery that took me by surprise, he walked instinctually through the water, as if he had traveled this route many times before. Perhaps I had underestimated this trusty little steed.

A few more steps through the water and we had reached the other side. By putting one foot in front of the other, as I'd done on the Everest Base Camp trek, we'd managed to cross the river, despite how terrifying it looked at first. There was power in tackling challenges one small step at a time.

Now we were in the world of the Gorkhi Terelj National Park and ready to start our journey in earnest. There was just one problem. Daylight was running out fast—it was already close to five o'clock, and the sun was starting to sink behind a nearby larch-studded mountain. In three hours, the sun would set and leave behind only stars, darkness, and cold. I still needed to find a suitable campsite, get the horses prepped for the night, and, in an ideal world, eat something after an entire day of accidental fasting. There had been so much to think about that I'd simply forgotten to eat.

I looked around. A short distance away, I spotted a small camp with a couple of *gers*: a perfect place to spend the night before venturing any farther—that was, assuming the owners would let me stay.

"*Nohoi horiooo!*" I shouted as I neared the camp, watching two dogs burst out of their enclosure, barking and baring their teeth. *Keep your dogs away!* This might not seem like the most polite way to greet a stranger—especially a stranger you're about to ask for shelter—but it's a necessity for travelers on horseback. Mongolian dogs will protect their herds against any intruders with ferocity, none of them are vaccinated against rabies, and I was not about to risk getting bitten. I was just hoping I hadn't mispronounced the phrase as *nökhör horiooo*, which I had the habit of doing, and which translates to "Keep your husband away!"

A shepherd raised his head from beneath the cow he was milking and called off the dogs (and not his husband, to my instant relief). He had a wide, smiling face, and his eyes lit up when he saw me. I hopped off the horse and, in my broken Mongolian, asked if I could pitch my tent at his camp. He continued smiling and, without saying a word, grabbed the ropes of my horses and led them away. I took that to mean yes. Then he pointed me to the *ger*, inviting me to enter.

I pushed open the doors, which were painted in intricate patterns in orange, pink, and blue, and was greeted by a middle-aged woman—the wife of the man outside, I assumed—and a little girl, who must have been their daughter. Entering their home, I was careful not to break any of the traditional rules of Mongolian hospitality. I was keen to demonstrate my gratitude and respect to this family. As was customary, when crossing into the *ger*, I lifted my right foot high so as to step over the door ledge, not onto it. I then turned left and walked around the room in a clockwise direction to shake the hand of my host's wife. I was relieved that there was another woman at camp, and that I would be staying with a family.

The furniture in the *ger*—a couple of beds, cupboards, and tables—was arranged around the walls of the structure, while the middle was occupied by a stove with a fire flickering inside it. Above us, on the ceiling, a series of wooden beams painted a burnt orange led toward a round window at the very top, giving a view onto the darkening sky and the many constellations it was unveiling, one by one.

The man came back inside. He introduced himself as Sukhbataar Tenjing, and before sitting down, he offered me a tsai, a creamy, salty milk tea into which he dropped a few buuz—Mongolian dumplings. Grateful for the luxury of the tea, I held the warm cup in both hands and told the couple about my plans to reach Khagiin Khar Nuur. The man gasped, said that it was very far from there, and, in a mix of Russian and English, offered to guide me all the way to the lake.

"*Bayarlaa*," I said. "*Gantsaaraa*." Thank you, but I will go alone. *Damn! I did it again*, I realized a moment too late.

The wife pointed at herself, then pointed at me with a scared expression. "*Chono*," she said, pretending to tremble. *Wolves*. She would be scared of the wolves. She pointed at me again and gave me a thumbs-up. We all laughed.

When I eventually motioned that I needed to go outside and set up my tent, the family wouldn't hear of it. Instead, Sukhbataar prepared one of the beds and, pointing at it, instructed me to sleep there. We all went to bed in our day clothes to keep warm, and at nine o'clock sharp, the solar-powered light inside the *ger* went out. As I lay there in the darkness, waves of uncertainty flashed through my mind about what the coming day's trek might hold. But the night's silence also held the loud, clear call of the unknown, which lulled me, eventually, into deep sleep.

The next morning, my hosts forced a few more cups of tsai into my grateful hands, and I squeezed a banknote into theirs. Sukhbataar helped me get the horses ready, and before I knew it, the chestnut horse, the black horse, and I were on the road again. I was ready to keep riding now, alone, and to feel like my adventure had finally begun in earnest.

chapter twelve

my *khiimori*, the wind horse

The trail I followed led me along the Terelj River, past grazing cows and barking dogs, and past a few more *ger* encampments and settlements. Every time I rode by a camp, I hoped that nobody would ask that dreaded question, *Gantsaaraa?* Alone? What if someone saw that I was alone and decided to follow me? I struggled to rid myself of these thoughts, trying hard to replace them with anything that I felt like I could actually control. *How many miles have we covered so far? Where shall we stop for lunch? What will I eat?* Keeping my mind occupied with these questions, before I knew it, I had left all settlements behind and was crossing into Mongolia's vast wilderness, inhabited by bears, wolves, and the few nomads who still chose to live in the most remote areas of the country.

The south of Mongolia is flanked by the infamous Gobi Desert, an arid and wind-swept expanse of sand and rock, where the native, twin-humped Bactrian camels roam in temperatures that have a range of about 140 degrees Fahrenheit between the seasons. The north of the country, where I was, is home to the open steppe, mountain ranges, and endless boreal forests. North of here, the majestic taiga stretches all the way into Siberia, eventually giving way to the vast territory of the Arctic. If you headed north of here in a straight line, it's not beyond the realm of possibility that you could get all the way to the Arctic Ocean, fifteen hundred miles away, without ever running into another human being. This was what I had come here for, this sense of being engulfed by the vastness of the natural world, away from loud traffic and busy streets and shopping malls and trash TV and social media. As much as it felt terrifying to zoom out and imagine myself, a tiny bundle of human flesh, roaming around such untamed, unforgiving country, what had driven me here was stronger than fear. It was the deep desire to be alone, as alone as I could possibly be, and perhaps to prove to myself that I could survive out here on my own, with nobody to guide, support, or embrace me.

Being out in these wild places, with nobody to answer to, I felt all the familiar layers of culture and conditioning begin to peel back. I became a part of the natural world, and yet the natural world remained indifferent to my struggles, my challenges, my achievements, and my mere presence. Out here, I was free to let go of the pressures of social media, which had only been increasing since my social media channels started growing. I was far from snarky comments and anxieties over engagement stats. I no longer had to worry about publication schedules, or brand partnerships, or what anyone on the internet thought about me. And, very importantly, thanks to the absolute lack of a cell signal, I could not be tempted into texting Nadir and picking up our situationship. To this landscape around me, I was just a living being that breathed in the oxygen, left footprints, and made the occasional rustle. I might as well have been the third horse in my herd. The question became not "what I am," but "whether I am." I knew in that moment that this was what freedom felt like. This, right here, was what I was searching for.

It was a sunny, cool summer afternoon that flocks of pine buntings and warblers soared through. I crossed a couple of streams and rode along an established trail. Once I got into the rhythm of the day, everything began to feel calm. In the last hours of sunlight, I finally stopped to set up camp in a wide meadow of a valley, the grass carpeted with purple Mongolian Gentiana and white edelweiss flowers that were animated by a touch from the cool breeze like a flight of butterflies. Ahead of me was a fir-covered mountain, stretched across the valley like a fallen god.

I walked up to a small rocky outcrop to pitch my tent, then watered the horses and sat down to eat and enjoy my warm tea. I'd been so distracted by all the chores and by a large bruise appearing on my hip thanks to the chestnut horse throwing me off earlier that only now did the beauty of where I was strike me. Evening was drawing near, and the whole valley was bathed in warm, golden light. My horses grazed nearby. A stream flowed through the heart of the valley, the last of the sun's rays reflecting off its surface like diamonds spilled across the landscape. Opposite me, in the distance, a mountain rose lazily from the ground, covered on one side with a lush forest, the other side barren but for a vibrant green carpet of grass. Way up ahead, somewhere in the direction where I was going, hills groaned into mountains, an endless sea of green covered the landscape, and no signs of roads or towns were to be seen anywhere on the horizon. There were no voices or sounds of traffic, only a deep and ancient silence, broken occasionally by the sounds of crickets chirping in the grass and birds singing in the nearby trees.

I had finally made it. I was alone.

The next day, I woke as the sun's first rays danced across the orange tarp of my tent. I poked my head outside. The horses were already grazing, and I was still alone, still surrounded by the same humbling landscape. I had been so exhausted from a very long day that I hadn't even had time to think up terrifying nighttime scenarios; sleep had come almost instantly.

I steadily packed up camp, gathered the horses, and started getting them ready for the road. We shadowed the river all day, and all around us rose gentle hills, some topped with giant granite boulders that took on the shapes of animals and fantastical creatures if I looked at them long enough—as was traditional in Mongolian folklore, with some larger boulders having names like "Turtle Rock" and "The Old Man Reading a Book" and "Praying Lama Rock." Traveling at the slow pace of a horse's walk, I was able to squint and bring them to life in my mind's eye. I wondered how many generations of passersby had imagined these boulders to be those same living beings.

The established trail sometimes gave way to giant meadows blossoming with tall grasses and seas of purple and white flowers, or led us straight into thick forests, where we walked between tall, whispering larch trees.

After hours of listening to the sounds of the natural world, the roar of engines jarred me, gradually getting louder and more distinct. I realized that it was coming toward me. I turned around and saw two motorbikes heading in my direction. They were closing in on me and not slowing down. The horses got spooked by the roar of their engines and bolted. The saddlebags were not made to be used at full canter, and I pictured them ripping apart. There was no way I was letting that happen. I pulled the reins and issued the calmest, most assertive "*Whoa, whoa*" I could muster, hoping to communicate the universal horse command for *stop*.

The horses stopped.

But the boys on the motorbikes didn't. They looked both entertained and confused, but I was in no mood to laugh. They had not backed off when they had seen that my horses were panicked by their loud motorbikes. And just their mere presence was enough to send my mind spiraling into anxiety. These could be kind and polite boys, for all I knew, but I couldn't take any chances. They got off their motorbikes and approached me.

Channeling all the anger and confidence I had, I yelled in English, "What the hell do you think you're doing?! You scared my horses with your loud engines; did you see what happened? Seriously, what is this?" I glared at the boys, trying my very best to look enraged. "Seriously," I repeated, "what were you thinking? What the hell!"

I didn't know whether they understood any of what I was saying, but that wasn't the point. With my whole being—my gestures, volume, and tone—I was trying to put myself in a position of power. I wanted to show these boys that I would not be messed with, and that I could stand up for myself. I knew I couldn't afford to send anyone the wrong signals out here, and that open hostility—as feigned as it might be—was my best line of defense.

It seemed to work. They both looked shell-shocked. To their eyes, I was some crazy white lady losing her mind in the wilderness. One of them looked at me apologetically and muttered, "Sorry," in English.

"*Bayartai*," I said, bidding them a curt goodbye. Without smiling once, I turned around and rode away. It didn't feel good to put on an angry show like that. It was uncharacteristic of me, and I felt guilty for staging the whole confrontation. But when your safety is on the line, sometimes you need to make choices that feel out of character in the interest of self-preservation. It was important to have these tricks up your sleeve and to know when to use them. If I had been challenged by someone more dominant than those two, I would have likely acted differently: more docile, conciliatory, appeasing. But given the age of these boys, I'd judged that I could afford to put myself in a more powerful and hostile position, leaving them with the unshakable belief that I did not wish to be approached.

A couple of hours of riding later, I spotted their motorbikes in the distance. They were riding in the opposite direction of where I was going this time, and only then did the tension in my shoulders melt away.

That afternoon, I spotted a potential campsite on higher ground, close to some giant boulders that lined the hilltops, wearing the evening mist like a necklace. It was the perfect vantage point, overlooking the entire valley but close enough to the brow of the hill that I could see over the other side. I untacked the horses first and led them down to a nearby stream, where they dropped their heads and sipped the water quietly. All was fresh air, birdsong, and the vivid green of high summer. My eyes scanned the horizon. There was no sign of human presence anywhere. I felt like I could have been the only person left in the world. If, for some reason, the rest of humanity got wiped out at that very moment, I'd be none the wiser.

I was captivated by this notion of being the only human left alive, and out there, it proved to be easy enough to believe. I'd had no cell signal at all over the past few days, and my satellite messenger had stopped communicating with the outside world that morning. As a safety precaution, I had programmed it to send regular waypoints to a map that my mom had access to. But despite my best efforts and constant tinkering, the device was now stuck on a message that said, "Make sure you have a clear view of the sky." If nothing else, I certainly had that.

I walked to the very top of the hill and climbed up on the boulders. A massive, seemingly endless coniferous forest stretched as far as the horizon. The taiga. One of the wildest ecosystems on earth, it is a vast and mysterious place: the land of winds and ice, where trees battle some of the coldest temperatures to survive. The taiga was also one of the most plundered natural habitats—logging was causing widespread destruction all across it, from Scandinavia to Siberia, with massive swathes of taiga being lost to the timber industry every year. I gazed over this immense, primeval landscape, which brought to mind the soldiers of Genghis Khan, who, hundreds of years ago, might well have stood on the very same spot and looked at the very same view. Yet it could all now disappear within a few short seasons, because of modern logging machines and humanity's insatiable hunger to build, buy, and consume.

There was power in this place. I could sense it with every atom of my being. That vast space is not an abstract view. It's an interconnected web of organisms and beings. The trees form extended families and speak to each other in a secret language we will never understand. The soil moves around on the feet of the myriad tiny insects that travel across the forest in search of food. The wind dances in between the branches and the leaves, carrying messages for the animals that live there. Wolves leave their tracks on the damp topsoil, and birds observe them from high up in the canopy. In this landscape, everything is interconnected and everything is life.

I drew it all in in one deep breath and my whole body tingled. I was overcome with a profound sense of wonder and awe. I knew I wasn't simply looking at a pretty landscape; I was looking at the manifestation of that force which is Life itself. A grand mosaic of existence, an eternal energy, a spirit of life that never ends but keeps transforming into ever-new life. The fox dies and its carcass feeds the wolf. The tree falls and offers its nutrients to the soil. The human breathes her last and, in Mongolian tradition, is left on a hilltop in a sky burial. The body falls apart and gives sustenance to the crows and vultures. I paused my thoughts. Isn't this what they speak of when they speak of immortality? Everything becomes something else. There is no death. There is merely transformation in a massive and cosmic cycle that was here long before us, and will be here long after we're gone, churning everything that once existed into everything that will ever exist. Call it reincarnation, immortality, or particle physics—in that moment it all felt like part of the same grand scheme.

As I understood this for the first time in my life, a wave of euphoria came over me. There was no need to fear anything, because life prevailed. I let out a scream, in part to double-check that I was really still there. It traveled on the breeze for a short distance but faded all too quicky, absorbed by this vast place. So I screamed again, louder this time, spurred on by my profound solitude. My voice echoed through the valley and disappeared into the vastness. I screamed once more, even louder, and as my voice ricocheted off the slumbering boulders, I pictured a red wave of fear and doubt leaving my body. Every scream purified me, and the longer I went on, the lighter I felt, like a ghost roaming these lands. I imagined that I was overcome by *khiimori*, the wind horse of Mongolian folklore, believed to be the human spirit. Just as the horse and the wind could not be tied to the earth, the same was true of the soul. I was a part of all this blossoming life, and there, in this moment, I truly felt it: *I am alive.*

This buzzing euphoria lasted well into the next day. And I knew, without a doubt, that my purpose was to follow this faint trail that plunged into valleys, pine forests, and boggy clearings to wherever it would lead me. It had rained heavily here the week before, and the mud hadn't fully dried out. Sometimes the horses' hooves dug deep into the soil, which swallowed them up to their ankles.

At a crossroads that had been marked on my paper map, the trail diverged in several different directions. To the left was a safer and more commonly frequented loop in the national park. To the right, the distant Khagiin Khar Nuur—the Black Lake I had in my mind. I remembered the words of Sukhbataar, the nomad who'd hosted me on the first night: "It's very, very far."

Given all the delays I'd experienced on day one, and the time I had spent fixing my pack issues most afternoons, I was already behind schedule—and it would take me another four days to reach the lake. The physical and mental effort of the expedition was already taking a heavy toll on me. My body was not yet used to sitting in a saddle for so many hours, so my muscles had turned sore. The physical effort that went into tending to the horses, setting up camp, sleeping on a thin pad, and repacking all the gear twice a day left me exhausted at the end of each afternoon. Not to mention the constant hum of low-level stress. I felt drained already and knew that I would want to take a couple of days at the lake to recover before turning back around. Neither the timing nor the way looked promising. Still, I turned the horses right, toward the lake.

The trail swiftly became overgrown with brush and tall shrubs. The way underfoot grew increasingly boggy, and the horses kept sinking into the deep mud. All the beautiful open scenery from the past few days felt like a distant dream. This path grew murky and narrow, and there was no relief in sight. In that moment, I wished I could have turned to a companion and asked them for advice on what to do next. But I was alone, and I alone would bear the consequences of any decision I made. Up until this moment, solitude had been nothing but a blessing. Now, however, the burden of sole responsibility began to weigh heavily on my mind.

As if on cue, dark clouds rolled in, covering the blue sky with a dense gray blanket. Thunder. The horses tensed and pricked up their ears. More thunder, at first grumbling and extended, then hitting loudly and violently. The clouds were getting thicker and darker by the minute. If we got caught in heavy rain on this boggy path, it could turn into a swamp, and then we'd be in real trouble. I had to think on my feet. I looked up at the sky. The dark clouds were rolling in our direction of travel, toward the lake. The first flashes of lightning appeared on the horizon. I turned in my saddle and looked at where we'd come from. Blue skies. The choice was easy. I turned the horses around.

Returning to the crossroads, I took the left turn this time, embarking on a loop of the national park. I didn't love the idea of changing my original route, but I knew that I needed to follow the good weather if I could, and that it could take me a week to reach the Black Lake in those boggy conditions. On this trail, the valley opened up once again, welcoming us back into its lush embrace. Small clouds cruised through the sky, and the air was calm, save for a gentle breeze that had accompanied us since the beginning of the trek. To the right, somewhere in the direction of Khagiin Khar Nuur, the storm kept brewing, lightning flashing menacingly in the distance.

It may have been the height of summer, but nighttime temperatures could plummet to bone-chilling lows. Yet the days and even the cold nights passed all too quickly. Out here, I didn't feel in control of my time at all. I felt like time was carrying me on its rolling waves, pulling me along, refusing to let me count the minutes or the hours. The day simply moved on, just as I moved on, just as the horses did. We all moved in unison, together, and to quantify this relentless onward motion as a set number of seconds in a minute would have felt like betraying the natural order.

Every now and then I ran into people, mostly local herders. It always surprised me, people living all the way out here. But in traveling to these remote places, I quickly learned that the "middle of nowhere" to one person was the center of everything to another. Keeping a low profile, I nodded at the herders and moved on without stopping for conversation. I wished I could be more social—if I had been a man, I wouldn't have hesitated to stop by for a tsai, or even a cup of airag, the local moonshine made out of mare's milk.

But I wasn't a man. And that meant I couldn't afford to take any unnecessary risks. So I rode solo and quickly learned to cherish my solitude—I was free to pursue the things that made me happy. Climbing the big boulders at sunset. Treasuring the trees that gave me respite from the sun in their shade. Observing the fresh water running in the streams, the waking light of day, the stars illuminating the night sky. Watching my horses from inside my tent in the morning. Making dinner. Wolfing it down and, every time, realizing I had been so much hungrier than I had thought.

Out here, the rules were different. I had not taken a single shower in about a week. I had not brought soap to wash with, so whenever I needed to clean my hands or face, I splashed myself with river water or rubbed my palms with grass. No soap, no shampoo, no deodorant, no shaving. I don't remember missing any of those things at any point. I didn't wear any makeup, instead letting my skin absorb the fresh air. My lips became parched and a little burned from the strong sun, but this made me feel raw and alive. I tied my hair into a simple braid. I didn't pack a mirror, so the only way for me to know what I looked like was to take a photo of myself. I wore the same clothes day in and day out, because the size of the pack didn't let me bring more than one set for daytime use and one set for sleeping.

I felt as if there was a wildling inside of me whom I'd never really gotten a chance to meet before. The things that took up so much of my time back in the city now felt superfluous. Here, I had to focus on the things that really mattered: food, water, shelter, putting one foot in front of the other. Sinking my bare feet into the long, cool grass, I realized that so many of the things I had thought mattered didn't, and that a whole new understanding of life was building within me.

I got to role-play a hermit. A feral woman. There was nothing I *had to be*, nothing I had to do. The gaze of other people could have no bearing on how I felt when there were no other people; there was no gaze—except that of my horses. In my Mongolian solitude, I was free to think of myself in relation to the natural world, to the cosmos, and not in relation to other people, to heartbreak, to disappointment, to man-made pain. I could romp around in mud-covered jeans, sing '90s pop hits completely out of tune, and stare into the distance while doing absolutely nothing, while thinking of absolutely no one. This sudden aloneness—the most intense and profound I had ever experienced—jolted me into a state of such physical, emotional, and spiritual freedom that I felt myself drawn deeper and deeper into it. *How did I ever exist among people?* I asked myself as I contemplated my dirt-encrusted nails and relished chewing on a long stalk of grass.

With no relationship to keep me tethered to another being, I felt like I had been set loose in the world. I no longer felt the obligation to exist in relation to another human, or express my emotions in a way that included someone else. I was no longer obliged to say, as I had been with Nadir, "I'm having a great time, *but* I miss you," or "I'm loving my solo adventure, *but* I wish you were here." This time, there were no caveats to every feeling, no half happiness, no unfulfilled girlfriend duties, and no guilt. I could just *feel*, without restriction, without "buts." For the first time in my life, I was free to feel *my own feelings* and not give a damn about anyone else. *How fucking liberating!*

All alone out there, I had left the very notion of loneliness behind when I set out on this journey, along with all the other social constructs I had shed, like an impractical winter coat on the first warm day of spring.

I was alone and free.

This remoteness did have its drawbacks. For several days running, I had no contact with the outside world. My satellite device still wasn't working. I wondered whether my mom was getting worried by now and I wished I had a way of letting her know I was doing fine. But, more importantly, if I ended up in an emergency situation, I wouldn't be able to let anyone know. In hindsight, I realize that fear was my constant companion. It was there just like the birdsong was there and, like birdsong, I knew I couldn't choose whether it was there or not, but I could choose whether or not to listen to it.

It's a common misconception that people who are brave are fearless. The bravest are the ones who have experienced fear to the deepest core of their being and fought through it. If courage is all about overcoming fear, then fear is the very foundation that courage stands on. The two cannot exist without each other.

A week into the trek, I was riding into another gentle morning, along a wide path. To the left of me was a long valley. To the right, a rising hill. Higher up, just above us, hundreds of white, gray, and tan cashmere goats nibbled the blades of grass beneath their hooves, and I wondered how many of them it would take to make a jumper.

I was jolted out of my daydream by the chesnut horse as we

rounded a bend. A few goats were standing around on the track. A sudden gust of wind blew in our direction, carrying their scent with it. The combination of these two factors spooked the horse. Perhaps he had never seen goats before. He bucked beneath me. I held on tight and tried to calm him. "*Whoa, whoa*," I repeated. But he threw me off his back. I fell, hitting the hard, rocky surface with an impact that I had not expected in falling from such a small horse. I felt pain spreading over my forehead, shoulder, and hip. In a state of shock, I was still holding on to the reins, trying to preserve what little control I had over the horses.

The next thing I remember, I was looking at my saddle lying in the middle of the track. I had no idea whether it had fallen off or whether I'd removed it myself, but there it was, in a neat pile. For a few confused moments, I simply walked in a circle, holding on to both horses, trying to regain my senses. All I could think in that moment was, *I am okay, I am alive*, repeating it to myself like an incantation. Then my head began to throb, and I realized I felt dizzy. I wanted to sit down, but I worried that if I did, I might lose consciousness. I was sure I had a concussion, and therefore knew that I might not be thinking straight. It was only much later, when I took a video of myself, that I realized I had been bleeding from my eyebrow. I was extremely lucky that I hadn't hit my head any harder.

Fuck. Still nothing, I thought as I looked at the screen of my satellite messenger, still stuck on the same "clear sky" message. I wished I could text someone for help. But I was still alone. And alone, I had to figure out what to do next. I looked at my map. If I traveled another thirteen miles, I could cut across a valley and reach a village with a road. I knew I needed to reach other humans. *What if I faint?* The panicked thought crossed my mind. *What if I fall asleep and don't wake up tomorrow?* I needed to be close to people who could help monitor whatever state I was in.

This, I felt, was the right option, but it would mean quitting the trek.

I stood there, battling with myself in my own head. Quitting the trek was not something I had even considered before. And yet, here I was, about to quit. About to trade in my newfound love of solitude for the company and safety of other people. I'd just had a small, tantalizing taste of what life could be when you lived away from social expectations, and that had been snatched away from me in a single buck of my horse.

The bruises on my body were nothing compared to my bruised spirit. The little voice returned. "You came out on this life-changing adventure and you're giving up because of a tiny fall?" *Weak, defective, useless*. The words I had heard in my own head so many times returned, whispering in a choir.

"No," I snapped at them. "This isn't going to be the end of me." I forced myself to turn in the direction of the village, toward people. As I plodded wearily for several hours, leading my horses behind me, I wondered whether I had made the decision to quit out of cowardice or bravery.

Once I reached the village just before sunset, I stayed in my tent at a small, informal campsite. The owners called Mendee, and he summoned the truck driver. The next day, the driver came, put my horses in the back, and grabbed my saddlebags. He opened the passenger door for me to get in.

It was over.

It took me a week to recover physically from the trek. I returned to Mendee's camp and rested and slept well, and within a couple of days, my wounds started healing and the symptoms of my mild concussion dissipated. But it took me much longer to come to terms with having ended the trek early. I existed in a limbo between sleeping and watching the chestnut horse and the black horse grazing in the pasture. I held two conflicting realities in my heart: relief at being safe and comfortable, and a visceral desire to step back into that wild version of myself I'd met in the valleys of Terelj. While I recognized that my decision had been the best one I could have made in that moment, what I regretted was having to bid an early goodbye to the awe and freedom that I'd experienced out there. I had trouble finding sense and meaning in the world outside of the trek. Suddenly, asphalt roads smelled like burnt, acrid waste. Traffic noise grated against my ears like a high-pitched scream. My professional ambitions felt like fiction.

I had spent long enough out there to make me question some of the most fundamental things I had been taught. In my twenty-eight years of living, nothing compared to this level of wonder and exhilaration. What did this tell me about my life before the trek? Were there other pockets of human experience that I had no idea existed? Emotional states I had never tapped into, that still awaited me?

I had a thirst for solitude now, and I wanted to lose myself in it again, float in its waters. After that first taste, I could have drunk a river of it. On the trek, I had peeked behind a curtain that separated the safe, conventional life from a wild, adventurous one. And I knew exactly which side of the curtain I wanted to be on going forward.

chapter thirteen

the real robinson crusoe

When I was a little girl, I learned about the story of Robinson Crusoe, shipwrecked all alone on a remote island. Since then, whenever my daydreams steered me that way, I wondered what it would be like to find myself on a desert island, living alone, at one with an island and the sea, fishing for my dinner and fending for myself as I watched the sun rise and set across an uninterrupted horizon. Beyond a love of palm trees and golden sands, enduring extreme survival situations is not your typical childhood fantasy, and, given my not-very-outdoorsy upbringing, I often wondered why this particular scenario had drawn me in.

Slowly, I recognized the root of my desire for this fantasy: the desert island scenario felt tantalizing, because on a desert island, I could be fully, authentically myself. There would be no pressure to fit in. No prying, judging eyes. Just like what I'd experienced in the wild embrace of Mongolia. Given the nomadic lifestyle I had been building for myself—in which I was becoming a desert island in my own right—I wondered whether a real-life Robinson Crusoe could offer me some guidance, some inspiration as to how I might continue shaping this journey that was becoming my strange new life.

I looked around. The small metal boat I was holding on to tore through water that was even bluer than the immaculate sky; I watched the jagged shore of the island recede to our right, where the sun had risen just a few hours earlier. My skin was prickling with sand and sea salt. Submerging my hand beneath the surface, I felt the cool cyan sea slipping between my fingers. I leaned back to take in the fresh smell of salty water filling my head every time I inhaled.

Several feet below my hand, visible through the glass-clear waters, were over two dozen dolphins, bounding through the water, racing our *qarib*—a small traditional fishing boat, not much more than a metal cradle with a cheap engine rigged onto the back. When I looked back up, expecting to see the unbroken blue on blue of sea and sky, there were dolphins everywhere, like birds, dipping in and out of the waves.

If I focused my mind only on the visuals, forgetting everything I knew about this place, I could have probably tricked myself into believing I was on some island paradise—Hawaii, or the Caribbean, perhaps. But that couldn't have been further from reality, because I was, in fact, in Yemen, and specifically Socotra, a remote and little-visited island tucked into the Gulf of Aden, surrounded on all sides by pirate-infested waters. On a map, Socotra looks like an ink drop, left by the invisible hand that drew the horn of Africa. Geographically, it *is* part of Africa, just off the Somali coast, but it has been owned by Yemen since the Yemeni unification in 1990. That this idyllic island is part of Yemen is enough to put off most travelers. The country has been ravaged by war for decades and is among the poorest, most dangerous, and most conservative places in the world.

But Sanaa, the capital of Yemen, is roughly a thousand miles away from Socotra, separated by a wide stretch of the Arabian Sea, and many of the country's problems felt a thousand miles away, too. Until recently, the island had not been reachable by plane, only via an overnight ferry from the shores of Yemen or Oman. Now it requires several flights, one of which must be chartered specifically to the island from Abu Dhabi—the result of Emirati meddling in the politics of the region. I had been lucky enough to get an invitation to visit Socotra from one of the few local tour agencies that operated on the island back then. A significant perk of the job: in exchange for a free trip, I would document my time there on YouTube. I didn't pursue collaborations like this very often, since I preferred the freedom of independent travel, solo and without a guide. At this point in my travel filmmaking career, I was receiving a modest income from the YouTube platform and from the occasional brand partnership. So although I had long since run out of my London savings, I now had the means—however limited and unpredictable from month to month—to travel the world on my own dime. But traveling independently to Socotra was out of the question. Given that it's such an inaccessible place, travelers are allowed in only with a guide. And as per my agreement with mine, I would document my time on the island while retaining total creative control over the films. In turn, the tour agency hoped that my YouTube followers would be inspired to visit Socotra. Even with new flight routes connecting Socotra to the outside world, the island is still exceedingly remote, and, at this point in time, it was accessible only through one scheduled flight per week. And that flight, as it turned out, transported me not just a couple of thousand miles but into a whole new world entirely.

Socotra is an island of prehistoric landscapes, an ever-changing topography of untouched mountains, sun-blasted three-hundred-foot-high sand dunes, pristine turquoise waters, and dragon blood tree forests that look like they might've been painted straight out of the pages of a fantasy novel.

Its people are proud Socotrans and have their own culture and language. But with the Middle East's lingua franca—Arabic—having made its way into schools, politics, and smartphones for many years now, the Sokotri language is being lost to the tides of time. Because it is a language that is in love with nature, this feels like a particular loss. Socotra's biodiversity is so vast that it is commonly dubbed the Galápagos of the Indian Ocean: 37 percent of this island's plant species and 90 percent of its reptiles are found only here, and nowhere else in the world. As Douglas Botting wrote in *Island of the Dragon's Blood*, "I felt intensely that I was living in a world so old that man had no place there." I couldn't have agreed more: an almost unbelievably beautiful, otherworldly place that could have come straight out of a fairy tale. I wanted to come here to be sure that it really existed. I had recently been traveling to some pretty offbeat places all across the Middle East, like Iran, Iraq, and Syria, so Yemen felt like it slotted right in.

That morning, crossing the azure waters in a rickety *qarib*, accompanied by a guide and a boat driver, I was on a mission to reach Shoab Beach. This remote beach was home to someone who, in my mind, represented a lifelong fantasy of mine: he was a modern-day Robinson Crusoe, living alone, separated from the rest of civilization, on an inaccessible stretch of land, on one of the most remote islands in the world. We arrived at Shoab's shoreline after an hour and a half of travel through the open sea.

I jumped from the boat straight into the lukewarm, shallow water that lapped at the white sand: it looked every bit my fantasy.

ALL PHOTOS ARE COURTESY OF THE AUTHOR, UNLESS OTHERWISE NOTED.

On vacation at the Polish seaside with my grandpa Leszek. I was six years old.

Posing on a college lawn at Oxford University (and definitely not playing croquet).

"Ready" for the altar on the morning of my wedding.

© Lukasz Bak

Filming a segment in the Karakoram mountain range for my travel show in Pakistan.

Admiring the epic views of the Himalayas during my Everest Base Camp trek in 2018.

The very start of my solo trek in Mongolia with my horses (just before we crossed the first river).

When my satellite messenger stopped working on the trail in Mongolia, I had no way to communicate with the outside world.

The third-rate magenta motorbike, which I named Cindy, that became my faithful companion on Socotra during the Covid-19 lockdown.

Learning how to gut fish during the first days of the Covid-19 lockdown on Socotra.

The moment Odyssey, the 2006 Land Rover Defender, became mine. Equal parts excited and terrified!

Hanging out in the back of Odyssey, now a full-fledged expedition truck complete with a tentlike roof conversion that serves as my sleeping quarters.

The day I picked up Vilk, and his first time in Odyssey.

Vilk, even as a puppy, has always been a paw-erful protector!

These vast landscapes stretched out all around us as Mathilde, Nick, and I made our way toward Prudhoe Bay in Alaska in our trusty Land Rover Defenders.

We were blessed with a dazzling display of the northern lights in the Yukon on our way to the north of Alaska.

Somewhere along the infamous Dalton Highway in northern Alaska. (I would put on shoes only if I absolutely had to.)

My oasis in the Carpathian Mountains.

The northern lights illuminating the way during my 320-mile ultramarathon in the Arctic Circle.

Taking a quick break to load up on calories during my Arctic ultramarathon.

Minus 4 degrees Fahrenheit, my hat and hair encrusted with ice—the reality of being two-hundred-plus miles into the 320-mile Arctic Circle ultramarathon.

But once we left the comfort of the water, conditions immediately felt arid—the air was dry, and the sun was unhindered by even a single cloud. The shoreline was like a cove nestled between high ocher hillscapes, patterned with rugged, unforgiving shrubs. As we walked up the beach, I spotted the only signs of habitation for miles around. A mere few hundred feet inland was a collection of dwellings made from a filigree of weathered driftwood on a foundation of stone. These had been hand-built fifty years ago by Hamid, Socotra's own Robinson Crusoe.

Hamid came out of his shelter smiling and waving to greet us. "*Aull gua'aresh?*" He uttered the traditional Sokotri greeting, which literally translates to "Is anyone sick?" Traditionally, the people of the island often went for long stretches without seeing each other, and this being an inhospitable place to live, away from modern medical care, sickness and accidents were once commonplace. When seeing your neighbor after a long absence, it was therefore considered polite to check whether their family was in good health and, indeed, whether they were all still alive.

"*Bishi di-gua'aour,*" I responded. Nobody is sick. Hearing my Sokotri reply, Hamid laughed heartily.

"*Mashallah, mashallah!* You speak Sokotri!" He switched to Arabic.

"*La, la,*" I protested, and turned to my guide to let Hamid know that I knew only a few phrases. I had always found it easy to pick up bits and pieces of new languages, which turned out to be a great conversation starter—quite literally—anywhere I traveled, including on one of the most remote islands in the world.

I didn't know when the last time he'd seen another person was, but he was evidently delighted by our arrival. Hamid was a slight man who could have been anywhere between sixty and eighty years old. I didn't ask because I was sure he wouldn't know his exact age. Old-school Socotrans didn't own birth certificates: they lived on an island that was a world unto itself, where everybody knew one another. They never needed a piece of paper to confirm that they existed. Their existence was all the proof required. Hamid's black beard was marled with gray, and his parchment-dry olive skin gave him the countenance of someone who had spent his life facing the sea. He wore a gray tartan *futah*—a wrap skirt traditional for Muslim men from the Yemeni part of the Arabian Peninsula—an unbuttoned short-sleeved shirt, the color of which might once have been lilac, that revealed a tanned and lean torso, and a sun-beaten turban covering his head. For a man who spent almost all his time in solitude, herding his modest flock of goats for a living, he was surprisingly friendly, keeping up an easy, playful flow of conversation.

He ushered us into his home, the mesh of branches sheltering us from the glaring sun outside. After my local guides caught up with Hamid on the goings-on of the island, we sat on his shale floor. Hamid busied himself making us a pot of tea, and a hush fell upon the dwelling. The only sounds were the beating of the waves and the occasional whistle of the wind as it squeezed its way through the driftwood walls into Hamid's home. When Hamid was here on his own—which would have been for the vast majority of the fifty or so years that he'd spent here—these sounds were his companions. There was no radio in his hut, no background din of traffic, no neighbors playing music late into the night. Aside from the occasional bleating of his goats, the ocean and the wind provided the background score for Hamid's life. I felt that if I listened to the wind through his walls for long enough, I would eventually hear his name.

I didn't know what I expected to hear from him. But deep inside, I wanted to *know* what it was really like for him to live here, alone. Did he cherish his solitude like Bibi Nigor, back in

Pakistan? Or did he struggle with the challenges it brought? On some level, I wanted to compare our experiences. I wanted to know whether I was crazy for entertaining thoughts about a life lived in isolation, away from people, away from noise. I wanted him to normalize me.

"Do you ever get lonely here?" It was an obvious question to ask of a hermit, especially since he seemed so happy to share his space with us, so eager to talk and have company.

"No," he insisted. "I live here with my goats for company. Sometimes people come and visit me. But I do not feel lonely."

I smiled and nodded. We were extremely different, Hamid and I: my life was being witnessed by hundreds of thousands of people, and I continuously shared the highs and lows of my existence with strangers from all around the world. But despite this, I felt a kinship with Hamid that I'd rarely experienced. On a very fundamental level, I understood what drove him to stay here, on this remote stretch of beach. Viscerally, I, too, knew the desire to be alone.

Remembering those moments of absolute, all-encompassing solitude in Mongolia, I wished I could tell Hamid that I knew why he was here; that I had felt it for myself, if only briefly; that he didn't have to explain. Because aloneness did not necessarily mean loneliness. Loneliness happened *to* you. You had no choice in the matter—and it was not a state that was dependent on your being alone. You could be in a lifelong relationship and still feel lonely. But I had always been taught that to "end up alone" would be the darkest scenario for a human life.

And yet, my recent adventures in solitude had brought me the kind of intense joy I'd rarely experienced in the company of others. If freedom and aloneness could feel so good, why did I always default to being in a relationship? To fall into the arms of another had become like a reflex for me. Why did I always seek refuge outside myself, when surely it could never be found there if I had already created a space within myself to retreat to? Then the answer to a question I didn't realize I had been asking for decades became clear: maybe, just maybe, any relationship was *not* better than no relationship. Maybe to "end up alone" was to taste this level of freedom every single day. And maybe there was only one way to find out.

"I built this house," Hamid picked up again, bringing me back out of myself, "and I like living here. I've lived here for fifty years. I live simply, catching fish from the sea—sometimes I buy rice and flour from the town, and meat and dates."

I took a glance around us. There was a modest supply of food in his rudimentary shelter, and very little else. I thought I had been living a minimalistic lifestyle over the past couple of years, shedding most of my material possessions in favor of a light backpack and the ability to live nomadically without the burden of things getting in the way. I was proud that I did not own more than a few pairs of shoes, or a single piece of furniture: it marked a significant departure from my old life. It was evidence of psychological progress, I thought, a sign that my values had shifted and that I no longer relied on material wealth to provide me with a sense of validation.

But looking around Hamid's house, I realized that my newfound minimalism was in fact just another luxury and a different form of privilege. I had *chosen* to give away my valuables. I had *chosen* to live out of a suitcase. At any point in time, I could just hop on a plane, move to any city in the world that caught my fancy, get a nine-to-five, and begin once again to amass furniture, books, clothes, and all manner of earthly possessions. Hamid didn't have that choice. He had never had that choice. To live out there, on his own, in a tiny shelter built of driftwood and stone, was a destiny that had been written for him since birth. "I don't need any more things," Hamid insisted when I probed him about whether he was comfortable living out here. "This is everything I need in this life."

Hamid was a fisherman and goatherd, and though he professed that he would never live anywhere else, it was also true that he lived here out of necessity for both professions. As he told us about his goats, he led us through to his pride: the guest room, which had a driftwood roof that rose onto a huge, porous rock. This room also served as his kitchen, where he enthusiastically prepared us lunch, frying up a heap of fish he had caught in the ocean that morning, with potatoes and spices we had brought for him from town, and which he gratefully accepted.

After we finished lunch, I took a Polaroid of Hamid and gave it to him, to his delight. He offered an infectious, childlike smile in return. As the sun began to descend, I felt a small sadness at the thought of leaving him alone there. Perhaps he felt sad, too, as he said goodbye a hundred times.

On the boat, I watched his shoreline disappear and imagined him alone, watching the sun set behind the sea, as he did every evening. Could the company of the natural world truly be enough to sustain a man for a lifetime? Watching the dolphins that were chaperoning our boat's return, I remembered Hamid's words. "It's a difficult life," he'd said, "very difficult." And those words came from a man who has never known anything different, never spent weeks or months in the comfort most of us are accustomed to.

Though my childhood fantasy of living a life like Robinson Crusoe might have been fractured by this comparatively short excursion, I couldn't help but wonder if we were any happier than Hamid, with all our comforts and luxuries. As we tore through the blue waters, the sun setting behind us, there was one thing I knew I would never want to leave behind, not even for the most perfect desert island: the deep and profound sense of gratitude that I got to *choose* whether I spent my time alone, testing my mettle, or in comfort, surrounded by the people I loved and who loved me in return.

I appreciated that there was a small possibility that Hamid was just a crazy hermit, an antisocial outcast maladjusted to living in the "real world." But there was another possibility, too. Hamid might have been a very wise man, living in a world much more real than the one I presently occupied. He had something unquantifiable, a quality that only people who spent long periods of time alone had. I wanted it, too.

"I don't expect I'll see you again," he'd said to me as we left. Somehow, I knew he was right. But a small voice inside me whispered, *That doesn't mean I won't return.*

The spring was approaching, the sun still gathering its strength. Less than a year after my visit to Hamid, I was back on Socotra. The same agency that had originally invited me to the island had asked me to come back to run—and document—a marathon, the Socotra Challenge 2020, the first-ever marathon on the island. I had returned there with a group of fellow runners, but without any training. We had arrived in early March 2020, just a few days before Covid-19 would be announced as a pandemic. At the time, the world was still unsure which way the scales would tip. So, in the first days of March, before the pandemic was declared, I did what many others decided to do: I went on with my life as planned and traveled to the island, where, for the following days, I would have no access to a cell signal, the internet, or the news. I ran the marathon and filmed it. Then, on night three, I was woken up at around midnight. It was Enni, the marathon group's guide, who by then had become a friend. He had rushed to our campsite on a motorbike from the island's capital after being summoned there by the local government.

"Look, guys," he announced to our ragtag group of runners. "I just got some bad news. They said the world is shutting down because of this coronavirus. All flights from Socotra have now been canceled, but there is one last plane that will leave in a few hours. If you don't take this flight, you may become stranded here for a very long time. So you better start packing."

Back then, "this Covid thing" seemed to most people like a dark cloud that would soon float away and leave behind a blue sky. The words *pandemic* and *evacuation flight* felt like a rude awakening to the seriousness of the situation. In shocked, hushed tones, we started discussing the situation and what we were to do now. Tension hung in the air, clinging to us like condensation as we tried to figure out what was happening in the "outside world." One thing was certain: everyone was hopeful that this last flight would take them back home.

Home.

The word was carried on the lips of my fellow runners like a spell. *Home. Get home. Go home. Be home.* That one word, on repeat, *home, home, home*.

I had only been planning to stay on Socotra for a couple of weeks before continuing my travels. I had no *home* to return to.

My life had become one long adventure in *avoiding* home. Everything I had once built in London and Brussels was gone. My parents were living their own lives. My grandparents lived in Poland, but, after seventeen years away, it seemed as much of an arbitrary choice as any other place in the world. It didn't help that my family was still bewildered by my choice to abandon my perfectly nice married, corporate life. In the three years since my defection, we had not spoken to or seen each other regularly. Every time we did, they asked me about Leo. They pressed me to *return*, as if I had left for a quick, mad jaunt around the world and would soon be back to London to resume what in their minds was a "normal" way of life. In their minds, this nomadic phase was just a glitch in the system. My family didn't make me feel seen, and didn't make me feel like I was *home*. In my eyes, there *was* no home.

As the people around me planned their returning routes, discussing how they would continue to France, or Canada, or the United States, all I could think was, *Where should I go?*

I mentally listed all the countries I had been to recently, all the people I knew, all the people who could maybe help me find a place to rent, to wait out whatever this new situation was. Every single name and location I came up with felt tenuous. I had no idea what the rules were in the middle of a completely new global scenario. Would I even be allowed to travel to any country other than the one listed on my passport? Every option I thought of slipped through my fingers. *What do I do?* I asked myself, desperately. And then an insane thought popped into my mind.

What if I stayed?

What if I didn't take the last flight off the island?

I thought of my time with Hamid the year before. I thought of the elation I'd experienced when I was able to sit alone with the natural world, something that the island seemed to encourage. Suddenly, the answer was so simple. I could just not go *anywhere*.

My heart started pounding with the excitement of having found such a simple solution to a critical, complicated problem. I turned to Enni. "I want to stay," I blurted out without thinking. I needed to get the words out before they morphed into something too daunting. I thought that by turning this rash, wild intention into something tangible, something that really existed in the world as an utterance, I could tame it. Make it feel like less of a wild and uncalculated leap.

Enni looked at me, taken aback. "Okay," he replied. "You do know you could be here, on an island in Yemen, for many months? Nobody knows how long."

"Yeah. I know," I said. "But I have nowhere else to go. I want to stay." And with those words, my mind was made up.

A few hours later, I stood in the departures lounge of Socotra's tiny airport, watching the people I had gotten to know over the past week checking in their luggage and grasping their passports and boarding passes in their hands like their most prized possessions. Everyone looked relieved to be going home, grateful at the prospect of being reunited with their families in a world that suddenly felt volatile.

"Are you absolutely certain that you want to stay, Eva?" Several people asked that same question. I hugged them goodbye and smiled, nodding my head. "I'll be fine," I replied each time, reassuring them but not quite managing to reassure myself. I had absolutely no idea whether I would be fine.

Watching everyone disappear behind the security gates, I was filled with uncertainty and doubt as my mind threw up a rolling list of questions. Was I doing the right thing? How long would I be here? From this moment on, my fate was tied to a remote island in one of the world's most dangerous countries, now completely isolated as a pandemic wreaked havoc on the world I knew. Was this the cost of not having a home to return to?

I was not alone in having made the risky decision to stay. Enni stayed, too, as did his brother, Fede. A couple of their friends decided to remain on the island as well. All in all, we were three Italians, one Croatian, and one Pole. We were an eclectic group of stragglers who hadn't made it home and decided to spend the first few days of our self-imposed island stay together, getting our bearings within this new reality.

Though I had imagined myself sitting alone, staring out at the island from its high dunes, for the time being we had to remain in Hadiboh, Socotra's small capital, which felt more like a chaotic rural town than a capital city. Here, we awaited a formal verdict from the authorities on whether we would be allowed to stay on the island long-term (though, with the last plane already having left, our fates seemed sealed, no matter what the bureaucracy might decide). Unlike the rest of the rugged island, Hadiboh was a crowded and dusty amalgamation of dirt tracks, hastily erected buildings, and spontaneous trash dumps. Skinny goats grazed amid discarded plastic bottles, men milled about simultaneously restless and dazed, and motorbikes sped past, sending clouds of dust high in the air. As much as Socotra felt like a wide-open space, Hadiboh was the very opposite: stifling and ugly. Over time, we started to jokingly refer to it as the worst town on earth.

The moment that last plane had left the island earlier that morning, Socotra had become cut off from the rest of the world. And since all traffic to the island had been halted—both air and marine—and nobody was showing signs of sickness, the local government concluded that Socotra was free from "corona," as they called it. They did not initiate a lockdown of any kind, and allowed people to carry on with their lives as if nothing was happening. The island became one of the few places in the world with no known cases of Covid-19, and would remain this way for several months.

But in order to adhere to the protocol, a local official invited us five foreigners to the local hospital to get checked out for any symptoms. "It's an official requirement," he said almost apologetically. As I filled out a health questionnaire and let a seemingly indifferent doctor examine me, I wondered what was next for us.

"No corona," said the doctor, barely looking at me. "*Yallah*, you can go."

Where?

For the time being, we had to stay in the soulless, goat-nibbled "capital" of Hadiboh. Government officials wanted to be able to reach us in case we had to be somehow shipped off the island after all. We dropped our backpacks on the floor of a dank storage room that acted as the office of a local travel agency. This was not quite what I'd had in mind when I had decided to stay on Socotra. I had been lured in by the fantasy of living in one of its wild places, not in one of the most miserable towns on earth.

"We'll have to sleep here for a few days while they figure out the situation," said Enni, his voice soft with resignation.

"Home sweet home," I laughed in response, trying to make light of the situation. But my bravado was starting to waver. I looked around. The room was dark, cool, and tiled. It smelled faintly of mold. A few pieces of furniture had been arranged haphazardly around it, but aside from a few cupboards, a desk, and two chairs, there was nowhere to sleep, and there was nowhere to cook. There was at least a toilet: a hole-in-the-floor kind of affair, without a flush, but with a sizable pail in the corner, and with running water, which descended forcefully from a water container sitting on the roof. My eye caught something moving in the corner of the toilet. I squinted. A moment later, two giant cockroaches shot out from behind the water pail and started racing around the bathroom. They were everywhere in this little room we would now be trapped in for God knew how long. I screamed and, with a whole-body shudder, shut the door of the toilet. My body still convulsing, I turned to Enni.

"Are we actually going to sleep here?"

He nodded, lifting his shoulders toward his ears and opening his arms in a very Italian gesture meant to communicate *I don't make the rules.*

Scanning the room for signs of more cockroaches, I imagined sitting among the people on the plane headed out of Socotra. I wasn't sure where I would have gone, but, for once, I was starting to think that maybe I should have done the thing that everyone else did. Choosing to stay on the island was starting to feel like a big, and irrevocable, mistake.

chapter fourteen

romantic pirates

We had finally been officially discharged from stifling Hadiboh—and the cell-like office where cockroaches had become intimate friends—after five days there, and were free to roam the island on our own terms. There was still no talk of a lockdown on Socotra. There were no local cases of Covid-19, and with the island now cut off from the rest of a world that was enduring strict curfews and lockdowns, life here just carried on. People were out and about on the streets as if nothing had happened, and the few restaurants and shops continued to operate, customers coming and going. Socotra's remoteness was proving to be its biggest blessing in this regard. Only occasionally did I dwell on thoughts that this remoteness might someday backfire, that one day I might need to leave the island—whether I liked it or not.

The vast majority of Socotra is free, open space. The land belongs to the various tribes and communities that live there, but there are few fences, and no "Private Land" signs. A culture of hospitality meant that, provided we respected customs and asked the permission of locals, we were allowed to pitch our tents practically anywhere. We chose a tiny fishing village on the scenic northeastern corner of the island called Erissel to install our makeshift camp: it hit all the right spots, as it was accessible by car and within walking distance of a village, and was perched on a beach, which meant we could fish. To our delight, it also felt far removed even from the rest of the sparse population of Socotra. The villagers there were kind enough to let us use their old shelter made out of sticks and stones, much like Hamid's hut. In it, we stored supplies we'd brought from Hadiboh—potatoes, canned tomatoes, tea, rice, sugar—and created a basic kitchen setup, complete with a portable cooler, a gas tank, and a stove.

The beach where we would spend our days from now on was a luminous landscape of golden sand, miles of it until the eye could see no more, with only the stone-clad fishing village in the near distance. In front of the camp, the dark blue of the Arabian Sea was a constant reminder of how far removed we were from the mainland. Behind us rose the dramatic prehistoric mountain range that ran through the very heart of Socotra, like a sleeping dragon stretched out across the island, undisturbed since the dawn of time. The side of the mountain we were on was lined with enormous sand dunes that burst into two-hundred-foot-high waves of dust above the beach. On many occasions, I climbed these dunes and threw myself from the top, running at high speed, barely controlling my legs as gravity swept me down toward the beach. In those moments I was ecstatic and light, like the birds that graced the shore, as if my bones were full of air. I emerged at the bottom, my hair powdered with sand, ready to climb up again.

Our shelter was just a few feet from where the local fishermen departed early every morning for a day of toil in the elements, out on the sea. And every evening, just before sunset, when they came back with the day's catch, their young sons would run up to their boats that bounced on the shallow water and help their fathers pull them to shore. One of the boys would lead the undertaking and start chanting to get a rhythm going. The other boys would heave the boats a little closer, tugging hard every time the chant reached a high point. When I climbed up to the top of the nearby hill, sometimes I could see women walking back to the village carrying heavy loads of firewood on their backs.

As for us, our unlikely group was busy settling into our own routines. There was Enni, a tall, slim Italian who had spent the most time on Socotra out of all of us as a guide, and he naturally fell into the role of an impromptu leader. His brother, Fede, was a young man on one of his first trips abroad. Then there was Matteo, a mercurial, bearded Italian fisherman who'd spent most of his life on fishing boats, and Rob, a Croatian photographer, who was kind and honorable. Together, we were all that remained of our respective expeditions: Enni, Fede, and I had stayed on from the marathon. Matteo and Rob had decided to stick around after finishing a fishing expedition they had been leading.

Our first night on the beach had felt like one long sigh of relief. We were finally out of Hadiboh, and it felt like we'd broken out of jail. We were free!

"Look at us," Enni had said as we sat around by the shoreline. "We are such romantic pirates."

We'd burst out laughing at the idea, but, in truth, we all related to the sentiment. It was an impulsive romanticism that had led us to stay on Socotra, as opposed to choosing the more familiar option of traveling back home. We were each the captain of our own destiny, lured by the siren song of the Socotran magic.

Before the sun set that night, Rob and Matteo went out to fish. I hadn't expected to eat anything but rice that evening, and would have been quite content with that, but they came back with a pile of seafood fresh from the sea. We made a fire that lit up the stone shelter with a warm glow and feasted on grouper, coral trout, and yellowfin tuna, all barbecued right on the fire. This was what I had stayed on Socotra for.

As we sat back after dinner, the feeling in the camp was one of gratitude and excitement, and we talked and joked around until late into the night, until everything hushed and there was only the sound of the waves and the wind in my ears. I lay there under the stars thinking about a verse I half remembered from Khalil Gibran's *The Prophet*:

> But you, children of space, you restless in rest,
> you shall not be trapped nor tamed.
> Your house shall be not an anchor but a mast.
> [. . .] For that which is boundless in you abides
> in the mansion of the sky, whose door is the morning mist,
> and whose windows are the songs and the silences of night.

With nothing separating our skin from the night sky, we felt that by making the choice to stay on Socotra, we had done something rebellious, and so, even though we didn't know each other very well, and despite the uncertainty of the pandemic, as I drifted off to sleep, I felt safe in the company of this motley bunch. In a place as conservative as Yemen, to be a solo woman—even a foreign solo woman—was to attract attention. I was grateful to have company, and to feel protected by their presence.

But the world outside our island's borders seemed to have fallen into a vortex of chaos—a chaos that everyone we knew and loved had been sucked into. While we were in Hadiboh, family members told us about lockdowns and restrictions, about death tolls and skyrocketing infections and a race to come up with a vaccine. Some were scared, others quickly growing frustrated with this new reality.

With virtually no access to papers and TV, and very little access to the internet, we were living in what felt like a parallel world: most of our sustenance came straight from the sea, for free, and whatever we couldn't fish for—rice, flour, vegetables—we bought at local prices. Since we were wild camping on a beach, our accommodation budget was close to zero. Enni and Matteo sometimes traded the fish they caught for whatever other basics we needed. Without access to fancy grocery stores or products flown in on cargo planes from the other side of the globe, we were limited to the most basic of fare. But this being an island on the Arabian Sea, *our* simple fare, caught every morning on a fishing rod, would have made for a feast on any Michelin-starred restaurant table.

Days passed. I took walks along the beach, read e-books on my phone, cuddled up with a little brown-and-caramel-colored goat that I'd befriended and named Toffee, and helped the guys catch and prepare food. Matteo and Rob would set off on daylong fishing trips, sometimes together, sometimes alone. They spent long hours casting their lines into the sea and spinning, then repeating the action all over again. This was the slow and secure rhythm of our days for a while.

As sunrises and sunsets came and went, fishermen departed and returned on their rickety boats. Life was slowly carrying on, and I knew I needed to ensure that my new life carried on, too, however slowly. I made it a mission to document my days on Socotra in as much detail as possible—it was unlikely this experience was ever going to come around again, and I wanted to have a record of it. With my phone in hand, I snapped photos of our camp and filmed short little vlogs, which I would later post online in low resolution on trips to Hadiboh, as long as the island's unreliable internet was willing to cooperate.

But whenever I made my videos, out of the corner of my eye, I could see the rest of the group rolling their eyes at me as I chatted away into the camera. Admittedly, it felt a little awkward to film my vlogs in front of an audience, and the not-so-discreet scoffing didn't help. But I was glad to have something to do, and I kept myself busy trying to invent ways to keep my YouTube channel going despite all the technological limitations that came with being on a remote island. I tried to shut off the self-conscious discomfort that had started to bubble up and got on with my work. But, within a month, cracks were already forming in the group.

The five of us, brought together by circumstance more than by choice, were all headstrong individuals. Just the types of people who would consciously decide to stay on a remote Yemeni island during a pandemic, with no guarantees of getting out. Individualistic, stubborn, unwilling to conform. We enjoyed a short honeymoon period in this unusual situation, but the very real uncertainty of our future on the island and our strong personalities meant that tensions would soon start to arise.

We were three months away from the notorious *khareef* hitting the island. The *khareef* is an annual monsoon that brings high winds and hurricanes, frequent rain, and a white fog that shrouds the hills. When locals describe the intensity of the *khareef* winds, they explain that women avoid going outside for fear that their floor-length abayas will blow up to their chins, revealing their undergarments. Sleeping outside would quickly become a distant memory.

But there were bigger things to worry about than where we might sleep during the *khareef*. Socotra has no natural harbor, which is part of the reason for its inaccessibility through the centuries. This significant feature, or absence thereof, also means that during the windy season, as the gale-force winds batter the seas and all who sail her, there is no way to reach the island safely. All trade and passenger links between Socotra and the Persian Gulf are cut off between June and October in a normal year, which this year would leave the island even more isolated. During the *khareef*, the only way to travel here would be on a plane. But with the pandemic having brought air traffic to a standstill, we could not count on an airline to get us off the island in the near future.

Discussions began among us about the impact the *khareef* could have on our stay. If this pandemic situation didn't resolve itself by June, we could become stranded on the island until after the *khareef*, which would be another half a year. Part of our group grew convinced that we needed to find a way off the island as soon as possible. I wasn't ready to start thinking about that. I had nowhere to go. I had no home. All I had was where I was.

We began to explicitly disagree about what course of action to take. I often overheard whispered conversations in Italian among Enni, Fede, and Matteo, in which Oman, Saudi Arabia, and Djibouti were mentioned over and over again as neighboring countries via which we could potentially leave the island. They spoke in hushed tones about working with the Italian diplomatic service to be evacuated off the island. It felt wrong to me that these conversations were happening in a different language, without all of us present, without a sense of consensus, and in comparative secrecy. Every time I recognized the familiar whispers, my trust in the group eroded a little further. Eventually, as my patience was running out, I decided to confront them.

"Can I get some information on what you're planning to do?" I said to Matteo. "I hear whispers of contacting embassies but have no idea what's going on." Perhaps because of my anxiety, the words came out of my mouth a little more aggressively than I would have liked.

Enni rolled his eyes. "C*he cazzo*," he mumbled to himself,

gesturing in Italian exasperation with his hands squeezed into pinecones. "There is no information and no 'whispers,'" he said, looking at me in annoyance. "Nothing for you to know."

"Well, maybe you can tell me what you've been discussing, because it affects us all."

"What do you wanna know?" Matteo shouted, lashing out without warning. "There's nothing! Everything is fucked! We don't know anything!" As he screamed at me, I stood in silence, which seemed to make his shouts get louder and more out of control. His eyes were wide, his face was livid, and saliva was flying out of his mouth. Even as he screamed at me, I suspected this explosion had little to do with me and everything to do with the growing uncertainty about what we would do when the *khareef* hit the island. But perhaps what was worse than being screamed at was that as he screamed and screamed, the others did nothing to calm him down, siding with him in silent agreement.

"All I wanted was an update on what was happening," I said during a brief pause. "Why are you shouting at me?"

Matteo shrugged, his hands flying into the air, palms turning up toward the sky. "I'm shouting because I am angry. *Cazzo*, why do we have to discuss every single thing? Do you have a way of getting off the island?"

I did not.

The prospect of a conflict had been brewing for a while, but until now, the sources of friction between the group had been little things: minor disagreements about what course of action to take, eye rolls and gesticulations left open to interpretation, cultural differences in how we communicated, Italian fire brushing up against Slavic distance. I was more than happy to ignore these minor strains and explain them away: we had been existing in close quarters; we had no idea what the future would bring. I had always found rational, unemotional explanations as to why the atmosphere sometimes felt strained between us all. But that evening, the bubble burst.

I no longer felt like I fit in with the group, and I no longer felt like I wanted to be a part of it. We had been united by the uncertainty of our situation, but, increasingly, I felt like that was the only thing we had in common. Later that night, I lay awake, stuck with a feeling that our group's fragile dynamic had hit a wall and that there would be no going back. What I needed was to jump over to the other side of that wall, and keep going on my own.

I thought back to the last time I'd felt truly free, those treasured memories of Mongolia. I craved peace. I had begun to feel uneasy and uncomfortable here. I needed to get away from the tension and the testosterone. And then I saw it in my mind's eye: there were no horses on Socotra, but I could find my freedom on the back of a mechanical steed. I pictured myself riding around the island on one of the many cheap Chinese bikes the locals used. As I imagined how I might feel alone on the island on the back of a motorbike, I felt a familiar lightness of being return.

chapter fifteen

among the dragon bloods

"Don't look at anyone. Don't listen to anyone. Just drive," Sadeq told me. Sadeq had been born in Sanaa in mainland Yemen but had come to Socotra with his family to escape the war. With his small frame, an industrial amount of hair gel, and a shy, self-effacing smile, Sadeq looked much younger than the twenty-year-old motorbike mechanic-cum-instructor that he was.

I'd met Sadeq through a local contact, and he'd jumped at the opportunity to help me buy a motorbike and teach me how to ride it. So, with $900 that my mom sent me via a Western Union money transfer, I became the proud owner of a Baotian: a third-rate Chinese motorbike.

The motorbike came in a few boxes and had to be assembled from scratch. Once it had been put together, I was delighted to discover that it had a slightly vintage look, with chrome handles and pipes, its bodywork a dark magenta. It was an undeniably pretty bike, and because I had been craving some female company for weeks now, I decided to name her Cindy.

Sadeq took me out on training rides on a flat piece of land outside Hadiboh.

"Okay, now shift gears! Shift into first gear," he shouted over the rumble of the engine as my first lesson started.

"Where are the gears, Sadeq? I can't find the gears!" Clearly, he had overestimated my riding skills.

A few laborious days later, Sadeq had managed to teach me how to shift gears, how to turn, and, very importantly, how to stop. I still hesitated before making any decisions on the bike, my movements stilted and rash, my riding far from fluid. But it was a start.

"What if the police stop me? I don't have a license," I asked Sadeq, a little panicked, as it had only just dawned on me.

Sadeq burst out laughing. "You think I have a license?" he exclaimed defiantly. "In Yemen, nobody has a license! In Yemen, you get on your bike and you go!"

This statement did not manage to reassure me as I set off on my toughest lesson yet: riding Cindy through Hadiboh's busy, dusty, potholed streets. As I weaved through the alleyways, I knew this would almost certainly be the first time anyone had seen a woman ride a motorbike on the island. I was doing my best to focus on handling Cindy and avoiding goats, people, and potholes, all with an audience focused on my every move. I felt like a wild animal making my way across the savannah while a hundred humans watched intently, snapping pictures from their safari vehicles.

"I want everyone to look at you and think that you are very good," Sadeq shouted seriously from the back of the bike. "These guys here, they don't want you to drive the motorbike."

"Why not?" I asked, swerving nervously around some litter on the road.

"Because you're a girl. They think that a girl cannot drive a motorbike," Sadeq responded, audibly stifling his anger. "Here in Yemen, girls don't have anything. They cannot drive, they cannot go out." In conservative Yemen, Sadeq was an exception: a rebel with an acute sense of justice and an open mind. I often wondered what made him so different; perhaps it was his social media diet or having grown up with several sisters. Whatever it was, he repeatedly told me: "Don't look at anyone. Don't listen to anyone. Just drive." And I, a foreigner, could take the risk and *just drive*.

Because I was an *affrangiya*, as foreigners are casually termed on Socotra, my antics were tolerated here. A visiting woman, who is not bound by the strict cultural and religious rules of Yemen, is granted an otherwise unimaginable amount of freedom. Unlike local women, I could ride a bike. I could hang out with men by myself. I could choose to cover my head or not, but given the constant staring whenever my hair showed, I usually did. Yemeni women enjoy no such liberty. The country ranks among the lowest on all global rankings for gender equality. With limited access to education, health care, or work opportunities, and high rates of early marriage, as well as massive restrictions on personal freedom, women exist at the margins of Yemen's society. They are discriminated against, unrepresented in the government, and almost completely excluded from public life. All of this, in addition to the armed conflict ripping the country apart and the devastating poverty that comes with it, makes Yemen one of the most dangerous places in the world to be a woman.

Socotra felt like a small exception. Given the island's distance from mainland Yemen, its relative peace, and a slowly burgeoning tourism industry, women were granted more independence here; of course, *more* certainly did not mean equal, and it could still feel like a treacherous place, even for me. Whenever I ran errands in Hadiboh alone, I became the target of the local version of catcalls ("*Affrangiya! Affrangiya!*"), whistles, and unwelcome approaches.

So, like the local women, I took to wearing a long, black abaya whenever I ventured out by myself, but even that didn't help.

Sadeq took Cindy to his garage for some last-minute maintenance before I embarked on my first proper adventure with her. She reemerged with a shaggy pink faux-fur blanket where her hard seat had been. As if I wasn't attracting enough attention, Sadeq had sourced large stickers of pink, kohl-lined eyes and eyebrows and stuck them on the headlights to give Cindy a more distinctly feminine vibe. He also printed me a custom license plate, complete with the picture of a dragon blood tree and "Socotra Islannd" [*sic*] printed in the middle. "I am so happy," he repeated proudly. I suspected that his meticulous efforts in decorating Cindy had something to do with the fact that I was the only female rider on the island. He wanted everyone to know that this was *my* motorbike. A lack of professional motorcycle gear on the island meant that we had to improvise. We found a plastic fruit crate and fixed it to the back of the bike with a few yards of salvaged rope. Cindy was a uniquely Socotran specimen, endemic to the island, like many of the species that called it home. And I loved her.

The look was completed with a pink helmet Sadeq had found me, the plastic visor of which wouldn't stay in place and was so scratched up that I could barely see through it. The chinstrap kept loosening by itself and would have to be adjusted several times during the course of a single ride. But I had a helmet and a motorbike, I could move around independently, and I was now ready to escape the increasingly bad atmosphere of our group of five.

Back in Hadiboh, I stuffed a few basic necessities into my backpack and chucked my tent, my sleeping bag, and some food into the plastic crate in the back. Before I left, I hugged Rob, Enni, Matteo, and Fede goodbye, saying I wanted to visit a friend's family on a different part of the island. I was embarking on my own adventure now, and I wanted to leave with a clean slate, with no festering animosity, no grudges, just the beginnings of the friendships we had already made—what really mattered. Then, waving goodbye to Sadeq, I rode out of town. I could feel him watching me set off, cheering me on. "*Don't look at anyone. Don't listen to anyone. Just drive.*"

The gray concrete of Hadiboh fell away behind me. I took a deep breath. I was no longer stuck in second gear, half expecting someone in town to cut a corner or cross the street unexpectedly. I shifted into third, fourth, and then, with fifth, the breeze came like *khiimori*, the Mongolian wind horse, racing through my hair. The sun shone brightly from a deep blue sky, and I was finally on my own again, doing what felt like I was destined for, back in the driver's seat of my adventure.

I rode along the coastal road, heading westward. To my left, cliffs rose like towers toward the sky, and dusty orange boulders hung precariously above the road. To my right, the Arabian Sea defined the horizon, azure and calm, the occasional white ripple a giveaway of some small presence—a pod of dolphins, or fishermen on their boat. As the distance between Cindy and Hadiboh rolled out, I felt a new energy kicking in, that same old—yet ever-new—excitement of hitting the road, heading toward a place that was unknown to me.

I was riding to Diksam, a plateau deep in the interior of Socotra, home to the famous dragon blood trees. They're almost mushroom-like in appearance: a bare trunk crowned with a thick network of branches that look like gills, their leaves granting the tree its "cap." The dragon blood tree is native to the island, and is so called because of the bright red sap that seeps from its bark when cut: it looks truly wounded when injured. Its legendary resin, the "dragon blood," has medicinal and beautifying properties—the women here apply its dried and powdered dust as blush.

However, the tree is at risk of extinction due to the overgrazing of livestock and subsequent habitat loss, the often unsustainable harvesting of its coveted sap, and climate change.

I'd heard that there was a family here who, through generations of living in Diksam, had become the guardians of the dragon bloods, and apparently, they had hosted a female European researcher for several months. After the not-so-romantic pirates' infighting, I was hoping that this family might be open to hosting me, too. I'd tentatively called their eldest son, Salem, a few days prior to gauge whether staying with them might be possible, and he invited me over with enthusiasm. "You can stay as long as you like," he assured me, bringing up echoes of the Posh family in Pakistan. By the warm, welcoming, friendly tone of his voice on the other end of the line, I could sense that he was smiling.

I rode deeper and deeper into the island, gradually leaving the coastal road behind. The flat, sandy landscape of the coast gave way to hills, where the air became cooler and villages less frequent. Cindy's feeble engine struggled as the road inclined sharply, winding up toward the mountains. Up ahead, I could see the first dragon blood tree along this road. I was struck by how differently I experienced the world depending on how I moved through it.

On the motorbike, I could hear the world passing by and feel it on my skin, without windows or loudspeakers muting the reality of it. The air was soft and warm. I could reach out and touch the shrubs and trees that sprang up along the road. I noticed a group of giant boulders and a small settlement tucked just behind them, a lizard sitting on a rock.

After three hours of slow progress, stopping to take photos, getting lost, and asking for directions in my broken Arabic, I finally arrived on Diksam Plateau and parked the motorbike by the first house in the village. On hearing my bike, a man emerged from the building. He was a stocky man with a traditional *futah* tunic wrapped around his waist, and he rushed over to greet me with a big smile and a few English words. "Hello, hello, welcome Diksam!"

I had just happened to park in the exact right place: this was Mohammed Kebany, the host I had been looking for.

"I was born sometime around sixty years ago, in a cave in the mountains," Mohammed said, his words translated by his son, Salem, as we sat eating our first meal together. "I spent my entire childhood in the cave with my parents."

I'd set up on the Kebanys' veranda with a mattress and a tent, despite the women and girls' insistence that I should take a room to sleep in. But the nights were so perfectly warm out on the plateau, and I relished spending every single night sleeping outside, without a wall between me and the natural world. So I opted to remain as I was. And over the coming weeks, it was there, on the veranda, where girls from the village would come and visit me and we'd dance and sing together, and Mohammed, his wife, Fatima, and their sons, Salem and Abdullah, would come and share meals with me. It was during those meals that I would get to hear the tales about what it was like to live on the island in years gone by.

When Mohammed married Fatima, they moved to a cave much like the one Mohammed had grown up in. That cave was where he started his life as an adult and breadwinner, and he and Fatima started their family. Salem still remembered the days when they lived in the cave—and was quick to dismiss the lifestyle. "It's much better to live in a house," he said.

I looked over at Abdullah, the youngest Kebany, and I couldn't picture that boy living in a cave. A few minutes before, he had been showing me videos of Mr. Bean on his phone, and we'd giggled together as we watched his universally intelligible capers. *How could this boy live in a cave?* I thought, looking at him now. It seemed impossible.

But in Mohammed's eyes and heart, you could see and hear the nostalgia. "Us Socotrans, we are a part of this island," he continued. "Can you believe that in our language, we have one hundred words for rain?"

In Sokotri, a downpour that sends a thick veil of water to earth is called *kelle'h*. A thin drizzle is called *nisas*. Rain seen from far away is known as *nasab*. A downpour covering the whole island is an *e'meh*. There are words to describe a puddle of water that's found under a rock, words that name rain puddles of different shapes and sizes.

"Living in a cave, you're at one with nature. At night, you're close to the stars," Mohammed said, now reclining on a cushion, wearing the traditional *futah* around his waist, and a T-shirt with a puffy pilot-style jacket. He took his time speaking, looking somewhere deep into the dark mountains in the distance. "No lights, no cars, no cement," he continued, waving his hand at the small village in front of us dismissively. "Everything you ate was fresh and came from your flock. We drank milk and ate yogurt and goat meat."

Today, Bedouins who still live in the mountains can hike down to Hadiboh and choose from a comparative smorgasbord of products. Olive oil made in Syria, fruit imported from Oman, Nutella manufactured in Europe. The stock on the supermarket shelves was pitiful by European standards, but compared to the traditional Bedouin food selection, it could have catered to a king.

"Do you miss living in your cave?" I asked Mohammed.

"It was a different kind of life," he said simply.

Now most of the caves that used to be inhabited by mountain families serve as temporary shelters for shepherds or as enclosures for goats and sheep. With an increasing amount of money flowing to the island, the culture of cave dwelling is on the brink of extinction. Living in a cave in the mountains is now the exception rather than the rule.

Feeling stuffed with good food and beautiful stories, I lay back on my mattress that evening, the warm wind drifting over me as if I were a stone. Mohammed's tales were adding fuel to a fire I had been tending for a while. There was magic in this simple, "little" life. Increasingly, I wondered which life was the truly "little life": the one that Mohammed had lived, in harmony with nature—which, for all its challenges, was an expansive one—or the supposedly big life that I had once lived in the city, which had seemed intent on shrinking me down. As I went to sleep that night, I wondered what it would be like to live in a way that made me a part of nature rather than a mere observer, and what it would take for me to arrive at that state.

For two hundred thousand years of evolution, we dwelled outside, migrated with the seasons, moved across vast landscapes, and never once looked in the mirror. At our core, we are all feral creatures. *Romantic pirates*, I thought, and chuckled to myself, remembering the kinship that I'd shared with the guys on that beach in Erissel. As much as our differences might've forced us apart, the reason we had all decided to stay was that we were all feral people, happy to sleep outside, to gut fish with our bare hands, to let the sun carve its rays into our skin.

Lying there, I wondered what it would take for me to become a more feral creature, to become that wildling whom I'd glimpsed alone out on the steppe in Mongolia. Was it even possible as a thoroughly modern human being who (oh, the irony!) made her living on social media? What would happen if I started to shed more layers of social conditioning? After all, I had changed my life once before, and I knew that, despite the pain and the challenges, it had been the right decision to make. I also knew that that decision would continue to evolve, as, in turn, would I.

Radicalize yourself into living more wildly. The phrase clung to my brain as I gazed out onto the open expanse of the plateau that had become my temporary home. I wasn't totally sure what it meant yet, but instinctually, I knew this was something I needed to pay attention to. I needed to follow the voice within and trust that it would lead me in the right direction once more. So I did, the very next day.

I took off my shoes and kept them off.

I snapped my shaving razor in half.

I packed away my plastic tent and would sleep outside from now on, in the open air.

At first, when I walked around barefoot on the goat trails crisscrossing Socotra's mountains, every little stone stabbed my feet after almost thirty years of their being mollycoddled inside soft, protective shoes.

Initially, as I slept outside the protective covering of my tent, I worried that insects would crawl all over me. I remembered some factoid about how humans accidentally swallowed an average of twenty spiders in their sleep over a lifetime and imagined that I'd be ingesting many more. *Good protein*, I thought to myself, but I still spent the first few nights with a scarf draped over my head.

I watched with a mix of conditioned disgust and then fascination as the hairs in my armpits started to grow out for the first time in my adult life and I had nothing to mow them down with.

Despite the discomfort, I kept up with these experiments for days, then weeks. I had desperately needed time alone to allow this new emotional and spiritual growth spurt to come into being. I had needed solitude and space, away from the male gaze, to take me on this path of wildness.

With time, walking barefoot became easier. The calluses on my feet hardened as if they'd been waiting for the opportunity to do so for years. The cicadas that had given me insect-swallowing anxiety just a few days prior transformed into a lullaby I looked forward to every night. With no artificial light, my sleep became deep and restful, the first rays of the sun waking me gently at dawn.

Eventually, I stopped looking out for hazards. Something had clicked. I felt like I was stepping into a different version of reality. A reality in which the darkness of night always came when it wanted, and you could not stave it off with a light and pretend it was not there. A reality in which the sun prickled your skin, and your skin responded by turning a little red, a little damp with perspiration. And I realized that this new world I had entered felt so much more real than the world I had spent most of my life in. I thought of a comment that popped up over and over again under my videos: "One day, you will come back to reality." I presumed that people who wrote these types of comments meant that my nonconforming lifestyle had an expiration date, that it was a temporary fantasy.

In front of me, thousand-year-old dragon blood trees rose toward the sky. My body carried itself high, strong, and open. My hair, uncombed for days, fell to my shoulders in an unkempt, bushy mane. I felt free. But the comment continued to play on my mind. Out of nowhere, a new thought burst in, illuminating something I didn't know existed: *What if* this *is reality*, the thought asked, *and we have all been duped into believing that it isn't?*

What if we were meant to exist like this all along? Our hair wild, our skin sun-kissed, our bodies resilient? What if the everyday life we all knew so well, with its numbing comforts, was not a natural state but the product of having wandered off a path? I still had more questions than answers on that veranda, but all of a sudden, the notion of "reality" seemed very open to interpretation.

chapter sixteen

paradise lost

I found myself entranced by the voice of the muezzin coming from the village mosque as I sat out on the Kebanys' veranda every night. That the *adhan*—the call to prayer—was played from a tape every time didn't matter: it was still soulful and emotional, weighted and balanced. The anonymous voice behind the loudspeaker took his time with every syllable and left space for contemplation during every pause. With every verse, his voice rose and fell like the hills and mountains that surrounded us. I looked at the horizon as the *adhan* echoed, the black uneven line of the island's plateau distinct against the dark gray clouds, which hid the cool, bright face of the moon.

On a recent trip to Hadiboh I had found out about a women's cooperative that produced and sold traditional Socotran handicrafts. On my first visit to the cooperative, I had been stunned to discover a group of local craftswomen who were as proficient at their craft as they were proud of their skills. Grinning from ear to ear, they showed me an incredible variety of baskets, mats, and carpets, all woven by hand from dried-out weeds and grass. Each piece had been hand-braided over the course of many days, sometimes weeks.

"It's my only source of income," said Halima, a stocky, round-faced woman who never once took her hands off the mat she was weaving. "It's the only way we women can make money here."

It was true that weaving goods was one of the few opportunities for women to earn an income here: it could be done at home and was considered a "female" craft. Immediately, I knew I wanted to work with these women and share their craft with the world. I decided I would put a spotlight on their products and show them to my social media audience, gauge the reaction, and eventually find a way to sell and ship them overseas, with all profit going to the craftswomen.

But I couldn't do it alone. I needed a translator who could help me discuss the project with the women, and I needed a big car to help me transport the goods to a storage space in Hadiboh. This was why I approached Seif, a local businessman who had helped me sort out some formalities on the island early in my stay, and whose family members worked at the cooperative. He could help me translate, learn more about the crafts, and, given his connections in the local trade, eventually find a way to ship the products off the island. This was my hope, anyway.

Seif was a tall and well-built man, with a round face and searching eyes. He took great care in his appearance, always wearing matching colors and elegant ensembles—washed and ironed, I assumed, by either of his two wives. He was excited to jump on the project, keen as he was to spread the word about Socotra to the rest of the world.

On our second visit to the cooperative together, as I rummaged through the wares, I could feel Seif's gaze on my back. It was that piercing feeling you get when you know someone is undressing you in their mind's eye. I tried to brush it off, convincing myself that I was being paranoid. *I shouldn't assume that all men have bad intentions*, I thought, talking myself out of this visceral gut feeling, an internal alarm that was warning me that something was off.

Seif and I left the shop with a few select pieces I was planning to post on my Instagram in a bid to raise money for the collective. We put everything in the back of his large white Land Cruiser and set off for Hadiboh. Seif seemed to be in a particularly jovial mood, waxing lyrical about how much I was about to help the island and how many great projects we could cook up together. I listened half-heartedly, taking his words with a pinch of salt—he was, after all, a businessman.

As we were crossing a wide, sandy, isolated pitch on the way to the main road, Seif put his foot on the brake and brought the car to a slow roll. The car stopped. Why were we stopping? I looked over at him. In that instant, he grabbed the back of my head with his hand. With a forceful jerk, he pulled my face toward his. His grip on me was strong. *Fuck* was the only thought I had. *Fuck fuck fuck.* I tried to turn my face away from his and wriggle out of his grip, but he was stronger than me and held on to me firmly.

In a silent struggle during which time crawled, I tried pulling away again. But no matter which way I turned, his face was there. He pulled me closer. Seif's dry lips grated like sandpaper against mine. I was stunned. Paralyzed. *What the fuck do I do?* In the millisecond it took me to decide, a leathery tongue was already creeping between my lips. I tried twisting my way out of his grasp, forcing my head back and away from him. But he kept hold of me.

Then I yelped. My whole body convulsed with fear and disgust. This primal fear of mine caught Seif by surprise. He loosened his grip.

I knew I couldn't waste a second. Before he could tighten his grip again, I immediately pulled back and retreated as far as possible from him, backing myself into the corner between the seat and the door, trying to make myself small and distant, like a hunted animal that found itself cornered. And that was how I felt: hunted. The initial shock ebbed, and now came a wave of panic. I was out here alone with this man, trapped behind tinted windows and heavy doors with the child lock engaged.

There was silence. *What do I do? What's his next move?* Seif looked at me, self-satisfied, smiling carefree like an oaf, seemingly oblivious to the fact that he had done something wrong. As I stared at him in horror, I wanted to tell him that he was a pig, that I was disgusted by him, and who the fuck did he think he was? I wanted to tell him that what he had just done was harassment and assault, that I would tell his family, that he would face grave consequences, that there was no way in hell he would get away with this.

"What are you doing?" was all I managed to get out.

I wanted to run. I wanted to run far from this man, far from his car, far from this island. I wanted to run and scream. But all I could muster were those four words, uttered quietly, hesitantly. He screwed up his lips and raised his eyebrows, as if I were the one who had done something untoward.

As a solo female traveler, I was practically guaranteed to get accosted by men at some point. It's a sad truth, but an undeniable one. I had been propositioned on many occasions in all corners of the globe: from catcalls to explicit sexual invitations, from unwanted physical brushes to full-on groping. I had become convinced, in my travels as a woman, that men all over the world felt entitled to women's bodies.

Despite all these experiences, I had still considered myself "lucky." At least I hadn't been born into a culture where my father or my husband truly did own me. Suddenly, this thinking struck me as extremely backward: *At least I am allowed to wear what I want. At least the law in my country* might *protect me if a man chooses to assault me.* Warped, backward thinking, wrong on every level. Every single woman in the world should be free from male control and harrassment, just as she should be free from the male gaze and the possible threat implicitly contained within it.

A couple of weeks earlier, while I was elsewhere, Enni had been approached by a local shopkeeper. Without a single word of English but equipped with a stack of bills in his hands, the shopkeeper had started counting: $100, $200 . . . he counted all the way to $1,000. Enni stared at the shopkeeper blankly, and asked him, "What about it?"

The shopkeeper made the gesture of putting a ring on his finger and said, "Eva." Enni was very amused by the spontaneous marriage proposal but informed the man that he was not my father and could not give me away. The shopkeeper continued to insist, asking, "How much?" In the end, he offered $10,000 in dowry—or, as I preferred to call it, buyer's fees—before being sent away without a wife. When Enni told me about it, the situation initially sent us into fits of laughter—it was a shock, just too much to believe, so far from the social conduct of the world I had grown up in. But there was a much darker side to it. In so many places and cultures around the world, men still treated women as objects to be possessed. And the man sitting two feet away from me in the white Land Cruiser now was a part of the problem.

"I thought you wanted this," he said.

What reason could I have possibly given him to believe that? My mind raced as it searched for answers. I had been so careful. I rarely maintained eye contact with local men on the island for fear they would get the wrong message. I avoided smiling too much. I always wore loose clothing. I always inquired about their wives, their mothers, their children, and did my best to develop relationships with those women whenever I could. And, in truth, the majority of the men on the island approached me with respect and kindness. Some, like Sadeq and Salem, were just like brothers to me. But there were exceptions everywhere, and seemingly, all my social maneuvering had not been enough to remind Seif that he was married and that I was a human being, just like his mother, his wives, his sister. But perhaps this was giving more credence to how he saw the women in his life than he deserved.

"No, Seif, I do not want this," I responded as firmly as my shaking voice would allow. "I do *not* want this. Please drive me back to Hadiboh now."

I wondered if I should storm out of his car and run back to town on my own two feet. But I didn't know where we were, and I didn't know anyone there well enough to explain my predicament. I chose to sit silently in the passenger seat of Seif's car, hoping he would not touch me again. I was a fox caught in a snare, praying that the hunter would release me.

A silence fell over the car, so dense and loaded that it was hard to take a breath. Seif pushed the gear stick into drive.

"You will not tell anyone about this." His words came as a flat statement of fact rather than a question.

I hesitated.

"No."

The voice of the Egyptian singer Umm Kulthum boomed from the speakers. We did not exchange another word. When I got out of his car an hour later, my knees felt weak. *I'm lucky*, I kept telling myself. *I'm lucky that nothing else happened. That this was it.*

When I reached my veranda on the plateau that evening, I sat down in silence and stared at the night. You could hear the *khareef* approaching. The wind had started to pick up, barreling down the mountainsides and pushing around dust on the trails.

Tumbleweeds rolled down into my camp from higher up in the hills. Thick clouds rushed in regularly, darkening the sky further. They almost always brought rain. Most days, it trickled down from the sky, but sometimes it came crashing down, the very air became liquid, and the water beat the dry soil like a celestial drummer. Soon, every day would be like this, for many months.

In the darkness, my mind was gray, and I felt nothing.

It had started to become clear that the political situation on the island was becoming unstable. The relative sense of peace was beginning to rupture for the first time in many years. Due to its strategic location in the Gulf of Aden, a little speck right between Africa and the Middle East, Socotra was desirable real estate for all the superpowers in the region. With Yemen thrust into a devastating war that left it with few resources to care for Socotra's interests, the competing governments of Saudi Arabia and the United Arab Emirates were able to work their way onto the island. They mostly used subtle strategies to gain favor with the locals: building a clinic, subsidizing schools and sending teachers, installing a phone network, and establishing new trade routes. But inside some of the cargo containers, alongside flour and flip-flops, were weapons, high-tech military equipment, and army vehicles. The intention was not to educate and improve the lives of ordinary Socotrans. The intention was to garner enough soft power to eventually—potentially—seize control of the island.

Amid all of this, Yemeni forces were trying to hold on, too. The STC—the Southern Transitional Council of Yemen—had its presence firmly established on the island. This secessionist organization controlled much of southern Yemen in the Yemeni war and was backed by the United Arab Emirates. The political situation on Socotra was complex, with favors exchanged behind closed doors and a policy of intentional obscurity. The island had become a sort of battleground for a cold war–style conflict between regional superpowers, and things were about to get even more complicated.

Late one afternoon, I was sitting out on the veranda, watching the sun on its trek through the sky, when Salem arrived. After we exchanged *salaams*, he sat down on the mat next to my mattress and said, "Bad news from Hadiboh."

"What's happened?" I replied.

"One man got killed," he said, shaking his head. "There were some violent clashes this morning near the airport."

"Is this something that has happened before?" I asked, trying to discern whether this was a regular occurrence and therefore nothing to worry about, or whether it had the potential to turn into something to be wary of in a region that had been unstable for decades.

"It's completely new," he replied. "This has never happened before."

My heart sank. It had always been risky to stay on the island: it was Yemen, after all. But the quiet life I lived alongside the Kebany family in the mountains had lulled me into a sense of security.

Salem explained that this was the first time in almost fifty years that blood had been spilled on Socotran soil in a Yemeni political conflict. Despite the fact that Yemen had seen upheaval after upheaval in the past few decades, with bloodshed and violence becoming a regularity across the country, Socotra had always remained peaceful. This was the first time since 1974 that tensions had escalated into violence.

Mohammed, the Kebany father, walked by us and muttered,

"*Mushkila Hadiboh.*" Problems in Hadiboh. Seemingly reflecting the clouds forming in anticipation of the *khareef*, everything had started to feel threatening.

After Salem left, I sat dazed, absorbing the news. Until now, my stay here had felt indefinite, almost infinite. I, like the rest of the world, had made no future plans. For once, my restless desire to explore and experience had been sated. I thought of nothing but a long life sleeping under the stars. I had gotten used to living without running water, my feet had become tough like the hooves of a goat, and I had found unexpected freedom in throwing away my makeup and razors. This was the most myself I had ever felt.

But the reality was that the majestic, time-defying island that had enabled me to live this way was being rocked by modern politics. It was being pulled in two very different directions. There was its prehistoric, rugged, beautiful self, with its language that had myriad words to express the idea of rain. But it was also a place whose strategic location on a twenty-first-century geopolitical map had turned it into a battleground for Middle Eastern politics. It felt like my time on this beautiful island might be running out. A storm was coming.

Before I had time to worry about the implications of the clashes in Hadiboh, another battle started raging, and it was starting to feel like everything dark was being dredged up by these coming winds. This battle was being played out in the arena of social media. Throughout my time in Socotra, a few voices had popped up every now and again on social media to express criticism of my stay on the island. They were a small group who, as time progressed, became louder and louder in their allegations. Armed with the knowledge we now have regarding pandemics, it's easy to look back and say what we think we should have done or not done. Added to the fact that none of us had been in a global pandemic before, on Socotra, we had very little internet access—we were relatively detached from the reality almost everyone else was living at the time. But the one thing I did keep hearing was how dangerous it was to travel. I thought the safest thing I could do for everyone, including myself, was to stay put. In a lot of people's eyes, that was the problem.

This group of keyboard warriors accused me of various misdemeanors, often twisted into dramatic-sounding sound bites for the benefit of a bored, controversy-craving audience on the internet. I was accused of exploiting the hospitality of the local people—even though I was paying rent to the Kebany family, which my hosts were extremely reluctant to accept; even though the Kebanys had become close friends and urged me, half in jest, to find a local husband and stay on the island. I was falsely accused of spreading Covid across Socotra, even though the island had no documented cases at the time and I was virus-free. Videos from a trip to the hospital, during which I had been put on an IV after suffering from heatstroke, and shots of me taking antibiotics for an infected wound were misrepresented as depicting my having Covid by people who wanted to tear me down for reasons that were beyond me (and, given that Covid is a viral rather than a bacterial infection, my taking antibiotics for it would have been pretty foolish). What was initially a slow but steady social media trickle greatly increased, and I began to be accused of a whole host of fictitious crimes.

While the allegations were often on my mind (no matter how rational one might be, it's difficult to accept that someone on the internet might be spreading lies about you beyond your control), I mostly managed to push them to the side. Living in the mountains of a remote island, I had little internet access and little desire to be online, unlike the people frustrated and trapped indoors for months on the other side of the ocean. So I didn't know that anger was continuing to build in the background, until it all exploded.

Across the ocean, somewhere thousands of miles from my veranda, a small group of keyboard activists were busy planning a campaign. In their eyes, the campaign would spotlight my stay on the island as something unethical—immoral, even. Using lies, half-truths, and unfounded assumptions, they created an Instagram story that led an angry online mob straight to my account.

It is a widely known fact that once a person is convinced of something, it is pretty much impossible to convince them otherwise with words written on the internet. The comment sections of social media feeds have the unique ability to bring out the worst in people. Our emotions rising in inverse proportion to the size of the screen in our hands, we allow ourselves to utter things that most people would consider shocking in the extreme if they were vocalized in "real life."

I braced myself, and the battle of comments began. I did try not to look, but the clash raged on for a couple of days and it was impossible to completely ignore the haters versus the lovers, the accusers versus the defenders. I felt anxious, upset, and powerless to stop it, but I couldn't give this storm too much energy because, behind the scenes, there was something even more nefarious going on.

Worse than being vilified on social media in public, in a private WhatsApp message, a woman—who was not without social standing—was trying to blackmail me based on scenarios she had made up. In the midst of an exchange, I received a message that read: "If you don't leave the island now, I can resort to other means. New information about you is coming to light. I've been hearing about your wild nights with armed and married men on the island. You think you can profit from these stories?"

In short, this woman's intention was to incriminate me. I could only guess at her motivations, and the more sympathetic guesses were that she was bored and frustrated, trapped inside while I was enjoying comparative freedom on the island. But her intention was clear: to make up and spread a lie to as wide an audience as possible, painting me as a promiscuous Westerner who slept with married (and armed) men on the island and engaged in all manner of other madnesses. In light of my absolute celibacy during that time, and what had happened with Seif, the message left me shell-shocked.

Then the message just disappeared only a few moments later. A short blurb appeared in its place reading, "Message deleted." Did she realize she had taken things too far? I'll never know. All I knew was that I couldn't stomach accusations like that, let alone the fact that so many people actually believed them. My little world on the mountain had started to spin dangerously out of control, and had begun to contort into yet another cage. The Kebany family, as kind as they were, had no way to relate to my situation. Even though a million pairs of eyes watched my social media channels, I felt alone in the world.

Throughout the social media smear campaign, the looming *khareef* had been playing on my mind, and I knew I needed to try to find a way off the island. Having left on good terms with the other romantic pirates, I was still in touch with them, and we caught up regularly. After a few discussions, as a group this time, we decided to put out feelers to the local politicians and even the Socotran sultan. It seemed like no airplanes would be landing on the island anytime soon, so the marine route appeared to be our only option. But where would we go? Which country would let us in, if most international borders were still sealed shut?

Although marine traffic to Socotra was slowly opening up again, allowing for trade to resume, leaving the island was not as simple as hopping on a boat. Firstly, where would we go? Yemen was a no-go, because we would simply end up trapped on the mainland. Oman, its neighbor, had firmly sealed its borders to all foreigners, with no exceptions. Djibouti would not let us in either. Those were the three directions in which boats headed from Socotra, and none of them was available to us. Then, one evening at the end of May, my phone rang. The call was from an Emirati number. I picked up.

"This is Abdullah Al-Fatah." I knew the name immediately. This was the Emirati sheikh who acted as a liaison between Socotra and the United Arab Emirates. Everyone on the island knew his name. *How on earth do you greet a sheikh?* My minimal knowledge of court etiquette had grown somewhat rusty after months of living like a feral woman.

"Hello . . . Your Highness?" I asked, more than greeted, the sheikh.

His Highness, apparently unbothered by my rough manners, wished me a good day, and inquired how I was doing. It was polite of him to ask, and I thought to tell him about my experiments in becoming a feral being, the connection to the infinite I felt while walking barefoot on the raw ground, the fact that I was finally starting to feel comfortable with not shaving my armpits, my developing theory that humans were made to live more wildly, the anxiety that came with my being assaulted by a man in his Land Cruiser, and the dread I was starting to feel around everything that was still so uncertain in my life and my future.

"Doing well, thank you so much," I replied, limiting myself to a few words. "And yourself?"

"Good," he replied hastily. "So, you can pack your bags and drive to the city. Tomorrow you will leave on the cargo ship from the port. I'll see you in Abu Dhabi."

I momentarily lost my mental footing. I just about retained

my senses to ask one last, key question: "Should I tell my friends as well?"

"Yes, there are five spots available to you."

I thanked him profusely, and less than a minute after I'd picked up the phone, the call was finished.

I fell to the ground and let out a wild shriek. I was absolutely stunned to think that I would be leaving Socotra the very next day. Questions overlapped in my mind in a cacophony, and I did not know which one to address first. Had they given us a way to get off the island because of the rising political tensions? Was something more dangerous about to happen that they didn't want foreigners to witness? What would happen next? Where would we go . . . Abu Dhabi? Would the Emirati sheikh foot the bill? Was this really legitimate? Would it actually happen? I needed to get packing. I needed to start saying goodbye to everyone. I needed to start saying goodbye to the land. After I left, when would I next see the Kebanys? What would happen to Cindy? Was I *really* ready to leave?

I headed straight to Sadeq, my self-appointed motorbike teacher, for one final dinner with his family. After we ate and exchanged thank-yous and good wishes, I got ready to ride back to Diksam. I climbed on the bike and Sadeq turned to me with a sincere, solemn expression on his face.

"Eva, I have a question I want to ask you. I don't know what you will say, and you can say yes or no, but I know that I must ask you." I was taken aback by his sudden seriousness but was preoccupied with the prospect of leaving the island. I knew that the cargo ship had already arrived and I was keen to start talking to people about getting on board and ensuring that this was still a possibility.

"What if I ask you to marry me?" he said, leaning on the doorframe of his family's house.

There it was. The question I'd been half expecting from him for a long time. For a while now, and despite our entirely platonic relationship, I had suspected that Sadeq might be smitten with the idea of marrying a foreign girl. The question hung between us, so charged I was nervous to acknowledge it. How did you turn down a marriage proposal without hurting someone's feelings?

"What do you say?" he asked, his voice eager.

"Sadeq . . ." I started, and then hesitated. "Sadeq, you are my friend. You're like a brother to me. But you know I am not from here, and I am leaving. I cannot marry you."

I was trying to sound upbeat, but I feared the only effect I managed to achieve was of a cheerful dismissal. I couldn't gauge his reaction; his face was hidden in the shadows.

"But if you marry me," he replied, "I will give you all the things. You can stay on the island and travel on the island. You don't have to travel to other countries. I will give you all the things." He pressed on. It was clear that the proposal was a serious matter for him, that he had thought long and hard about how life might look for a Yemeni boy and a (much older) European girl.

The evening traffic was starting up. Cars and motorbikes appeared on the street, their headlights blinding. They drove past us, sending dust into the air that danced for a while, high above the ground.

"The island isn't my home, Sadeq. My home is somewhere else." As I said these words, I felt their full weight. In that moment, it hit me just how far from home I was. I didn't know what "home" meant, exactly, but I knew that Socotra could never be it. For all the beauty of the island, with its unique language, for all the kindness of the people who surrounded me, for all the friends I had made, the rudimentary ways of living, the nature—for all of this, I knew that this island belonged to its people, not to me. I was overwhelmed by the memories of the past three months, and by just how much the island had changed me. But now it was time to leave. I said my goodbyes, firmly but lovingly, to Sadeq, who accepted the rejection in silence. I turned on the engine and rode back to finish packing.

chapter seventeen

a cargo ship escape

I was standing on the watch deck of the *Ad Astra,* the cargo ship bound for Abu Dhabi. Its engine was thrumming somewhere deep in the bowels of the vessel, reverberating through my feet, through my legs, and up to the roots of my hair—an uncomfortable sensation I would become familiar with over the next seven days as we traced the edge of the Arabian Peninsula en route to the United Arab Emirates.

It was after sunset, and the first evening stars had already punctured the sky when the vessel was finally unmoored. With the monstrous groan of a thousand metal parts slotting into place, we started to drift away from the small dock on the northern coast of Socotra. The captain blew the horn to announce our departure, and the ship's roar pulsated through the warm evening air, hitting the mountains in the distance, and eventually disappeared into the darkness, echoing.

After seventy-nine days, I was leaving Socotra.

As we pulled away from the shore, I tried to make out the

contours of the island. Somewhere out there were Diksam, Cindy, and the dragon blood tree forest. The island was in darkness save for one giant mound of glowing sand—a massive dune that rose like a white mountain, catching the light of the moon. My legs twitched involuntarily, jerked awake by the memories of the thousand times I'd hurled my body downhill, down the slippery slope, down the sandy river. I looked up at the sky. A crescent moon hung above us, hopeful and full of possibility. Like me, the moon was beginning a new journey, and every day for the next seven days, it would grow a little fuller, get a little closer to coming full circle.

Both the offer and the decision to leave Socotra still felt so abrupt. Like a curveball, it had come out of nowhere and I'd had no time to do anything but act on instinct and catch it. Although we had been looking for a way to leave before the *khareef*, I had thought I would have more time to prepare, pack, and say goodbye to the island. In the end, less than forty-eight hours had elapsed between the sheikh's call and the ship's departure. Everything had happened so quickly that I'd barely had time to collect my possessions, let alone my thoughts.

I knew that sometimes life required us to let go of the reins and float on the tides of the unknown, trusting that wherever it was we ended up might just be the place we'd been looking for all along. But ten miles out to sea, still standing out on the deck, I began to miss Socotra terribly. The separation from the island brought a wrenching feeling I hadn't had time to prepare myself for. I had fallen desperately in love with Socotra the moment I'd arrived. As much as Pakistan had challenged, inspired, and awed me, I hadn't felt a connection to a place like this since Mongolia. The beauty of this island—like a paradise in every imaginable way—disarmed me completely.

I felt a sudden yearning to return, to jump into the dark water and swim ashore, but the distance between us was only growing with every passing second. The human heart was complex. You could both long for something and exhale with relief at its being gone. And so, there was solace in leaving the island, as well as regret. I was privileged because the political instability no longer posed a threat to me. I could now put distance between myself and the social media smear campaign instigated because of my being on the island. The *khareef* wouldn't trap me. All these worries were free to float away, and it struck me how easily they drifted from me, even though the day before, they had been central to my entire existence.

One thing remained vivid and visceral despite the expanse of sea rolling out between myself and the island: Seif's hands gripping the back of my head, his leathery tongue forcing itself between my lips. Shame and fear and disgust still sent my body into such a degree of stress that I shuddered whenever I thought of it, like a dog shaking its whole body to recover from a tense encounter. I didn't want that moment to continue to have such power over me. I wouldn't let it. I breathed out and, in my mind's eye, with the air that came out of my mouth, I imagined expelling the memory of Seif's uninvited lips on mine. As the ship continued sailing away from the island, I tried to reassure myself that I would never have to worry about this man again, but I knew that, beyond the rational understanding that I was leaving him behind, I needed to reassure every part of myself that I was free of him. I saw the experience with Seif as a black cloud, and every exhalation was a small part of that cloud—black. I breathed out over and over and over again, and I continued breathing until the black eventually turned white. I wanted to feel like that moment no longer had power over me. Like I was free to let it go.

The *Ad Astra*, our ship, was a six-hundred-foot-long cargo barge that crisscrossed oceans, transporting goods between different ports. On this voyage, she was heading into the Persian Gulf, stacked high with heavy metal containers that looked like giant Lego towers. We might've been allowed to hitch a ride, but we still didn't know how we were going to get into the United Arab Emirates at the end of the journey—or where we would go from there. Still, the words *I'm going home* crossed my mind. But as soon as I paid attention to them, they felt hollow: it was a thought I *wished* were mine.

There was some part of me that wanted to feel like I was going home. Leaving a remote island after nearly three months, heading toward a distant city, with the idea that from there I would fly to Europe—the situation had all the makings of a glorious homecoming, and I should have been excited. But all I knew was that I was getting closer to an international airport and, with that, closer to the question I was finding impossible to answer: Where *am* I going?

I watched the island until it became little more than a smudge on the horizon. By now the faint but appetizing smell of dinner was wafting from one of the nearby pipes. I opened the heavy metal door on the side of the ship and descended to the mess for dinner. The crew greeted me warmly. They were a mix of Syrians, Egyptians, and Filipinos, all of whom had spent most of their adult lives on board ships sailing across the world. Unsurprisingly, as women made up a mere 1.2 percent of the global seafaring workforce, the crew was all male.

In the mess, fluorescent lights flickered above our heads, thick metal walls separated us from the water, and a constant background whirring reminded me that we were breathing in air delivered via ventilation pipes. Osama, the chef, placed a huge, steaming plate in front of me with a smile. And so, back to the "real" world it was. A plate stacked high with french fries and chicken burgers, and all the knives and forks I could ever need, and a big flat-screen TV broadcasting a Hollywood blockbuster in the background, and satellite Wi-Fi . . . All of this suddenly felt too bright, too intense, too fast, too alien.

Under the bright lights and surrounded by noise, I longed for my veranda overlooking the silent dragon blood forest. My general mood wasn't helped by the first two days of sailing, which happened to take us over rough waters. From morning to nighttime, and all the way to the next sunrise, the entire ship rolled and pitched. Massive waves bounced off its fort-like walls, the surf reaching all the way to the stacked containers. Every time the waves launched us sideways, I watched these metal towers, expecting them to drop into the depths at any moment. And yet they resisted, restrained by cables that had endured much stormier seas than these. Unfortunately, my body-convulsing seasickness could not be restrained quite so successfully. Nor was it helped by the constant thick smell of diesel from the ship.

Several times a day, I made the short walk along metal corridors between the outside watch deck and the small cabin I shared with Fede, which had two beds, a small desk, a window, and a tiny toilet. On our first day of sharing the cabin, Fede came out of the toilet looking gravely concerned.

"I left some 'biscuits' in the toilet, but there is no bucket to rinse the loo." We were both puzzled. We had been used to squat toilets on Socotra, and they always came equipped with a large bucket or pail filled with water. You would pick up the bucket, tip it, pour water into the loo, and voilà—"biscuits" would disappear down the drain. How would we use the toilet on the ship if we couldn't flush it?

It took us an embarrassingly long time to figure it out, but upon closer inspection, I had a eureka moment. To the side of the toilet there was a metal lever. When pushed, it released a flow of water straight into the toilet. It was a toilet flush. After seventy-nine days on the island, Fede and I had genuinely (albeit momentarily) forgotten about the invention of flushing toilets.

Over the coming days, the seas finally calmed, and the *Ad Astra* moved lazily through the waters like we were sailing through a sea of syrup. I watched flying fish and dolphins slip through the air and the waves, this time hurrying me away from the island. Birds and even butterflies and bees flew over the surface. They cruised over the ship for a few seconds, found little of note, and buzzed away again to the open water. How had they gotten here? How far had they flown? Where did they rest? Where were they going?

Where was *I* going?

With days with nothing to do other than just sit around staring at the big ocean and thinking, everything always seemed to be leading me back to that question. After a couple of days at sea, the question morphed from something that should have been answerable with a single word—*Paris*, or *Berlin*, or *Warsaw*—into an existential crossroads. The truth was, I did not know where my physical journey would take me after arriving in Abu Dhabi, and the bigger question was: What was next?

I knew that my time on Socotra had given me a newfound appreciation for putting down roots, or at least having a place—a tent, a campsite, a veranda—to return to at the end of the day. A little sanctuary, a place of stability that was familiar to me, that was my own. Though I had started to long for that sense of stability, I could not imagine moving back into an apartment or a house, where the air would feel stifling and my skin would not be free to receive the rays of the sun. All those years ago, in London and Brussels, it had seemed like the most natural thing in the world to spend most of my time inside a concrete structure, inside four walls, opening and closing doors behind me, and watching the outside world from behind a double-glazed window. *How else would you live?* I would have thought back then. But a few years of wandering had reframed what a home looked like in my mind. I couldn't separate myself from the wilder world—and the wilder part of myself that I had only just found—and I didn't want to separate myself from the woman that wilder world had made me.

"Some experienced captains can tell the latitude and longitude just by tasting the mist that rises over the sea," the captain of the *Ad Astra* told me later that evening as we chatted in the navigation room. I turned his words over in my mind and let them settle there for a while. And then, somewhere in the middle of the ocean, it came to me: I knew what I was to do next. I wanted to continue to be that feral woman whom I'd met on Socotra, to live wild until the day came when I could taste my direction on the mist. I wanted that intense connection to the natural world that had already set me free so many times. And I wanted to feel like I belonged somewhere, for somewhere to feel like home. I wanted the freedom *and* I wanted the belonging; I wanted both. And to make these two seemingly contradictory realities possible, I just needed the stars to align.

chapter eighteen

a new odyssey begins

She looked like a car that a six-year-old might draw: a giant boxy frame, all clunky right angles and no finesse, propped up on four bulky tires. In order to plonk yourself in front of the steering wheel (assuming you were able to slam the heavy door behind you), you had to squeeze yourself into a space that could have passed for a chair-shaped coffin. No air-con, no air bags, no fuel economy to speak of. Changing gears was a workout. The use of earplugs was highly recommended at speeds upward of twenty miles an hour. Everyone told me that, being the most unreliable car in the universe, she would break down *all the time*. And yet, I fell in love with her at first sight.

In a world where sales of electric vehicles were surging and advanced driver assistance systems—with everything automatic or requiring only the touch of a button—were expected in every new vehicle, this sixteen-year-old navy blue manual Land Rover Defender looked like a vessel from another time and place. She was a misfit, and for that very reason, we were the perfect match.

But we made an unlikely pair. She was a "manly" car. A huge, gas-guzzling 4x4 you would expect to see covered in mud, with a burly army type behind the wheel who could perhaps wrestle a grizzly without a can of bear spray. I, on the other hand, was a thirty-year-old woman who'd had her license (after barely passing the test) for less than five years, and whose blood pressure spiked whenever she spotted a stick shift in a car. I had no idea what the differential lock did or how to engage low gears if you found yourself off-roading. Apparently, this was all basic knowledge for any self-respecting off-road driver, but I was distinctly *not* one of those.

I did know one thing, though. When I drove the truck for the first time, I couldn't help but grin from ear to ear. She was loud and uncomfortable and absolutely ridiculous, but she made me feel free and alive, like together we could go anywhere. Like I was embarking on an adventure every time I sat behind the wheel. And with her size, standing eight feet tall and allowing me to gaze out at the road from a throne-like perspective, she was an intimidating beast. Inside her, I felt invincible. I coughed up most of my savings and bought the damn truck. In anticipation of our journeys together, I named her Odyssey.

It had now been almost a year since my return from Socotra, and four years since I'd left London. Against all odds, all five of us romantic pirates had come out the other side of that increasingly disconcerting situation unscathed. After seven days at sea, we'd arrived in Abu Dhabi—going no farther than the port initially, as first we'd had to quarantine on the ship for another week. From there, with air traffic having partially resumed during those summer months, I'd made my way via ghostly, empty airports to Germany and, from there, back to my maternal grandparents' in Poland. Equipped with Covid-19 tests and masks, I had kept myself busy with shorter local trips, but as the pandemic quieted down, I started craving bigger adventures once again.

The feral spark that had flared inside me in Socotra continued to flicker throughout that year. I wasn't quite ready yet to move into a tent in the mountains and become a full-time forest witch, but I had started to dip my toes into some outdoor skills and wilder habits. I conquered my fear of camping all alone inside a dark forest—a setting that, thanks to *Grimm's Fairy Tales* and horror movies, seemed to me like the epitome of terror. (I got so scared of bears that night that I ended up eating an entire supersize bag of marshmallows I'd mistakenly brought along with me, out of fear that the sugar would attract a mama and her cub.) I learned how to make a fire from scratch, with birch bark for kindling, and I started to learn about map reading and navigation. These were things that a Boy Scout would learn at the age of ten, so I had some catching up to do.

But the feral fire burned much deeper, beyond bushcraft mastery. Back on the island, I had wondered what would happen to my life if I *radicalized* myself into living wildly. I had wondered who I might become and where this internal pivot might take me. Part of this process was a continuous letting go of some of the beliefs I had grown up with, like the notion that I needed makeup to be beautiful, or the idea that a woman couldn't be happy without a partner or children to complete her. But there was still one big thorn left in my side that I needed to pull out, and the only place where I could remove it was in Poland.

I needed to free myself from some serious spiritual shackles, and that process included formally leaving the Catholic Church. I had been raised Catholic, and though my family lacked fervent religious conviction, baptisms and communions were mandatory rites of passage—for no reasons other than "because that's how it's done." For many years, I was simply a passive Catholic: a member of the

Church if anyone bothered to check the diocesan records, but one without faith. My belief in a higher presence teetered somewhere between absolute nihilism and a genuine desire for *something* to exist out there, as long as it was not a bearded man in the sky.

But when I came back to Poland from Socotra, leaving the Catholic Church became a mission of the highest priority. By staying a registered member of the Church, I was part of a spiritual membership that stood for things I could no longer support. It was this Church that had once upon a time burned witches at the stake, that relegated women to a lesser role in society, that confined and controlled their bodies. Its crimes against women had been going on for centuries, and I could no longer turn a blind eye to that. Apostasy, as it's known, is quite possibly the gravest sin you can commit in the Catholic doctrine. It means severing all your formal ties with the religion, and even sounds like a sin: *apo*stasy . . . the first two syllables rising high in outrage, the last two a whisper, as if the whole word should not be uttered loudly. When I told my family about my apostatical aspirations, I got a mixed response. None of them were particularly religious, and none of them attended mass every Sunday. Still, as in every small town anywhere in the world, the question *What will the priest think?* was at the forefront of everyone's minds, regardless of their devotion. But I explained all my reasons, all the usual suspects: the issue of women's rights, all the secret crimes committed by priests, the dark history, the oppression, the cruelty. In the end, they all understood. But there was one more reason I did not share with them—something that felt too intimate to speak out loud, something a little too woo-woo, too spiritual, for them to be able to appreciate how much it mattered to me.

When Leo and I married in Poland, we had a Church ceremony. It was a symbolic ceremony, not legally binding in the eyes of the law, but symbolically binding in the eyes of the Lord, and in my own. I couldn't deny that, despite the divorce, I still felt bound to Leo in a way that was constraining some ethereal part of me. Since going our separate ways, we had never had this divine contract dissolved. So as soon as I arrived in Poland, I visited the priest who had married us and asked him for a formal annulment. When I told him the purpose of my visit, he looked disappointed.

"Are you sure you will not be getting back together?" he asked.

Yes, I was sure.

Once the priest had gauged my certainty about the situation, he became stoic and empathetic, saying that if my and Leo's paths didn't align, and we weren't willing to align them, there was nothing that could be done, and our spiritual contract would be rescinded. Then I submitted a letter that declared my wish to formally cut ties with the Catholic Church. Whatever spiritual ties had lingered between myself and my old life were now cut.

When I left the priest's rectory and my feet hit the pavement for the first time as a freshly baked apostate, I truly felt as if a weight had been lifted. The thorn had been removed, and I leaped into a sprint. I ran all the way down the street with my arms outstretched, a huge grin stretching my cheeks, unbound, just as I had arrived in this world.

Odyssey, the navy Land Rover Defender, became the project that would usher in a new era of exploration for me. It felt in some ways as if I had come full circle, to start this project in the town where I had been born, in the company of my family. But in deciding to live an unconventional life, I had to accept that not everyone would understand me. I now discovered that even those closest to me might question my choices for far longer than I might like them to.

"What do you need such a big car for?" my grandmother asked when I proudly showed off my new vehicle on the driveway.

"I'm going to turn her into a mini-camper," I said enthusiastically. "Like, a home on wheels!"

"And you're going to . . . live in it?" she queried. I could almost hear her mind trying to wrap itself around my grand vision.

"That's the plan! There will be storage, and a small kitchen, and some room to sit . . . and to sleep, I'll have a rooftop tent. That way, I can sleep in a different spot every night but still be self-sufficient," I explained cheerfully.

She inhaled dramatically, lifted her hands to her face, and covered her lips. "You'll be sleeping in a tent on top of your car every night?"

"Ye-es?" I hesitated. "But don't worry, it's safe."

Grandma made a round of the truck with her hands behind her back, mumbling to herself. "Unbelievable" was the only word I could make out. After her round was done, she stopped and looked at me.

"It's a very nice car, but . . ." She paused for a moment, looking between me and Odyssey. "I was hoping you would stay. What's all this travel for? How much longer are you planning to keep it up? You could just come back and find a nice job and a nice boy here."

I sighed, a little more impatiently than I would have liked to. I hadn't had much of a chance to reconnect with my family on a meaningful level after the divorce. They had accepted my decision to travel the world, but acceptance did not mean approval. "YouTuber" was not a job listed in their mental directory of respectable professions, and traveling the world was not what they deemed a sustainable life choice. I didn't blame them. This lifestyle was too far from anything they could have possibly related to. Where I saw excitement, they saw danger. Where I saw freedom, they saw chaos.

"Grandma . . . I am not coming back. There is nothing for me here." I paused. "I want to keep traveling until I find a place that maybe one day I can call home. But why would I live in Poland if I can live anywhere in the world?"

"Because this is your home," she insisted. "You grew up here. Your family is here. Your roots are here."

I shook my head. There was no version of reality in which I could imagine moving to Poland over all the fascinating places in the world that I had yet to see.

"I hate Polish weather. Maybe I'll move to Mexico," I joked, trying to brush it off, but Grandma was not amused.

"Mexico! My child . . . Mexico, with all the drugs and cartels! God, give me strength!"

For now, all I knew was that I was moving into Odyssey and I was planning to spend a few weeks in Poland, building out my mini-camper and making it livable, before setting off again. This time would be different from all the other times I'd set off on long journeys, because this time I would be traveling overland.

To convert a standard truck into an apartment on wheels would take some time. I needed to remove the old seats from the back, design a completely new interior, and then actually build it. With no DIY skills, I had to recruit help. My uncle, Andrzej, came to the rescue: a professional carpenter, he had harbored travel dreams of his own and was all too happy to help me shape Odyssey into the expedition truck of my dreams. We didn't exactly have palatial dimensions to work with. The space was about seven feet by five feet, and into this we needed to squeeze a kitchen, a wardrobe, an office, a living room, and an emergency bedroom (in case of storms). I did not need a high-end, Pinterest-style van and was not interested in becoming a van-lifer. My priority was to have a truck that could take me anywhere and provide me with basic shelter. I just wanted to have the freedom to roam without worrying about finding a bed for the night.

We stripped everything down to the absolute basics. I would use a simple camping stove to cook on, take my showers in rivers and with buckets outside, go to the bathroom at gas stations or behind bushes, and wash my dishes with plain water anywhere. Otherwise, I was all too happy to be spending all my time outside. After a few rounds of sketches over the family dining room table, we finally figured it out: the interior would consist of a seating platform with storage that would be long enough to sleep on in case I couldn't use my rooftop tent, a desk-slash-table-slash-fridge container, standing cupboards, side cupboards, and hanging cupboards. Most of our design was based on creating as much storage space as possible so that I could fit my entire life's belongings inside the truck.

We got to work. Admittedly, Andrzej worked much faster and more efficiently than me, but, perhaps to our detriment, I insisted on helping out. Andrzej sliced the plywood into neat chunks; I smoothed them down with sandpaper. He decided where to place a specific part; I drilled it into the metal walls of the car. Within a few short days, the sketch started to turn into reality and Odyssey was looking more and more like a tiny camper. Because the build was so small and basic, the process was swift, and we made good progress every day. One day, when I turned up at his house to keep chipping away on some cupboards, Andrzej said he had a surprise for me. I opened the back door of the truck, and the build was complete. He had worked all evening the night before to finish everything off. I couldn't believe it, and I was brought to tears with gratitude for all the time and effort he had put into making this dream a reality.

With Odyssey ready, there was now nothing stopping me from hitting the road. But leaving suddenly felt poignant. As much as

I hated to admit that my grandma had been right, during those few weeks in Poland, I'd felt more *at home* than I had in a very long time. Spending time around people I knew and loved felt like being in a safe bubble. It was only then that I realized how much mental exertion had been required from me every single day I was on the road. When you're traveling full-time, you might be having the best time in the world, but your subconscious mind is always scanning the world around you for danger and trying to figure out how to safely navigate whatever new and foreign environment you're in. You never know where your next meal will come from, or what tomorrow's journey will hold. Grandpa had said as much in his travel chronicles: "Whoever cannot adapt to this kind of life . . . in fact, whoever cannot come to love this kind of life, cannot be a true traveler. To be a true traveler requires strength of character." After several years on the road, I had come to understand this for myself now.

For the first time in years, I settled into a far more manageable, and less exhausting, emotional pattern. Every day, I woke up in my grandparents' guest bedroom, enjoyed a leisurely breakfast with them, and then headed out to run errands, work on the truck, and film videos. Every evening, I returned, chatted about the happenings of the day, and went to sleep in their guest room bed. It was late spring, and the meadows and forests around our town were in full bloom, green and fragrant. I picked wildflowers on my afternoon runs and unlocked an unexpected appreciation for the land that was, at its core, my motherland. Life felt idyllic.

During those few weeks in Poland, I saw my father regularly. We did normal father-and-daughter things: watched movies, ordered takeout, chatted about childhood memories. From the outside, it looked like a perfectly normal relationship. Underneath the surface, though, things still felt awkward between us, our bond hardened and strained by the tensions of adulthood.

I couldn't let go of the feeling that he didn't approve of my life choices. The memory of his having sided with Leo all those years ago still gnawed at me every time I saw him. And my response was to withdraw: I preferred to shield myself and keep an emotional distance from a man I suspected might reject me all over again at some point in the future.

"You know, for all his imperfections, your dad watches every single video you post on YouTube," an aunt whispered into my ear one day. "He is so very proud of you."

"Really? I thought he disagreed with my life choices," I scoffed, shrugging off her comment. But in that moment, something inside me shifted. Day by day, working on Odyssey in quiet meditation, I began to see that my and Leo's separation had reopened old wounds for my father. It reminded him of his own mistakes many years prior. I needed to believe that our lack of contact for over a year following the divorce had been a knee-jerk emotional reaction for him, his own way of shielding himself from pain. Over those few weeks in Poland, I forgave him for siding with Leo. In my mind, there was nothing more to be said. I needed to move on now.

But I had to hit the road if I wanted to follow the good seasons. For now, I just had one last mission in Poland. Given my grandparents' continued reservations about my lifestyle, I decided that, before I left, I wanted to demonstrate to them the ways in which I had, in fact, been making good life choices. So I sat them down. I explained how I made enough money to sustain myself, talked them through YouTube ad revenue and the paid partnerships with brands. I told them about the documentary I'd hosted in Pakistan and some of the travel films I'd made for various media networks. But most importantly, I told them how happy and alive I felt while I was on the road.

"I can't imagine doing anything else with my life. This is the only thing I ever want to do," I explained, impassioned. "I know it's different from my old life, but trust me when I say that this makes me so much happier."

The happiness argument they understood and supported. And while I couldn't exactly blame them if they never got around to accepting "YouTuber" as being a real job, the more mainstream the opportunities that came my way, the easier it became for them to wrap their heads around my career. Still, it wasn't until I started hosting travel shows for the BBC and National Geographic that they seemed to fully recognize that maybe I was onto something.

This is always the way. At first, while you're carving out your own unique niche, people will question your sanity. But when your niche becomes so successful that it eventually lands you in the mainstream, they will start coming around. That's when you'll hear them say, "I always knew you had it in you."

But we were a Slavic family, so phrases like *I'm proud of you* or *I always believed in you* didn't cross our lips very readily. In order to find that level of affection, I had to look beyond words and into their eyes. A barely discernible glimmer, a gentle softening, a slow and approving blink. That was how I knew I finally had their blessing.

chapter nineteen

finding meaning without god or children

Fat raindrops hit my windshield with such force that they created tiny liquid craters within themselves. My sixteen-year-old wipers could barely keep up with the steady deluge of rain, swinging feverishly from side to side, smearing the water across the windshield instead of wiping it off.

I could have bought a brand-new car, but where would the adventure be in that? I thought, trying to encourage myself during the first of many learning curves that I would endure throughout my elopement with Odyssey. It was the first day of my trans–eastern European expedition, and I could hardly see the road ahead of me. Until now, I had been a passenger whenever I'd been on the road. As I traveled the world on planes, trains, and buses, it had always been drivers and pilots who had been responsible for making sure that whatever vehicle we were aboard was running smoothly. If a bus broke down in the desert, as one did while I was crossing the Sahara in Mauritania, the driver typically was competent enough to fix it, or at least had the number for a replacement bus, which eventually came. Pilots had ensured that all my flights had taken off and landed successfully—even the one into Lukla. If I missed a flight, I could catch another. I was a passerby, never attached to my mode of transport, free to find whatever I needed to get me from A to B. But now there was a new letter in the alphabet to consider: O.

In this new scenario with Odyssey, the responsibility that came with the many miles we covered was on me and no one else. In the off-roading world, there is a saying that goes, "If you want to go into the bush, take a Land Rover. If you want to come back from the bush, take a Toyota." "Landies" weren't considered the most reliable of vehicles, and clearly, I was in the camp that *wasn't* making it back from the bush. I was firmly in the driver's seat in every sense of the word. There was no other car I could wave down, there was no opting for an easier alternative, there was no switching. Whatever happened, I was stuck with Odyssey. Perhaps that's what is meant by the saying "The things you own end up owning you."

Over the next few months, I drove Odyssey on what was essentially a six-thousand-mile test run: a warm-up trip to see how the rig held up, and whether this less glamorous cousin of van life was something I could sustain over an extended period. And so I drove from Poland through the Balkans, the entire length of Turkey, into Georgia, across the Black Sea on a shady cargo ferry, into Ukraine, and then back to Poland. There are too many adventures to recount from this time, and most of them are well-documented on YouTube. As much as this trip taught me about camping and car maintenance (a special thanks goes to my transmission, which fell apart and resulted in a saga of obnoxiously expensive repairs), it was the next trip that would turn out to be a formative chapter in my life.

After completing the test run, I concluded that I did enjoy the lifestyle of a glorified traveling hobo, with pockets just deep enough to cover fuel expenses. I decided it was now time to take things one step further. All the travel I had experienced up until this moment had felt like a jumble of countries: I had jumped from one place to another, staying in hotels and Airbnbs and guesthouses along the way. It was an exciting lifestyle, but after four full years of almost nonstop travel, I could feel the slow onset of exhaustion. I was drained, and I knew that I needed to change something in order to keep traveling long-term. By moving into my truck, I hoped to reclaim predictability, stability, in my life, if only an iota of it. The open road would inevitably bring its own surprises, but I'd still be able to retire to the familiar environment that was my trusty truck at the end of each day and sleep in the same sheets—*my* sheets. This warm-up road trip convinced me that not only could I avoid a lot of the mental fatigue that came with nonstop travel by driving my home-on-wheels, but that I really *wanted* to continue traveling overland. It was a novel realm of travel for me, one that would allow a journey of epic proportions.

Tired of the fractured monotony of jumping on planes, I wanted more continuous daily progress, where I could feel the measure of each moment by the turning of my wheels. I craved a road that would guide me for thousands of miles in one direction. I wanted to see what it would be like to cross an entire continent and observe it changing from one corner to the other, from one season to another. I wanted an odyssey. But where?

Until I knew where exactly I wanted this grand adventure to take place, I was keen to continue exploring closer to home, so I drove to the Carpathian Mountains to film a video with a couple I'd met via Instagram, Kasia and Leszek. They ran a small *agroturystyka*, a bed-and-breakfast, on their mountain farm there. The Carpathian range is almost a thousand miles long, spanning eight countries—

all of eastern Europe—in a giant, soft arc from Czechia in the west, to Ukraine in the east, and Romania in the south.

I was driving up to the Polish side, an untamed tangle of peaks called the High Tatras, Gorce, and Pieniny, home to lynxes and some of the last bears and wolves in Europe. It is the setting of many Polish legends, a place of magic and mysticism. I had always wanted to learn more about the lives of the people who lived in this remote location—who, through the centuries, had come here to escape persecution, hide out in the forests, and live far from the constraints of modern society. The closer I came to the mountains, the thicker the snow became, and soon the world around me was one of whiteness and glass-like ice—putting my driving skills with Odyssey to the test and reinforcing something I had already come to learn on my travels: that living away from society and modernity in isolated locations often brought the reward of stunning beauty, but it was always hard.

After climbing the ascending white road for many miles, I was welcomed by Kasia and Leszek and finally settled into my mountain hut for the night—enjoying the contrast of a snow bath and a warm fire and wondering what it would be like to live like this, in a wooden house I had built for myself, in the middle of a forest somewhere. One day. But not today.

The next morning, I filmed with Kasia and Leszek and met their alpacas and horses. With a little daylight left, I had a couple of hours to spare before heading off to my camping spot for the night. I was enamored with the dramatic landscape here, its wildness, the quiet crunch of magic beneath my feet. Kasia took me for a walk in the nearby hills to show me more of the area and a tiny plot of land that was for sale. As we made our way through a forest and up a steep incline, we arrived at a long and open private meadow that we had to pass through before getting to the plot. It was white and framed on all sides by tall, ancient beech trees. I looked at the dilapidated wooden hut that lay in the middle, then turned around and marveled at the High Tatras, a mountainous panorama that spread across the horizon.

"Wow. I could live here," I said to Kasia, astounded at the beauty and peace of the location.

"Who knows," she said with a mysterious smile, "maybe one day you will."

I laughed in reply, hopefully conveying my sentiments of *Maybe in another life*.

I had no plans to settle anywhere. "It's beautiful here, but I don't think I could live in Poland," I told Kasia. If you had the freedom to live anywhere, why would you choose to return to the same old boring place? But walking back to my truck, I did realize that just talking about the idea of living here had brought to light all the unknowns that remained in my future. I was over thirty years old, and I couldn't help but wonder if I should have more of my life set in stone. *Yes*, I thought, *most people would probably think I should*. But "should" had never made me happy in the past. I had to trust that my future would arrive in good time, when I was ready to live in it. It was the unknowns that brought flavor to life, and I knew all I needed to for now: Odyssey was my home, wherever we were, and our journey together was only just beginning.

That night I car-camped between silver firs in the mountains. It was a cold night, even in the car, and I could see my breath as I opened a map on my phone. My fingers moved across the screen, shifting the map along with them. I zoomed out, tracing the contours of continents, then zoomed in, recognizing the outlines of mountainous places and the shaded areas of tundra and desert. I wasn't thinking, just scanning. I was trying to feel out a possible orientation, a place that would draw me in and keep me grounded for a little while. As my eyes took in the entire globe, squeezed onto an absurdly small screen, I hoped for an invitation, imagining the stars above my camp aligning like an arrow, pointing me in a new direction.

Lying there looking for inspiration, I was also navigating the aftermath of another relationship having slowly come undone. We'd met on my travels, and our relationship had been a good one, calm and steady—the opposite of what I'd experienced with Nadir. But as I crossed the threshold into my thirties, the things that had felt malleable and uncertain in my twenties began to galvanize me with sudden clarity. The foremost of these was that I was definitely not interested in becoming a mother. The issue of children was something that had haunted all my relationships, strained them and drawn a big question mark over them. But this relationship was the only one in which my choice not to have children, and his desire to have them, was the direct cause of the breakup. And though we parted ways amicably, a bitter taste remained.

Choosing to be a child-free woman automatically shrinks your dating pool. And it comes with a whole lot of judgment and commentary that has nothing to do with dating. People have claimed that I can never be a "real" woman without the experience of childbirth. I have been told that I will never know true love, that I will regret it, that in not having children I am doing something that goes against human nature, that I will end up alone on my deathbed with nobody to care for me. (Perhaps it's just me, but ensuring that one will have deathbed care doesn't strike me as the best reason to have children.) People have taken it upon themselves to inform me that I am selfish and arrogant and that my choices will lead to the extinction of the human race.

Every woman in my position has likely been on the receiving end of these, or very similar, comments (as have possibly many men). But, steadfast in my convictions, I have found them easy enough to brush off. After all, the thought of having a baby has always filled me with dread. Picturing myself as a doting mother is an incongruity that I simply cannot process. I know myself well enough to recognize that if I ever became a mother, I would end up stymied by depression, resentment, and regret; I would feel trapped. What would possibly induce anyone to think I should be a mother when that's my starting point?

It's not just that I feel at peace with my choice not to have children. I feel positively ecstatic at the prospect of spending my life "selfishly," unencumbered by parenting duties, school pickup times, and sleepless nights. If this means I've missed out on a *type* of love that exists in the human arsenal of emotions, then so be it. It's a sacrifice I'm willing to make. I believe I have found other loves in its place.

That said, the decision not to have children doesn't come without its own set of existential challenges. When I decided to leave the Church, I gave up my shot at the paradise of the pious. But when I chose not to have children, I opted out of the secular version of life after death; I brought a death sentence upon my genes. It's not always easy navigating the meaning of life as a child-free, nonreligious person. To refuse both God and progeny is to refuse all the conventional meanings of life. I can no longer lean on spiritual guardrails, with their boundaries between right and wrong. My life is no longer a part of God's grand plan. I no longer participate in the noble mission of keeping the human race alive. In both a religious and a generational sense, I have thrown away my keys to the afterlife. Which means that all I have is the here and now.

With no future salvation or damnation to keep me accountable, the present became my only reference point. I realized that my whole personal story—my baggage, all my traumas and achievements, all my tears and hopes and dreams—could be wiped out at any second, with no opportunity for atonement. With these realizations came a transformation. My focus sharpened. I understood that the weight of my entire existence was borne solely by me. No second chances. All I had was right here, right now.

To me, that's what "being present" is all about—it's not about hedonism or complete disregard for the impact of your actions. Rather, it's the acceptance that you get to enjoy only a short ride in this rodeo, and if you don't want the weight of existence to pull you off the bull prematurely, you'll need to find your own meaning beyond the divine and beyond building a legacy—possibly, even beyond romantic relationships. And enjoy it while the moment lasts.

When I bought Odyssey, I made a pact with myself to embark on a relationship detox. It was time I took control of the wheel and picked a lane just for me. I was becoming more myself with every passing year, with every passing realization. Now I was ready to confront what had always been painted as the worst-case scenario for any woman: I was in my thirties, single and childless, with no plans to change those things.

In my journal, I wrote: "I don't think my story will end with 'and they lived happily ever after.' I think my story will end with 'and she continued to seek, forever after.'"

My index finger swiped westward on the map, until it crossed the Atlantic Ocean and its tip reached the shores of North America. The road-trip motherland. A huge landmass, it stretched north for thousands of miles, where it widened and expanded, until it became like a giant leaf nibbled by a cosmic caterpillar, a shredded territory of lakes and islands. I moved my fingers, shifting the map south, where the rigid block of the United States stood its ground until being whittled down, North America eventually turning into a thin, funnel-like strip just below Mexico. A thread held these two giants together. From there, the continent of South America began, shaped like an elongated heart.

The Americas.

Exhilaration fluttered in my stomach. What if I could drive all the way from Alaska at the very top of North America to Argentina at the bottom of South America? The Pan-American Highway: a nineteen-thousand-mile route that binds two massive continents into one iconic mega–road trip. My mind started spinning up a web of thoughts all at once: *It's perfect, it's too long, it cannot be done, it will be the adventure of a lifetime.*

It will be the adventure of a lifetime. I could almost feel the wind through the open window as I crossed the vast open spaces of the Americas, turning off to stop at a diner along Route 66, then disappearing into the desert, then cruising down the endless southern road in Patagonia. I could see it. I could *feel* it.

The impulse that had led me to buy a sixteen-year-old off-road truck instead of a nice new car was the very same impulse that would lead me to believe that traveling across the Americas alone in said truck was the best idea I had ever come up with. It may not come as a shock when I say that I rarely get to the stage of rationalizing myself out of adventures. For me, it's all or nothing, and usually I go with all. Since I was not beholden to a biological clock and was under no obligation to be a responsible adult, the world fell wide open at my wheels.

Within a week, I had figured out my route along the Pan-American Highway and booked my truck onto a cargo ship that would haul it across the Atlantic Ocean. I would be getting on a plane this time.

chapter twenty

drug mule or spy?

I glanced at Odyssey, then back at the border officer. "Look," I said, "this might take me a few hours, you know, to take everything out." I was hoping this would convince him to change his mind and let me off the hook. "This truck is basically my house, so there's a lot of stuff in there."

He smiled, self-assured. "Don't worry. We've got time."

That meant *Get on with emptying that truck so we can inspect every nook and cranny of this very suspicious foreign vehicle*. Every single item inside my little home on wheels had to come out, go through a scanner, and be subjected to a manual inspection by two border officials.

As it had been much cheaper and logistically easier than transporting it straight to the United States, I had shipped my truck to the port city of Veracruz in Mexico. I'd spent a month touring Central America in Odyssey, bouncing from the azure cenotes of the Yucatán Peninsula to the humid rainforests of Guatemala and the golden sands of Belize. Rather than the notorious drug cartels everyone had warned me about, I found locals who pointed me to wild campsites tucked away from the main roads and invited me to their homes for food. But I couldn't linger in Central America: my plan was to drive all the way to northern Alaska, and if I wanted to accomplish this mission, I had to follow the seasons.

I had just arrived on the US side of the notorious Nuevo Laredo border crossing marking the boundary between Mexico and the United States. Over the past three hours, I had been driving toward it through a region of hills and plains covered in Mexican white oak, cacti, and mesquite, and down one of the most infamous stretches of the Mexican highway system, known to many as the "highway of death," where vultures hung in the yawning blue sky. A local acquaintance, Primi, had told me that while he was driving on the same stretch of road just eight months prior, he'd been chased by unknown assailants—most likely cartel members looking for an easy target.

"Probably human traffickers or organ traffickers," Primi had told me a couple of nights earlier, over a family barbecue he had invited me to. He was still visibly shaken. "I have no idea what they would have done with us if they'd caught us. I just floored it and managed to get away."

Flooring it wasn't exactly an option in Odyssey, which had a top speed of sixty miles per hour. But I had to brave the highway if I wanted to enter the United States, and I had to enter the United States because I had someone very important waiting for me there. A few weeks earlier, I had reserved a male puppy from a litter of German shepherds that had just been born in the hills of Montana. Though I had always loved dogs, my plane-hopping lifestyle had made it impossible to own one. But after my warm-up road trip in Odyssey, I realized that my days of superfast travel were done. I wanted to go at a more deliberate pace, overland. A dog would make the perfect companion and would help me to slow down. I could raise him on the road, train him to protect me from strangers, and finally enjoy a male companion who wouldn't bring unwanted drama into my life.

Picturing the adventures I would get to share with my new puppy, I steeled myself and got on with the drive through the infamous desert stretch. I shared my live location with Primi on the Mexican side of the border and with my mom on the other side of the ocean, and dashed down the much-feared stretch of highway without stopping. My hands were moist with sweat as they gripped the steering wheel until my knuckles went white. But I was about to find that the real trouble would come after I had *left* Mexico.

Once I crossed the bridge over the Rio Grande that separated Nuevo Laredo (in Mexico) and what I presumed was the original Laredo (in Texas), I queued up behind a line of enormous pickup trucks with Texan license plates and breathed a sigh of relief. Surely cartels would not be so brazen as to steal my kidneys right in front of the American border force. I was moments away from my American dream. Smiling as I relaxed into being stateside, I drove up to the border post and passed my well-worn passport to the officer. After leafing through its pages and pausing several times to look more closely at the stamps from Yemen, Pakistan, Afghanistan, Iran, and Syria, he gave me an orange card and told me to turn my car toward the inspection bays.

Orange felt better than red (was there a red?), but it wasn't green. I watched the Mexican pickups just glide on through, sure that my pit stop on the border would be a quick formality. I had a valid visa and a valid reason to enter the United States, and I was not transporting anything illegal. So when the inspection officer asked me to "please empty your car for inspection," he caught me by surprise. Border control seemed to suspect I might be a drug mule: Why else would a young foreign woman travel alone in a big truck across such a dangerous border?

I was willing to bet that this border did not see too many solo female travelers in big expedition vehicles. The officer stood a couple of paces away and watched me intently as I began the tedious process of emptying my truck of all my possessions. Piece by little piece, with my hands open and movements calm and slow to prevent the officer from thinking I might be trying to hide something, I moved every single object out of the car and placed it on the scanner nearby.

"There's a lot of femicide in Mexico, you know," the officer said suddenly. "Aren't you scared of traveling alone?"

"No, not really. I've been doing it for a while."

"Are you sure?" He looked at me sideways. "I have a feeling like you don't know exactly what you're talking about."

Standing there wearing loose hippie pants, a tight-fitting tank top, and a mountain of jewelry, I wondered what gave him that impression. "Well," I replied, "I think I've learned how to stay safe over the years. There's danger around every corner if you look for it, but I'm pretty good at avoiding it. Call me naive if you like—"

"Yes, I think that's what you might be," he interrupted. "You got to be careful, ma'am. This isn't a very safe place."

I got the impression he wasn't interested in swapping travel experiences as much as letting me know *his* opinion. I was indeed starting to feel more nervous right here on the American border than I had when visiting some of the world's most dangerous countries.

On the other side of the scanner, two more officials were going through every single item and bag I sent through. Each object was thoroughly examined with rubber gloves and awarded a great deal of time and attention: every book and every T-shirt in my car was a potential class A drug-hiding device. Then I watched in horror as a balding, middle-aged man pulled out a little orange bag and began to pry inside. *Holy shit.* I needed to think fast.

"Excuse me, sir, may I?" I ventured, pointing at the little bag and looking at him hopefully, but trying not to sound too desperate for fear I could inadvertently raise an alarm.

"Um . . . yes, go ahead?" He seemed a little surprised.

I walked up to him and whispered in his ear, "I am so, so sorry. . . . I completely forgot. . . . There are some . . . um . . . erotic toys inside this bag." I could feel a lava-hot flush spread across my cheeks. "You may not want to take them out in public," I said, remembering the last time an official had caught me smuggling a vibrator across an international border in the Islamic Republic of Iran. I'd pretended it was a neck massager and had—reluctantly—been let go.

The officer chuckled good-naturedly.

"Oh, okay! It's all right. Don't worry about that. We see far worse things out here."

He kept chuckling and put the bag to the side. It dawned on me that if someone wanted to smuggle drugs across the Mexico-US border, a pouch with sex toys might actually be a great spot to hide them in.

I breathed a short-lived sigh of relief, assuming things couldn't get any worse. Then a tall woman dressed formally in a white shirt and a dark blazer approached me. "Ma'am, may I ask you to please leave your things and come with me?" she said in a calm, firm voice.

"Um . . . sure. Shall I take my car keys?" I had no idea where we were going or how long we would be gone, or whether my truck was safe out here.

"Leave them with the officers," the woman replied. "I'll need you to put your hands behind your back, ma'am, and go inside that building right there." She pointed at the dark door leading inside the immigration post. My heart started racing. *Oh God, what have they found?* I could only assume it wasn't the vibrator that had gotten me in trouble.

"Okay, sure," I muttered, confused. I felt anxious at the prospect of leaving Odyssey and my entire livelihood in the hands of strangers at a notorious border crossing. Scenarios raced through my mind. What if someone decided to frame me and stick drugs in the car while I wasn't looking? What if my things got stolen? But all I could do was put my hands behind my back as instructed. The woman then grabbed my wrists in a surprisingly strong grip and led me into the building of the United States border force.

Inside, we entered a long, featureless white corridor illuminated by fluorescent lights and lined with countless white doors, each with a tiny square window at the top. It reminded me of interrogation and torture facilities in movies about dictators and their regimes. Eventually, we stopped in front of one of the many doors and I was led inside. Another officer was there, waiting.

"Ma'am," she commanded firmly, "please take off all your jewelry, empty your pockets, and take out your wallet. Are you pregnant, ma'am? Are you on your period? Are you currently using a tampon?"

This was not the line of questioning I had been expecting. I realized I was about to get searched. And I mean *searched*. I still had no idea what they were looking for, or if they had a good reason to believe that I was guilty of anything. At the same time, the whole setup felt so intimidating that I did not dare ask any questions: the formality of this sequence of events and the dazzling whiteness of the lights sent me into instant submission.

"Ma'am, please go up to the wall, place your forehead on the wall, your hands on the wall, and spread your legs."

Oh. God.

The official then subjected me to a pat down. Her firm hands did not miss an inch, checking every part of me, from the top of my head, via my privates, all the way to the bottoms of my feet. A pat down like this has a way of making you feel like you have relinquished control of, and autonomy over, your body—like someone else has the right to push you around, stick their hands where they shouldn't, and put you in your place.

I was then instructed to sit down in front of a table, and three new people walked in. They immediately whipped out their badges (exactly the way they do in films) and introduced themselves as FBI agents. I felt like I was having an out-of-body experience. I was watching Eva, a character in a movie, get detained at an international border and thrown into prison for a crime she had not committed.

And then the questioning started.

What do you do for a living? Who pays you? How much money do you make? What kinds of projects do you do? Why did you travel to Iraq, Pakistan, Afghanistan? Do you know anyone in Guatemala? Does anyone ask you to travel to these places? Are you employed by any government? What's the name of your mother's ex-husband?

The questioning continued, with the same questions being asked over and over again, as if they wanted me to slip up and give them a different answer. From the line of questioning, I eventually deduced that they suspected me less of being a drug mule than of being a spy. After an hour passed, one of the FBI agents suddenly asked me to stand up and took a photo of me, the camera flash going off so violently in the cell-like room that it momentarily stunned me. In that moment, I understood what some cultures meant when they claimed that a photograph could steal a part of your soul.

It was a lonely and unnerving experience, and I felt an acute vulnerability, the kind that only comes when you know that you are truly on your own. There were no friends waiting outside to witness what was happening. In an instant, I had become just another anonymous suspect in a bureaucratic system. And although all the officers had been civil with me, I knew that they suspected me of something, and thus they were not on my side. I knew I was powerless here.

I was led out of the cell and into a hallway and placed on a long metal bench. A few seats away sat a Mexican man, slightly younger than me, with the bottom half of his head shaved and the hair on the top half pulled back in a ponytail. He looked dejected. I saw that he was handcuffed to the bench, and I couldn't help but wonder what he had done to deserve it. Perhaps not that much, because, before I knew it, an officer approached me with a pair of handcuffs of my own. He asked me to hold out my wrists and locked them inside the two metal cuffs, attaching them to the side of the metal bench. Things were going very wrong very quickly, and I still had no idea why. In all this time, nobody had offered up an explanation for why I had been detained and handcuffed. I had to know.

"Am I being arrested?" I finally plucked up the courage to ask.

"No, you're not being arrested," the officer said in a dull monotone, as if this was a question he answered several hundred times a day. "This is just for your own safety. And for my safety, too."

I sneered at the suggestion. What could I possibly do to this tall, muscular man wearing a gun belt inside an American border post? And my own safety? Wearing handcuffs around both of my wrists, thereby being incapacitated, did not make me feel the least bit safe.

Handcuffed to a metal bench in the soulless hallway of the American immigration post, wearing my harem pants and minimalist sandals, a Buddhist mala-style necklace dangling off my neck, I was sure I was about to get kicked out of the United States.

As I examined my newly acquired bangles, I was certain that my plan to drive across the Americas was about to end before it even began. There was no way they were letting me into the country after the car inspection, the body search, the interrogation, and now the cuffing. My passport was in the hands of an FBI agent, and I was waiting to either be thrown into a cell or handed my passport and asked to turn my car around and drive back down that terrifying highway into the heart of Mexico.

If I wasn't allowed into the United States, I wouldn't be able to drive the length of the Americas. Years of my life were about to be thrown up in the air: I had planned to spend a long time on the road, traveling the two continents, with an entire year in the United States alone. Now I was certain that this was as far as I would get.

It all felt so hopeless. I was just a nameless cog in this impersonal immigration machine, and the machine didn't give a damn about my journey of a lifetime. My mind started flicking through images of everything I was about to lose: the wide-open spaces of North America and all the adventures they held, the long road to Alaska, the little puppy that was waiting for me up north—this was the part that crushed me. I thought of the photo that the breeder had sent me a few days earlier. He was a small ball of dark fluff, with a black snout and two light patches around his eyes. He was looking intently into the camera, alert and ready to pounce. More wolflike in appearance than your run-of-the-mill puppy, he was all pent-up energy and mischief. The photo was accompanied by a note that said, "Here's your boy! I picked him because he is the biggest, most confident and fearless. . . . All the qualities I believe will make a loyal and protective dog for you."

I knew I could use a friend like that out on the road. But with what felt like my impending deportation, none of this would be part of my story anymore. I pictured my puppy and me heading out into the Alaskan wilderness together, hiking in the mountains in Wyoming and camping for days on end in Montana, just two friends on an adventure. All these possibilities felt like fantasies now, but I let my mind wander off to better places with better companions. While my mind was in Montana, the three FBI agents on the Texas border were walking my way again.

"Ma'am, please come with me," the youngest, blondest of them said. I smiled politely and looked suggestively at my hands, still cuffed to the bench. "Oh, I'm sorry about that," she immediately offered, looking a little embarrassed. I wondered whether she would have been this polite had I not been a white European woman.

I was uncuffed and led to a small desk in the corner of the room, where another border official was handling my passport. The man behind the desk stamped my passport with a loud thud and passed it to me, saying, "Welcome to the United States of America."

What?

After all of that, they were letting me in? I had been convinced that my only two ways out of this border post were Mexico or a prison cell. I rushed out of the building before they could change their minds. Breathing short, shallow breaths and trying not to smile too much lest I look shifty, I dashed over to Odyssey and threw all the possessions I had spent so much time removing back inside.

Hours had passed since I first arrived at the checkpoint. Now darkness had enveloped the plains. A torrential downpour beat against the metal roof of the inspection bays. I jumped inside the truck and drove off down my first American highway as fast as I could without arousing suspicion.

When I arrived in the town of Laredo, Texas, the streets were dark and nobody was out. Water ran deep on the roads, and I drove against the current slowly, barely able to see several feet in front of me through the downpour, against which my shoddy windscreen wipers were a feeble defense. There was no way I would be able to camp now. I was a bundle of nerves, and the weather was doing nothing to help me relax. I was a woman in need of a bed.

After a couple of miles, I spotted a roadside hotel. Without thinking, I parked Odyssey in front, paid an exorbitant amount of money for a "basic room," and somehow ended up with the keys to the wrong one. I walked in on a gentleman trying to enjoy a relaxing evening in front of the television. And I had thought this day couldn't get any worse. After some fumbling at the reception desk, I finally managed to get the right key, fell into my room, and collapsed on the bed, equal parts relieved and utterly exhausted.

Welcome to my American dream.

chapter twenty-one

the demon wolf

The man admiring my truck was as Texan as they came, at least to a European harboring Hollywood-inspired fantasies of the Wild West. He had a white handlebar moustache, sported a cowboy hat, and sat behind the wheel of an enormous pickup truck with enough room in the back for several horses. He looked Odyssey up and down. "You lookin' f'r company? I'm comin' right with ya, wherever you're goin' in that thing!"

Whenever I stopped in small Texan towns to take pictures or get gas, locals paused and gawked at my unusual contraption of a car. As amazed as they were at the sight of my truck, I in turn found myself amazed at Texas. Away from the clinical white rooms of inspections and interrogations, rich greenery climbed up gentle hills, and thick forests of oak, cedar, yaupon, and Texas ash tumbled out on either side of the road, lush and thriving. I crossed bridges over rushing streams and stopped here and there to dip my feet into their cool waters. As I drove, the blossoming greenery eventually thinned out, the hills flattening and giving way to an expansive grassland: the plains.

I was finally on the road, in the midst of the vast, open spaces I'd traced with my finger on the map. I was now staring down the wild horizons that had drawn me here, all the way from my camp in the Carpathian Mountains. And this road would take me farther than I'd ever driven before, a distance so long that it became difficult to imagine. From here, it was more than four thousand miles to Prudhoe Bay in Alaska, the northernmost drivable point in the United States, where I was heading. From there, I would turn back around and drive south to Ushuaia on the southern tip of Argentina, the farthest drivable point on the South American continent, which would amount to another nineteen thousand miles, at least, through Mexico and Central America, all the way to the very south of the Americas. The journey would take me a year or two, maybe more. I was trying not to plan any further ahead than was strictly necessary. It would take as long as it needed to. I had been making YouTube videos for several years by now, and consistently earned enough that I could rely on a stable income as I made the journey at my own pace.

Having spent my former career always in a rush, with never a moment to spare, I knew full well that being unhurried might just be one of the greatest luxuries I could get to enjoy. With Odyssey's top speed being sixty miles an hour, I didn't have much of an option anyway. For that same reason, I avoided the interstate highways, instead opting to cross the state on country roads. A blessing, as it turned out: these roads led me through Texas, eight hundred miles from south to north, passing remote settlements, farmland, and some of the most desolate landscapes I'd ever seen. I took it all in, my eyes wide open, my hand caressing the warm air outside through the open window. I drove by ranches so massive that their fence lines vanished far beyond the horizon. Dilapidated farms disappeared behind me, their signature metal windmills creaking lazily in the breeze—picture-perfect scenes that were framed in my rearview mirror. Once in a while, on the side of the road, a wooden farmhouse would appear, standing all alone in the midst of the vast, open Texan prairie. For miles in every direction, there was nothing else. Not a single tree, not another house, no shops or gas stations. I imagined living out here, hours from the nearest store or town, without any neighbors in my line of sight, in a place where the summer sun scorched the ground into a terra-cotta mosaic and high winds blew across the grasslands, pelting everything man-made with clouds of suffocating dust. It was a life that required grit.

For hours, I drove without seeing another soul. Just as I had hoped might be the case, having been drawn here by the promise of America's open roads, their legendary status cemented in the books I had devoured about them, from Jack Kerouac's classic *On the Road* to Jon Krakauer's *Into the Wild*, about the idealist Chris McCandless's desire to leave the civilized world behind and enter the Alaskan wilderness alone. These stories drew me in, thrilled me, terrified me, but also injected me with a strong enough dose of inspiration that I felt the urge to re-create them on my own terms. In the US, I could travel down the poetically named "freeways" (let's set aside the fact that they borrow their name from their lack of toll fees, and not some inherent sense of freedom), and without any country borders to cross, there was nothing stopping me from driving across an entire continent. *If American asphalt doesn't smell like freedom, then I don't know what does*, I thought as I drove.

Once in a while, I would reach a crossroads with a stop sign. Dutifully, I stopped, even though I knew there was nobody coming from any of the other directions, and that likely nobody else would come for hours. I looked to the right and to the left, taking in the emptiness. The only sounds were the rumble of my engine and the sighing of the wind. I shifted into first gear and let the road carry me for hours and hours on end, remembering my grandfather's words, typed out in one of his travel chronicles:

"I don't get anxious about the slow, snail-like pace. I simply get into my vehicle and I drive so far and for so long, in absolute peace, until I finally reach the destination that I have set for myself. I also don't let the discomforts bother me, be it a hard seat, heat, dust, or the lack of water. All of this, in its own way, is beautiful and wonderful."

What would he have made of my journey? Over the past year, I'd managed to reconcile with my family, which had been a huge relief to me—as if a weight had been finally lifted from us all. During my short stint in Poland working on Odyssey, I had restored cordial relations with my father and managed to convince my grandparents that the life I was living was not as unreasonable as they'd thought. My mom was still cheering me on from the sidelines. I now felt a bit more seen, like a new line of communication, of understanding, had opened between us. But how could one explain their choices to someone who was no longer among the living? All I had of my grandfather were opaque memories and the pages he'd inscribed with his way of seeing the world. But the more of his writings I read, the more I realized that his perspective didn't always align with mine: back in Poland earlier that year, I'd read a passage in one of his chronicles that outlined his hatred of solitude. "When I'm immersed in sightseeing, or taking photos, or capturing films, I forget about solitude," he'd written. "This is what keeps me sane and allows me to forget just how much I miss my family. I don't understand people who leave their family home, their wives, children and loved ones, and go abroad for months or years—or those who never come back."

And here I was, one of those people.

I had been surprised to read these words, having always pictured my grandfather as the independent, solitary type. So much of my travel storytelling was inspired by him, but as I made my own way in the world with no intention of going back home, it was becoming clear that we were very different people. If he were still alive, it's possible that he would have looked at my travels with a mix of pride and bewilderment, excited to see me explore but worried that I might be lonely without a partner and without children to come back to. Perhaps he would have placed me alongside those people he didn't understand. It was a bittersweet thought: bitter, because it carved out another inch of distance between me and the man I'd always admired; sweet, because this journey was mine, and mine only.

Odyssey and I motored down into a massive canyon somewhere in northwest Texas. As the sun set, the walls of rock glistened red all around me. Sparkling as the sun's rays reflected off them, they were at first orange, then coral, then maroon. The face of the rock was dotted with verdant bushes that grew in its crevices, their vibrant green seeming to heighten the crimson of the walls that towered all around me. Like an artery, for miles, the canyon went on, illuminated and vast, with not a human, not a car, not a house in sight. I didn't want to distract myself with capturing these scenes on camera. I breathed in the cool air of the red afternoon and let the beauty of this solitary journey hold me like an old friend I hadn't seen in a long time.

Over the next two thousand miles, I made gradual progress north, through the arid plains of northern Texas, slipping into baked New Mexico for a few hours and then driving out into rocky Colorado. The road led me into Wyoming and its endless rolling hills of green. I drove all day every day, stopping wherever I spotted something of beauty or of note, or a roadside diner, or whenever I needed gas. At night, I boondocked on dispersed campsites, by riversides, in forests, and on hilltops. Every day followed a similar rhythm: pack up, drive, find a spot at which to camp, cook, and sleep. But no two days were ever the same. Some days, I got to wake up deep in the forest, with only songbirds for company, far from human settlements and the sounds of traffic. Perhaps counterintuitively, it was in those wild and remote places that I felt safest, falling asleep to the lullaby of the trees, tucked into the cocoon of a hidden campsite. Knowing just how sacred private property is in the United States, and how easy it is to buy guns, I steered clear of "No Trespassing" signs—but encounters with real people and landowners always left me feeling reassured. "That's a cool truck!" I would hear at almost every gas station. Usually followed by, "Where are you from? Do you need any help?"

Other days, when I had a lot of driving to do and not much time to dedicate to veering off my route, I camped in Walmart parking lots, waking up to the metallic sound of shopping carts being wheeled around on concrete. But on the best days, those spent at a slower pace, away from other humans, I would cook a simple meal of pasta and tomato sauce, spice it up with some chili, and sit on the ground with a wheel for a backrest and relish the silence, the simplicity.

The farther north I drove, the more frequently I saw signs warning campers about bears. In Wyoming, my campsite host looked at me in horror when I told her I had gone for an afternoon jog along a local trail without any bear spray and immediately pressed a can of it into my hands. It had expired, but it's the thought that counts when a five-hundred-pound grizzly is charging you. I was so used to camping alone by this point that sleeping in wild places felt safe, and, reassured by the general kindness of Americans, I was seldom troubled by thoughts of murderers and rapists. But as I drove farther north, all of a sudden every rustle of leaves and every oddly shaped track on the ground made my hair stand on end. It would take another few months of wild camping before I got comfortable with being a visitor in bear country.

Every bear warning sign brought me closer to Montana. Soon, I would get to meet the puppy that had been chosen for me. For months now, something inside me had been nagging at me to get a dog. I'd always been sure that my life would eventually be filled with animal companions—yet, when I'd pictured that life back in Pakistan, in Bibi Nigor's smoke-filled home, I didn't imagine one of them appearing quite so early on, while I was still traveling. My rational mind was still questioning the decision, but my gut knew the answer. No matter how much more complicated travel would get with a canine companion, I trusted that I could figure it out. And since I would be overlanding for the next two, three, or who knew how many years, we would grow up together on the road, living in the truck and spending our time outdoors. It sounded perfect.

But when the day to pick up my puppy finally came, I got cold feet. Freedom had been one of my main drivers and one of my most richly prized sources of joy, contentment, and peace. What if getting a dog snatched all of that away from me again? *This is a really, really big decision*, I started questioning myself. *I mean, I won't be able to fly with this dog. I won't have the same freedom as I have now. I can't just leave him somewhere and head off on a side quest. What am I doing?*

I pulled over by Montana's rushing Blackfoot River, listened to the dark water as it coursed over boulders, and took deep breaths to try and calm myself down. It wasn't working. *None of your actual human relationships have worked out*, I told myself. *You don't even want kids. What makes you think you can take care of a dog?*

And this wouldn't be just any dog. He was a working line German shepherd, the same breed they used in the army and in the police force to sniff out drugs, capture criminals, and protect the general peace and well-being of the human race. These dogs were not only smart but also extremely high-energy. They required a strong handler and could easily become a liability without the right training. But the basis on which I had made the decision that I needed a dog so specialized was not just some whim. Intuitive feelings were always difficult to explain, but it was intuition that had told me that one day, my safety would hang in the balance, and my dog would tip the scales. The little voice that urged me to get a dog also urged me to get a dog that I could train to protect me. I hadn't questioned this feeling initially. I knew my intuition had always been right thus far. So I stopped questioning it once more and listened. I turned the ignition back on and drove on in the direction of my puppy: one of the most high-maintenance breeds, absolutely *not* recommended for first-time dog owners.

After some weeks of driving, I finally arrived at the address that Ginny, the breeder, had given me. There was no going back now. Her house stood in the middle of a wide, flowering meadow of sedge, blanketflower, and fireweed, surrounded on all sides by the lush hills of Montana in early summer. She had invited me to stay at her place for a couple of nights while I was getting used to the puppy. I readily accepted her invitation, hoping that I could learn from her.

Ginny was in her sixties, her blond hair framing a friendly, pretty face. There was something about Ginny that made me feel like I'd known her forever. As she welcomed me, I spotted a pack of puppies romping around in the backyard.

"You ready to meet your boy?" she asked.

As soon as I was through the gate, the puppies hurled themselves at me, smashing into me with playful affection. But one puppy did not join the bounding pack. He was sitting firmly by Ginny, seemingly scoffing at the idea of his siblings approaching a stranger so carelessly. There was no fear in him; he just sat there, calm and collected, watching me intently. Immediately, I knew this was my boy. Although a few weeks older now, he had the same eyes as the tiny puppy in the picture I'd been sent all those weeks ago: steady and confident, with an intense gaze that made it almost impossible to break eye contact. Around his eyes were two lighter patches set on a big and serious head of silky black fur. His coat was a dark sable: a black overcoat peppered with caramel brown, and a sandy undercoat peeping through, soft like the feathers of a chick. He was noticeably bigger than all the other puppies, with stocky legs and big paws, and huge triangular ears that stood at attention at all times.

The puppy watched me intently as I approached him. He gave my hands a sniff with his shiny black nose, then wagged his tail. I picked him up and pressed him close to my chest. His tiny body was warm and soft, and he smelled of moss and grass, like a wild baby animal. In that moment, my cold feet instantly melted away.

Vilk. The name I had chosen for him at the sight of his picture seemed to fit him perfectly. In Polish, *wilk*—pronounced *vilk*—means wolf. But to spare him the same woes I had experienced as a teenager with English speakers mispronouncing *w*'s, I anglicized his name. He would be Vilk. And he was just like a wolf pup: alert, dark, and a little feral.

When I left Ginny's home a couple of days later, Vilk and I were already a bonded pair. He followed me everywhere I went, his little tail wagging happily, his needle-like teeth nibbling on my fingers whenever he sat in my lap. He was clumsy and playful and still very much trying to figure out the crazy world he had been brought into. In that sense, we had a lot in common.

But taking care of a nine-week-old puppy as a first-time dog owner who was living in a truck was never going to be easy. To cushion the transition, I rented a tiny forest cabin in Montana for a few weeks, expecting that Vilk and I would need some time to adjust to each other. The cabin had no running water, no stove, and no electricity, and with a week of low temperatures and torrential rain that followed, my fantasies of skipping around meadows with my new puppy in tow were quickly doused with cold water. Instead, I found myself stuck indoors most of the time, and while this in itself didn't make life hard—normally, I would just read a book or edit a video—the presence of Vilk changed everything.

Vilk was an uncontrollable ball of energy, gnawing on every single surface he could find to soothe his gums while teething, chasing my ankles whenever I dared to move from his side, and perennially finding novel ways to get up to all kinds of mischief. All of a sudden, I found myself responsible for someone else's potty and sleep schedule. I woke up every two hours at night to take him out to pee. I had to remember to feed him, to watch him, not to let him run away into the forest, which, this being Montana, was presumably prowled by grizzlies. One night, I left Vilk's food outside the cabin, only to find the bag ripped open and the kibble scattered everywhere within a two-mile radius the next morning. Chicken kibble was presumably a fantastic bear attractant, and finding pieces of it strewn around outside the cabin would keep me on my toes for several weeks. By then I had at least purchased a can of non-expired bear spray, which I brought along every single time I left the cabin from that morning on.

Only a few days earlier, I had been an independent solo traveler in charge of my own time, relishing my solitude. Now, every waking moment was dedicated to someone else. Between one day and the next, I became a "dog mom." My independence evaporated into thin air. I could barely leave the cabin to go to the bathroom because Vilk would start whining and barking whenever

I wasn't there. If I wasn't watching him like a hawk, he would swallow rocks and gravel. I couldn't go for a run or a jog—he was too young to come along, and there was no way I could leave him alone, for fear he would chew through the door. Simple things like grocery shopping became logistical nightmares: I could not take the dog into the store with me, but I had nobody to leave him with. I didn't take a shower for about a week, I could barely pick up the camera to film videos, and every few hours I burst into tears, overwhelmed. My decision to get a puppy had started to feel like a trap. I started to feel like perhaps I had made a mistake. I'd just started to relish my solitude and freedom, and now what? A surge of regret welled up inside me. *I should never have gotten him*, I thought, and immediately felt a pang of guilt. Still, I couldn't deny that life had been much less complicated in the pre-Vilk era. Without him, I would already have been en route to Alaska, my days uncomplicated, my life belonging to me, and me only. How would I ever manage to reach Alaska with this little demon wolf demanding something of me every five minutes?

I wavered between regret over getting Vilk and a deep sense of shame about the regret. I became convinced that there was something wrong with me: after all, millions of people around the world had raised puppies—millions had raised *human babies*—and somehow ended up fine. Why was I struggling so much with this tiny creature? I started to entertain the idea of giving him back to Ginny. I could tell her that I simply didn't have what it took to care for a dog, apologize, and say I had made a mistake and that I was sorry. Surely she could still easily find a new home for a young purebred German shepherd from a quality litter.

But just the thought of giving him away—this beautiful little furball who was already sleeping in my bed—seemed even more unbearable than the thought of keeping him. Every time I pictured handing him back to Ginny, my heart ached. After all, Ginny had told me that she had chosen him for me on a full moon. There was something magical about this. As my wolf, he had become a part of my pack. As much as I wavered, I also knew that our fates were tied together.

So I did the only thing I knew I could do in that moment: I started googling. I found an internet forum called "Regretful Parents," where the parents of real human children shared their struggles and regrets. From there, I stumbled upon another forum specifically tailored to pet parents, titled "Puppy Blues"—probably a better fit for my specific struggle. I read the stories of other dog owners who had also wrestled with the many challenges that came with puppies, and was somewhat reassured by the fact that some were finding it even harder than me. Many of them talked about regret and guilt and a feeling that they'd lost their identity and independence. As I scrolled down, devouring the posts, I felt seen. I wasn't the only one struggling, which meant that maybe there wasn't something wrong with me and that this was just a tough period I needed to get through.

The online discussion inspired me to share my own feelings publicly; I felt like there weren't enough people visibly talking about their challenges when it came to the first few weeks of dog ownership, and I thought perhaps sharing mine might make others feel seen and supported, as well as hopefully garner me some advice. When the video about my puppy blues went live on my YouTube channel, I received an outpouring of support. Some comments claimed snarkily that I was too selfish to ever take care of another living creature, but the vast majority of people could relate to my words, and reassured me that things would get easier and that soon I would have a best friend by my side (rather than a chewy, hyperactive hellhound).

I wasn't the only one. With that knowledge came relief, a release of all the fears and apprehensions I'd had. "Ask your friends for help. Doesn't everyone love puppies?" said one veteran puppy owner. I wasn't used to asking for help, but given that a furball weighing twenty pounds was pushing me to the verge of a nervous breakdown, I decided that something had to be done. I needed help. I needed a moment to myself. I needed some breathing space. I needed to recalibrate. I reached out to Ginny, asking if she could watch Vilk for a few hours. She agreed without hesitation.

With Ginny taking care of Vilk, I took a day off puppy duty and went running. I had now been trail running for a couple of years, getting out several times a week to give my body a shakeout. It was more useful than therapy, I claimed, perhaps a little too self-assuredly, but a long run always helped me clear my head. Comforted by the knowledge that my puppy was in good hands, I sprinted down a long forest trail, passing through meadows and over hilltops. I stopped at mountain creeks and jumped over tree roots and hurled myself downhill through the rustle of the last year's leaf litter like a madwoman. I could smell pine sap and wildflowers. As the endorphins spread through my body, my joy finally returned. "Thank you, thank you, thank you!" I screamed. My euphoric yells were probably an effective bear deterrent. I was overpowered by gratitude: I was thankful for this run, thankful for a strong body, thankful for the freedom to be here, and thankful for a new chapter in my life.

On my return, for the first time since getting Vilk, I took a shower. A shower in a small wooden shack in the forest, with some cold water running out of a single pipe—it didn't look like much of a luxury, but when I turned it on and the cool water flowed down my body that warm June afternoon, and I washed my hair and my body, scrubbing myself clean with a bar of soap, I felt like I had baptized myself.

The run and the shower were enough to restore me for a lifetime with Vilk.

When I picked him up later that day, tears welled up. He ran toward me and crashed into me with all his might, ecstatic to see me again. He was so small, so soft, so perfect. My heart melted at the sight of this trusting furball—I was already his entire world. As he nibbled on my hands, his miniature fangs leaving tiny marks on my skin, I promised myself that I would do everything in my power to make our life together a great adventure. He was now part of my story.

Over the following days, weeks, months, and years, I would come to see the idea that there is only one "valid" type of unconditional love—the type you feel for a child—as small-minded. People often dismiss any assertion that we can feel unconditional love toward animals. In my mind, that reflects a limited view of love, and a limited capacity to feel love. We can love anything unconditionally if we open our hearts and our minds. And Vilk had opened mine. So no matter how many times he needed to go out at night, no matter how many rocks he tried to swallow, no matter how much of a nuisance he could be when he didn't know what to do with his hurricane of energy, he was mine and I was his. And together, we were one wolf pack.

chapter twenty-two

to the north of alaska

I'd grown up under the impression that by the time I hit thirty years old, I would have life figured out. Perhaps, on my last day as a twenty-nine-year-old, I would receive some mystical almanac from an older mentor, filled with details on exactly how I should navigate life as an adult. After all, the religious had their scriptures. Every car had a manual. There were encyclopedias, textbooks, university courses, and online workshops to teach people how to be anything under the sun. So when my thirtieth birthday came and went, and nobody handed me the adulting almanac, I started to wonder whether I would remain forever uninitiated into maturity.

I was camping by a hidden pond somewhere in the mountains of Oregon as these thoughts wandered in and out of my mind like leaves caught in a whirlwind. Vilk romped around gleefully, wet and covered with sand from the lake bed, his paws leaving muddy footprints on the no-longer-clean new blanket I'd laid out. He'd adapted to our nomadic lifestyle as if he'd been born into it, and over the past couple of months we'd become very close. Although I still felt overwhelmed from time to time, for the most part my puppy blues were (mercifully) just a memory now. The situation had required me to make a mental switch in order to overcome my initial doubts. I encouraged myself to focus on all the things he could teach me: how to be joyful, how to be in the moment, how to live for living's sake. In the end, it proved quite astonishing how much I could learn from a five-month-old dog. But as much as my canine guru was teaching me, if we were outside the confined space of the truck, I did still have to monitor him around the clock to ensure that, for all his worldly wisdom, he didn't wander off to snack on deer poop.

While Vilk played in the water, I was busy trying to clean my only frying pan with a pinecone. I looked down. There was so much dirt gathered under my fingernails that only a good brushing session could get it all out. Alas, not only did I not own a dish sponge, but I didn't own a nailbrush either. I had been doing my business in holes I dug in the ground. My legs were covered in bruises from Vilk's constant pouncing, mud was crusted all over my clothes and bedding, and I hadn't worn shoes in days. The unshaved hair in my armpits was about an inch long, and every time I raised my arms, the simple audacity of its being there made me giggle.

What the hell am I even doing? I thought to myself. One of my closest friends, a fellow YouTuber, had just moved into her own house with her husband. Another had found out she was pregnant and was unexpectedly happy, even though she'd never wanted kids before. By comparison, my life was an unpredictable heap of chaos, made even messier by this puppy I had brought into the mix. It had been easy to rationalize myself out of "adulting" thoughts when I was in my twenties, since the universe more or less seemed to agree that your twenties were for having fun. But I was now a thirty-one-year-old woman without a life plan, and that seemed a more controversial proposition.

I thought of the few exceptions I knew—adults without kids who lived as they pleased—and considered them rebels who had somehow managed to cheat the system. They inhabited some parallel world where they got to enjoy the freedoms of adulthood without having to abide by any of its rules. Adulthood meant responsibility, or settling down, or commitment, or any number of those heavy concepts. It was very serious business, or so we were told. And I had so internalized this narrative that I still felt, subconsciously, that the rare and rebellious exceptions to that narrative were other people, not me. And surely these exceptions must be unhappy, deep down. That was what the people in my comments section seemed to think as they followed my overlanding trip across North America. "Sure, spend your whole life avoiding commitment," wrote user6723, "and good luck finding a man." "You'll see, real life will catch up with you," claimed the_tank_inator. "She lives in la-la-land, a trainwreck waiting to happen," yankeeboy1 chimed in.

I watched Vilk splashing around in the pond, digging up rocks and moving sticks from one place to another in an intricate game only he understood. He looked up at me and bowed playfully, inviting me to join him. Barefoot, I sauntered to the edge of the water. The trees were in full leaf and were reflected on the surface of the pond, crisp against the blue sky. I stepped in. The morning water had cooled after a chilly night. My feet sank a little into the sand at the bottom, the granular softness enveloping my toes. I felt the sun's rays prickle my skin. I lowered my nose to my arm and breathed in deeply. My skin smelled like only bare skin under a warm sun could. Not like perfume, but like a human body immersed in nature, a little sweet, a little salty. Living outside and practicing what were questionable hygiene habits by modern standards, I could smell myself. The scent was subtle and a little earthy, with notes of sweetness, like summer. I licked my arm, curious to see how it would taste. Salty. All around was the magic of trees, their silence, and the feeling of divine wilderness. If this very moment were to last forever, it would be a good forever.

By the water that mirrored the sky, I was beginning to see what adulthood might look like for me, and that it—I—needn't be any different from this exact moment. My coming of age was slowly coming into being on this long, slow journey of mine. Though I could not quite see it as it was happening, I could sense it: I was growing up on the road, in my own very particular way, and Vilk had just started to guide me.

Some aspects of life would not bend to the slow pace of this process of internal transformation, and one was the seasons. If I wanted to follow the plan I had concocted to drive the Pan-American Highway, then I needed to get a move on. The height of summer had come and gone, and I needed to reach the north of Alaska, several thousand miles away, before autumn kicked in. Up there, in the Arctic, autumn ushers in the cold, the rain, and very short days—not ideal conditions for an overlanding trip. While at the planning stage, I had connected with a couple of fellow travelers via Instagram who were also en route to Prudhoe Bay. They had invited me to join them, convoy-style, to drive the northernmost section of the journey together. I was hesitant at first: I had planned to travel the entirety of the Pan-American Highway solo.

A stubborn part of me insisted that I did not *need* company, and that I should make the trip—and film it—completely alone. I had looked forward to driving the length of Alaska by myself and showing that a woman traveling solo could complete the trip safely. The promise of that deep and remote solitude felt enticing. But Nick and Mathilde seemed friendly, and I would still have the majority of my time to myself. Besides, if this road was as dangerous as I had been warned it was, then it might be wise to have some support, just in case. So I replied to their message, and we decided to meet up at a campsite in the far north of British Columbia, about fifteen hundred miles away, a couple of weeks later. I got out my map and traced my fingers along the long blue line of the road, ambling far north through forests, mountains, and stretches of remote land. It was a *very* long blue line. I'd better get driving.

The prospect of driving over five thousand miles to the top of Alaska and back to the Lower 48 (the contiguous states that constitute the landmass of the United States and exclude Alaska and Hawaii) admittedly filled me with a little dread. It was a very long way to go in a creaky, now seventeen-year-old, not particularly fuel-efficient truck that had already broken down catastrophically a couple of times. It was a very long way to go at the end of the season, with temperatures dropping and the increasing likelihood of some roads being covered in ice. It was a long way to go with a young puppy who required nonstop care and attention. It was a long way to go only to say I'd been there and then turn around and drive all the way back again.

As I'd hoped when I first got Odyssey, it was proving to be a great relief to have my entire life so neatly packed into a compact metal box: I didn't have to lug my suitcase anywhere; my entire (modest) wardrobe fit neatly into a cupboard inside the truck. I didn't have to book tickets and worry about hotel reservations because my car was also where I slept, and it was all familiar to me—I didn't have the mental exhaustion of constantly assimilating to new places. Perhaps most importantly, I didn't have to rely on anyone else or experience the low-level anxiety that often induced. Odyssey gave me freedom, agency, and self-sufficiency, and allowed me to travel more or less at my own pace.

But as much as overlanding made some aspects of my life easier, I was now realizing that I had inadvertently added a host of new concerns into the mix. Rather than filming specific places and topics, as I had done on my earlier travels, now I had—almost unwittingly—turned my entire life into a YouTube show. I filmed every day, every step of the way, sharing my personal life much more deeply than ever before. This meant that my mind had no respite from thinking about the channel, the videos, the next story. It was beginning to feel like I could never fully "switch off." And then, of course, there was Vilk: a reckless puppy sharing my tiny home, who had a habit of disappearing into the woods, eating old animal poop, generally causing mischief, and requiring near-constant supervision.

I didn't know what to expect from the journey, but I did know that it would be an odyssey through some of the most hostile territory on earth. For perspective, the majority of all Canadians live within a hundred miles of the US border. This means that as you go farther north, towns and settlements become few and far between. Eventually, you find yourself on a narrow road winding its way across British Columbia's mountains and forests. That's where, via the Yukon and Alaska, you enter an icy tundra prone to blizzards and storms and subjected to twenty-four hours of darkness in the winter, and mammoth swarms of mosquitoes and lurking grizzlies in the summer. You can expect gas stations to be a rare sight in the Yukon, and from there, things get progressively worse.

Few people means few amenities, and that includes emergency mechanics, vets, and hospitals. Good planning helped me to prepare for some of these challenges. I had come a long way from the girl lugging about sacks of potatoes and cherry tomatoes on a packhorse in Mongolia, and now I preplanned my meals with expert precision. Ensuring that I stocked up on groceries before leaving the Lower 48, I filled Odyssey with plain, healthy food I could simply heat up on the road. I pinned potential camp locations on the map and sourced the numbers of towing services and mechanics along my route just in case Odyssey decided to stop cooperating. To preempt this, I changed the oil, upgraded the tires, and fixed a few small mechanical issues at a car shop in Washington. But even if everything went according to plan, it would be a long and tough journey.

It took me over a week of driving to reach the meeting point I had agreed on with Mathilde and Nick. Along the way, I was filming my trip religiously, documenting it every step of the way for my YouTube channel, motivated by all the unknowns that lay ahead and by being able to show girls and women everywhere that they, too, could embark on adventures of their own.

By the time I finally reached the lake in northern Canada where I was meeting my new travel companions, I still had no idea what to expect. We had agreed to spend a few weeks traveling together without knowing whether we would even get along. We did know that we had a few things in common. We drove old and impractical Land Rover Defenders. All three of us lived in our trucks full-time and had chosen this life for the adventure. When we finally met, there was an instant connection. They were a little younger than me and laid-back, and they had been pursuing their expedition for a while. "We've been planning this trip for a few years; it's been our dream," explained Nick as we spent the first evening sitting around a crackling campfire deep in the Canadian wilderness. "Back home, we both had great jobs, but we always knew that we wanted to do a big adventure."

"And when else would we get to do it?" Mathilde chimed in. "It seemed like the perfect moment, while we're in our twenties, before we have a family."

A few months earlier, Mathilde and Nick had quit their well-paid jobs in Brussels in order to pursue an ambitious dream: to drive their Land Rover Defender, called Albatross, around the world. Not only would they drive the Pan-American Highway, but they would then ship the truck to Australia, Asia, and Africa, driving each continent in turn.

As I was journeying up to meet them, I was thinking how the mental preparation was just as important as the logistical groundwork: when all else failed and you were stranded on the side of the road with no provisions, doubting the mission, the mind was all you had. It was on this road that my concept of the "expedition mindset" came about. An expedition was a journey, a process. An expedition was an attempt to do something extraordinary, regardless of the outcome.

You anticipated that you might want to give up, and along the way you might. But you also committed to striving: doing your best in the name of something bigger, whatever the mission you had set out for yourself. With the expedition mindset, you understood that whatever it was that you were embarking on was a journey of ups and downs that would eventually lead you to a place in your mind that you had never been. Nick and Mathilde's expedition mindset would have to take them much farther than mine this time.

The next morning, we packed up and got going. Our direction was toward Prudhoe Bay, deep in Alaska, and I found that the farther north we drove, the bigger the world became. We left British Columbia behind and entered the land of giants—the much-revered remote Yukon. Every valley we passed through looked like it had been flattened out by a God-size palm: a panorama of width and space, and prehistoric vastness. The ribbon-thin road we drove wound its way through ageless pine forests that went on, uninterrupted, for hundreds of miles in every direction, rising gradually into the distance as the terrain undulated, unhurried. The enormous taiga of the Yukon was home to caribou, moose, wolves, and grizzlies who roamed these lands without the nuisance of human presence.

Even sitting inside a car, on a man-made road, I could still sense the timeless power of this place and couldn't help but think that humans, myself included, really had no business being here, in an environment so wild and expansive. Yet here we were, a convoy of metal cans on rubber wheels, crossing this vastness and hoping that it would let us pass.

But what was troubling me had little to do with the enormity of the taiga or even the ferocity of its inhabitants. I was growing increasingly anxious knowing that the Canadian road would soon come to an end, and I would need to once again cross the American border to enter Alaska.

On an overcast day in mid-September, we approached the outpost of Little Gold, the northernmost border crossing on the American continent, which stood on the frontier between the Canadian Yukon and Alaska. It was the polar opposite of Laredo, Texas. Standing on the side of a long and desolate mountain road in one of the wildest places on earth, this was a tiny human outpost struggling to hold on to civilization amid the mightiness of nature at her most untamed. This border crossing was so remote that they shut it down for nearly half of the year because of the extreme weather that hit this region every winter. We had not seen another car for hours.

"You're right on time," the Canadian border official greeted me. "You do know we are closing for the season at the end of the day today?"

"Yessir, we've been rushing to get here," I replied. As the Canadian official stamped me out, I rolled over to the American side and wondered whether I would once again experience interrogations and pat downs. But the US border official barely checked my documents and, with a bored *Get me outta here* look on her face, stamped me into Alaska. I tried hard to restrain myself but couldn't resist a scream of relief as soon as the inspection station was in my rearview mirror. We were in Alaska.

As soon as we crossed the border, the overcast sky threw down rays of sunshine. The forest that surrounded us lit up in an orange glow, with specks of green and bursts of yellow turning the canopy into a painting. We were now a mini-convoy, and that meant we camped, ate, and took breaks in all the same spots. Over the course of the next few days, we drove and boondocked, our thoughts and compasses pointing steadfastly north. Mathilde and Nick were our chefs and cooked up delicious curries and casseroles. I cleaned up and took on fire duty, Vilk helping me to collect the sticks and ward off any bears that might be lurking in the trees. It had taken us a few days to get used to making plans as a group. Although I had been hesitant to give up my autonomy, it was transpiring that traveling together had more pros than cons. To joke around and share our impressions of this vast, wild place while sitting around a campfire together as the deep northern night approached meant every day on the road ended on a high note.

The three of us were on a mission together: the Arctic Overlandys (a play on the word *Landy*, a way of referring to a Land Rover) en route to the Arctic Ocean. The road we followed finally led us to the city of Fairbanks—the last bastion of urban life in Alaska. After stocking up on groceries and fuel, we passed by the last traffic light we would see for about a week.

To get to Prudhoe Bay, we would have to tackle the Dalton Highway, a roughly four-hundred-mile road that connects the oil fields of Prudhoe Bay to the lower forty-eight states. "This road is a way to reinvent. This highway is an act of living," Joy Mothertrucker, a legendary female trucker who spent many decades driving the

Dalton Highway, had said. I would come to see that she had been onto something. The road is only partially paved, with many stretches washed out by violent rains and fierce snowfall every year. It crosses a vast and largely uninhabited wilderness; aside from a few Indigenous communities that call it home, there are no towns or villages to speak of. At the 240-mile mark is the picturesquely named Coldfoot, a settlement with the only gas station along the entire highway. In sum, you didn't end up on the Dalton Highway by accident. The only people who came here were the truckers who serviced the oil fields up north, and travelers like us, en route to the Arctic Ocean.

"I don't think I'm ready for this," I said, looking at Mathilde and Nick as they started up Albatross, their white Defender.

"We're doing it! Let's go get it!" shouted Nick gleefully, his window cracked open. He slowly rolled toward the highway. Now all I had to do was follow behind. I turned the key in the ignition, smiling, and . . . nothing. A couple of lights went off on the dashboard, but there was no sound of the engine turning over. I tried it again, reinserting the key into the ignition and turning it. Silence. It appeared to be Odyssey who was not ready this time. We were already in the north of Alaska, far from mechanics who would know about my odd European car, and I could not get it started. There was nothing in my line of sight now, as Mathilde and Nick had already disappeared down the road, expecting me to catch up. I took out my phone and called them. "Guys, Odyssey won't start," I said, grateful that we still had a cell signal. Grateful that I had listened to that little voice inside that worried about Odyssey on such remote roads. Grateful that I had made the decision to share this journey with others. Grateful that I had someone to call.

Within a couple of minutes, they came back. Nick had some basic mechanical skills and was hoping to put them to use. "It could be something really simple or something really serious," he explained. Great. That was a reasonable range to work within. "It could be that your starter motor is shot. That would probably be the worst-case option, because it would mean that you'd need to source a completely new one from Europe. But let's start with the really simple option," Nick suggested. And with that, he disappeared underneath the truck, investigating its soot-covered belly. After a couple of minutes, I heard a faint "Okay, can you try starting her again?"

I jumped behind the steering wheel, hoping for a miracle. I was not one for prayer or manifestation, but a string of affirmations slipped out of my lips as I turned the key in the ignition once more.

The loud rumble of an old-school diesel engine filled my ears like the sweetest birdsong. She was back on. "What did you do?!" I shouted in Nick's direction, elated, struggling to believe that the vehicle was running again with minimal intervention.

"Oh, there's a cable that sometimes slips out of its socket in Defenders. We had the same issue a while back. You just need to slip it back in and everything goes back to normal." It sounded very simple, but I would never have figured it out on my own. I made sure Nick showed me *exactly* where that socket was. This "fix" would come in handy in my future travels and was a good experience to add to the tool kit of my expedition mindset.

After that false start, we were off. The firs and spruces of the taiga began to thin out, and with every valley we entered, the landscape became even wider, without any trees to give a sense of scale. We were crossing into the arctic tundra, a place so cold and hostile that no trees grew there. This was the domain of the toughest among the living: the plants and creatures that held on to life in spite of the blizzards and the extreme cold, and in spite of the night that fell there, its darkness unrelenting for several months every year.

The only other vehicles we saw were the trucks made famous by the American TV show *Ice Road Truckers*, which provided a lifeline for the far north. Every time a truck passed us, it sent a torrent of dust and gravel in our direction—though most of the truck drivers slowed down politely to try to spare us cracked windshields. For the entire four hundred miles, a wide silver pipe tracked the highway: this was the Trans-Alaska Pipeline System, transporting a river of oil south. Aside from the occasional truck and the pipeline, sticking out like a sore metallic thumb in an ocean of wilderness, nothing out there reminded me of our human world. To take in that enormity, to sleep in her embrace, tiny humans on the outer limits of the tamed world, was to see our lives from the perspective of the nonhuman.

"We live a life of extraordinary luxury," I said to Nick and Mathilde one night as we sat by our campfire, which flickered gently in the cold, still night. They looked at me and nodded, knowing exactly what I meant. To have chosen to live like this against everyone else's better judgment had been hard. But I had chosen it, and now it was mine. From where I sat, in the Alaskan night, I suddenly saw that making that painful decision to break from my old life, choosing this life for myself, had been my first true act of adulthood. The divorce, the grueling first hike in Nepal, the lonely trek in Mongolia, the separation and subsequent reconciliation with my family, the baptisms by fire on social media, the three-month "quarantine" on a remote island, the acceptance of responsibility that came with getting Vilk—these had been my rites of passage to enter into an adulthood that was my own, challenges I'd had to go through in order to find myself right there, driving one of the most remote roads on the planet in my expedition truck that I'd bought myself with income I'd made by traveling, with my dog sleeping in the back of it, under my loving care. Just us: a small wolf pack searching for the experience of being alive.

We reached Prudhoe Bay on a foggy September afternoon. Deadhorse, the only town in the area, sits between the end of the road and the frigid Arctic Ocean. Bear sightings here are a regular occurrence, and the most feared bears of all, polar bears, have been known to wander into town. In Deadhorse, the custom was to always leave your truck unlocked and leave the keys inside in case someone ever needed to jump in and get away from a bear.

To call Deadhorse a town is generous. In reality, it is a glorified industrial park perched on the roof of the world. The unpaved main road is lined with shipping containers that have been turned into dwellings and prefab accommodations for the workers that service the nearby oil fields. Pipes, fences, and metal surfaces fill the empty spaces. There are no parks, no cinemas, and no restaurants—nothing that you might expect to find in a typical town. The only shop sells souvenirs and snacks but no fresh food, not even a loaf of bread: after all, all the oil field workers have their canteen, and since so few outsiders ever come here, there is no need to feed or entertain them. When we visited, the atmosphere over Deadhorse was heavy and dark, with the wind howling constantly and fog obscuring the landscape, making it impossible to glean anything beyond the steel walls and the oil field machinery, which emerged out of the mist like huge metallic monsters. We might as well have been visiting a space station on another planet.

The town reminded me of the summit at Everest Base Camp, in that it was the ultimate proof of why the journey mattered more than the destination. I had only one item on my Prudhoe Bay bucket list: to jump into the Arctic Ocean. But this being an oil field, the coast was closely guarded. We were told it was not possible to simply drive up to the beach and jump into the water; the ocean was locked behind barriers and checkpoints. So, after parting with nearly $100, we booked ourselves on a "tour" operated by the only tourism agency in town. This tour—essentially just a minibus ride—was the only way for us to get a permit to access the coast. Shuttling tourists between Deadhorse and the frigid waters of the Arctic was presumably the agency's main gig in a town that didn't have many other attractions.

Mathilde offered to stay behind with Vilk, so Nick and I took the shuttle alongside a few other American tourists, all of whom had flown to Prudhoe Bay for reasons completely incomprehensible to me—and also, I think, to them. After fifteen minutes, our tour group was plonked onto a rocky black beach. In front of us, a peaceful and dark body of water stretched out into a wall of mist. When you heard "Arctic Ocean," you imagined an ocean of quite some magnitude: remote, dramatic, frigid, with powerful waves crashing into thousand-year-old icebergs, killer whales diving beneath the surface. The Arctic Ocean as I saw it in Prudhoe Bay was placid, seemingly more of a pond than an ocean.

"Well, at least it looks like it's safe to get in," I said, glancing at Nick.

Out of the twelve or so people who had come out on the shuttle, only two—Jason, a young man from Vermont, and I—decided to get into the ocean for a polar dip. The open road had made me realize that, more than anything else, I was in charge of my own fate, that I could take whichever turn I wanted to take, that I was free to live as I pleased, to surrender myself to every moment. In front of the Arctic Ocean, I was an adult with the freedom to make a decision, even if it struck everyone else as crazy. So Jason and I threw off our clothes down to our underwear and ran into the frigid ocean before we could change our minds.

When I finally got deep enough, I shrieked and let my body plunge underneath the surface, all the way up to my neck. As an instant shot of adrenaline surged through my body, my heart rate shot up, my breath was suspended, and my muscles seized up, gripped by the frigid water. I shrieked again, feeling as if every single cell in my body had been shaken awake by the sudden shock. Every inch of my skin was tingling and dancing, and my brain was momentarily seized by a rush of elation that was free of thought—in that brief moment, all that existed was pure feeling. And all I felt was, *What a miracle it is to be alive.*

chapter twenty-three

burned out

It crept up on me slowly, so much so that I failed to notice it for weeks. Like a patch of mold on the surface of a peach, my burnout settled on me and gradually spread inward.

I did not wake up one day and realize that I was burned out. There was no one moment when it all exploded in a dramatic flash. I did not spot the initial warning signs. When I first struggled to pick up my camera, I simply assumed I was very tired after a long five-thousand-mile trip. It had been an extremely intense couple of months, during which every day had entailed not only hours of driving but also finding places to stay, making sure I had water, feeding myself, feeding and training Vilk, filming, backing up footage, taking photos, posting on social media, working on the videos with my editor, planning the next shoot, and, of course, making sure that my small tornado of a dog didn't get eaten by a grizzly.

When I finally reached the Lower 48 after a month of roaming back from Alaska through a long series of wild campsites, I booked myself into a cottage in the Mojave Desert and spent an entire week sleeping, staring into the horizon, and struggling to form a coherent thought. My mind melted into the desert silence after weeks of being exposed to the incessant rumble of an old diesel engine and a poorly soundproofed cabin. My body felt very still after weeks of motion over the land, covering hundreds of miles at a time, with the truck in a constant state of vibration. It felt strange and new to be able to walk in and out of a house, sleep on a bed in a room separate from my living quarters, and stand under a stream of hot water cascading from the ceiling. And yet, there was no joy, not even relief, in my rest. I simply felt numb. I then numbed the guilt I felt regarding my numbness with a constant stream of craft beers and California wines. *I'm living my dream life. How can I feel this numb?* I'd think as another glass of red "crafted in California" by some artisan winemaker disappeared down my throat. *I thought I was long done with this oenophile bullshit*, I thought to myself while opening a new bottle. By the time I was on my third glass, my thoughts became fuzzy and soft. That was exactly what I wanted. By then, I should have seen that I was drinking to mask something that was happening underneath the surface.

I assumed I was in a state of exhaustion paired with some kind of post-adventure blues: the anecdotal dip in adrenaline that adventurers experience once they are done with their expeditions. I had nothing left in me. How could I keep driving south when all I wanted was to stay in the desert and let my thoughts dissolve into the sky? I observed the giant sandstone boulders that elbowed out of the hillsides, the coral pink sun setting behind them every afternoon in a dazzling display of warmth. As the days passed, I started to daydream. I pictured myself living out there, in the desert, on a plot of land much too big for a single person but just the right size for a hermit. "I would buy forty acres of land and install a well and build a small wooden shack," I wrote in my journal, fantasizing about a life that moved as slowly as my thoughts. I wanted to be a cactus: still, eternal. Instead, I felt like a tumbleweed, tossed around from one place to another, crumbling as it went, notable only because of its constant motion.

But there was no time to be still and commune with the eternal. My Pan-American road trip needed to follow the seasons—I did not want to be stuck in torrential rains in Costa Rica or the oppressive summer heat waves in Colombia. As ever, the seasons would not wait, not even for a woman who was the mistress of her own destiny. I was in a race with time, and always falling behind. As the pressure to get going again grew, my body and mind resisted.

As December approached, I reconnected with Mathilde and Nick. After our Alaska adventure, our routes had separated: they'd wanted to see some sights in the United States that I had already visited, and I'd wanted—needed—solitude. But when we talked again in the winter, they were about to cross into Mexico. If I couldn't make myself sit behind the steering wheel again on my own, I hoped those two could be my motivation. So, a couple of weeks later, we met on the other side of the American border and started our drive south with another couple heading in the same direction.

I continued to film for YouTube and capture photos for Instagram, but without any creative conviction. What drove me was a simple force of habit and a sense of obligation. If I didn't film new episodes, I wouldn't be able to make a living, and if I couldn't make a living, then I would have to find something else to do with my life. That was not what I wanted. This was a dream life, after all—*my* dream life. A life of freedom and independence that I had worked toward, made so many sacrifices for. A life that so many would kill for. . . .

And yet, increasingly, it felt like all the creative joy had been sucked out of it. I was *making content*, not telling stories anymore. The mere act of picking up the camera was preceded by drawn-out rumination, seesawing between a sense of moral duty and existential indifference. It wasn't a sudden, sharp hatred for the camera. It was a dull, droning voice that told me I had nothing to say, nothing to add. My energy had gone from electric to sluggish. Whereas once I'd been excited about seeing new places, I now felt dread and anxiety. One of the most insidious things about burnout is that it doesn't just deplete your energy and inspiration. It brings about a crisis of identity. You don't just lose your fuel. You lose your spark.

Around that time, someone left a comment under one of my videos that said, "Eva looks like she is just surviving, not thriving." My initial impulse was to deny it outright: "How dare you? I'm living my best life out here!" But another part of me stirred when I reread the comment. It was the dawning of recognition. By the time most of us acknowledge that we're burning out, it's usually too late. And I wasn't ready to acknowledge it yet.

I had embarked on the Pan-American Highway journey to give myself a sense of direction, unmoored as I had started to feel without a life plan, reaching an age when life seemed to be all about planning for the future. This yearslong road trip was an attempt at forging a new life plan, creating a new blueprint for myself. But it was becoming increasingly evident that assuming an established highway could provide me with a sense of direction had been an error of judgment. Our paths are never linear, and we can rarely follow one that is. Had I not already learned this lesson?

I followed Mathilde and Nick south all along the roughly eight-hundred-mile California Peninsula, from the United States to its end in Mexico. They set the pace; they provided the momentum. I simply tagged along, hoping that the open road would give me an idea of what to do next. For fear of being a killjoy, I didn't share much about my burnout with them. They were on their own journey, and the nomadic life was still very new to them. I did not want to plant seeds of doubt that might dampen their enthusiasm.

Halfway down the Baja Peninsula we camped out in the desert. Again I found that in its stillness I could see beneath the surface of things, and in its silence I could hear words unsaid. We were camping in a spot that was sheltered by three huge boulders that had stood there since time immemorial. It was just us, the silence, and a vast expanse of rock and sand; our world was still and imposing. It was a cool evening, and we huddled close to the fire. Above us, a spray of stars illuminated the sky, the cloud of the Milky Way clearly visible without any towns or villages nearby. We watched as the night drew down and distant stars studded the sky so thickly that, eventually, we stopped pointing them out.

In that moment, we were unhurried, unmoved. We were not being driven toward some goal. We simply sat around the fire, each of us lost in our thoughts, each of us a part of this still realm around us. In the silence, I could hear. In the silence, I could listen to all the words I wasn't saying, all the words I hadn't even allowed myself to think. And now I understood. With every atom of my being, I understood.

I needed to be still.

The thought dropped into the pool of my mind like a stone falling from the heavens above us. After five years of moving, rushing, flying, driving, climbing, sailing, racing, striving, losing, succeeding, finding, searching, aching, migrating . . . I needed to be still.

In the three months that followed, I stayed still. I moved out of Odyssey and into a cottage on the edge of town in the south of

Baja California, Mexico. Every morning, Vilk and I walked down to the beach, where we swam in the ocean, then sat in the sand, dripping wet, waiting for the breeze to dry us off.

It was paradise, but I struggled to find peace.

Burnout robbed me of something that had been fundamental over the preceding five years. It robbed me of the things that had saved me after my marriage had fallen apart. Burnout robbed me of curiosity. It robbed me of my desire to explore. It robbed me of my drive to create. As I battled it out in my head on that golden beach in Baja, I wondered whether those things, which I had assumed would always be a part of my core DNA, were now gone forever. If they were, who would I be?

But simply to be still just didn't seem to be enough. Moving out of the truck and into a cottage had helped stop things from getting any worse, but any improvement in my condition felt imperceptible. Living on the road, I experienced what can only be described as perpetual nomad syndrome: the anxiety and stress that came from having to find a new place to stay every day, from having to find water every day, from having to organize my route and drive hundreds of miles every day. It came from having to find my footing again and again, always in a new place, in a very complex and busy world. My perpetual nomad syndrome had dissolved into thin air, like time did in the desert, the moment I found my footing in my temporary new home.

But something still wasn't right inside me. I still wasn't creating videos—I simply couldn't make myself do it. Without that self-imposed momentum, I realized that I did not *want* to continue driving the Pan-American Highway. If I did it, I would be doing it for the wrong reasons: to prove a point, out of stubbornness, or because I did not want to give people the impression that I had failed. I knew there was no way I could travel for another fifteen thousand miles across South America with this level of existential dread. All desire to travel this road had left me, and all it had left me with was desire's exact opposite. So I made the decision not to continue. Instead of driving south, I would take a break from the noise and then head back north. That idea of forty acres in the desert was still rolling around in my mind every day. If I had no more desire to travel, if this was it, then maybe I could buy land in the United States and set up a homestead.

Before I did anything else, I had to tell my audience that I had decided to quit the Pan-American project. In my mind's eye, I could see the comments rolling in: "What a failure"; "I knew she couldn't do it"; "She's too weak to complete a journey that big." I gave myself another few days to think about it and prepare myself before making the news public, but I ultimately realized this: I was allowed to change my path, to shape my dreams, even to bury them altogether and seek new ones. I thereby gave myself that permission. I told an audience of millions of people that I was no longer driving the Pan-American Highway. Instead of the regret I'd imagined I might experience, I actually felt a huge wave of relief the moment I hit "publish." That was how I knew that quitting had been the right call.

As expected, some people retaliated by calling me weak and indecisive. But the vast majority seemed to understand the decision. With that out of the way, I felt like I had the blessing I needed to take time off, and I hoped that somewhere along the way my creative will would come back.

While in Baja, I was resolutely single and not looking for any liaisons. Relationships were not on my mind. In my journal, I wrote that I might be open to dating someone if they fulfilled a set of criteria. The list that followed went on for two pages and included items such as "Must love Vilk like own child," "Must not want human children," and "Must feel like an anchor in the storm."

I was strolling on a beach in a new part of Baja that I was exploring when a tall stranger approached me. "Cool rig," he said with an American accent, eyeing Odyssey. We chatted for a moment about the car, and after a while he asked if he could take me out for dinner. I'd not been asked out for dinner in many years. In fact, nobody had ever invited me on a date quite so directly. Taken aback, I mumbled, "Um . . . sure, I guess."

And that was how I met Noah.

It was love at (almost) first sight. Within a few days of our first date, we were already making plans to live a quiet life in the mountains together. He would build the house, I would film the process, and this was how we would live. He was tall, mesmerizingly handsome, with the brightest blue eyes I had ever looked into. He did not want children, did not believe in all the things that everyone else believed in; he was a wild man who had set off into the world in his truck, just like I had. He was a misfit, too. Together, we fit exceedingly well. That we were so similar—in our independence, our wandering natures, our love of solitude—made us an unlikely match in many ways, and also made the fact of us meeting so surprising. But somehow we had found each other, by a stroke of serendipity.

As is often the case when two people fall in love at first sight, our lives smashed into each other's at the speed of light. We wedded our plans: we decided to travel back north together, cross the United States by car, and then move to Europe. It was all madness, crazy-in-love madness. We started to discuss marriage almost immediately, not because either of us was passionate about having a wedding, but because a legal marriage would allow us to live together anywhere we wanted: he could eventually get a European passport through me, I an American one through him. We both wanted a life somewhere wild and solitary, just the two of us and a few animals and nobody else.

Being with Noah felt like the universe was giving me permission to take a break from work. For once, I could pour my energy into a relationship and not just my career, and I could feel that it was healing that depleted part of me. Everything that had not aligned in my previous relationships suddenly made sense with Noah. Since I wasn't filming videos during my self-imposed burnout break, I had a lot more time than usual to dedicate to another person. After all that time traveling with Nick and Mathilde, I also had proof that relationships *could* work on the road, in very close quarters—as long as you were traveling with the right person.

We decided to turn our plan into reality. We eventually left Baja, drove up to the United States, and traveled across the country. I started filming again—slowly at first, without putting too much pressure on myself. With a new travel companion, and a few months' rest, and flying high on the flames of a new love, I felt my burnout dissipate. We spent a couple of months on the East Coast, getting ready to uproot our lives and move to Europe. Noah prepared to sell his house and most of his possessions—something he had been planning to do for a long time, but it was only now that he had the impetus to go through with it. I watched as lawn mowers, tools, and knickknacks were shipped off to buyers after Noah had put them up for sale. Our future together was materializing as his belongings dematerialized, piece by piece.

Without hesitation, we headed to Italy together—a country of romance, a place where we had both dreamed of living at some point. So why not right now? I shipped Odyssey across the ocean once again. Vilk flew inside a crate on the same airplane as me. Drawn by the culture, the food, the beauty of the landscape, and fantasies we'd both harbored of living in the Italian countryside,

Noah and I moved into a charming cottage in the mountains of Abruzzo.

And so it was that two independent, freedom-seeking nomads who had spent many years living on their own terms abruptly halted their travels. All of a sudden, we were living in one place, making our decisions as a couple, and no longer experiencing the excitement that came with troubleshooting the challenges of being on the road. We were static, a little bored, and stuck inside four brick walls. I'd moved to Italy without fully considering what this would mean for myself and for my work: I was no longer filming videos on the road, and whenever an opportunity to travel arose, I felt like I was abandoning Noah. I was trying to juggle work, Noah, and Vilk, which meant that none of them got sufficient attention—just as things were really beginning to happen for me career-wise. In these months, I was offered my first presenting gig with the BBC for their *Travel Show*, and National Geographic had reached out, ushering in a new era for my career.

With all this, and after so many years spent living on the road, I was also struggling to adjust to a sedentary lifestyle. Specifically, I couldn't get used to living in a house with doors, separate rooms, and brick walls. When Noah and I moved to our cottage, I woke up in a California king–size bed, blended my juice smoothies with my endless supply of electricity every morning, and enjoyed the invention of central heating on cold days. My perpetual nomad syndrome was gone, but I was experiencing withdrawal: all the things that made life easy and convenient when living in a house made me feel like I was betraying my true self. In my mind, conveniences became over-the-top opulence, and the comfort of living in one place turned into a fear of missing out. Instead of traveling or filming, I was now sitting in front of my laptop all day. I pictured myself growing dull and indifferent without the hardships and excitement of the road to wake me from my existential stupor. The walls of the cottage shielded me from the elements, and . . . I hated them for it. Day by day, the house felt more like a cell than like a romantic Italian haven. I hungered to be outside and away from what, to me, seemed like excessive comforts. I stared out the window at the mountains—one of which haunted me with its uncanny resemblance to Ama Dablam—and felt as if they were pitying me in my new life. I longed to be washing my pots with a pinecone picked up off the ground, not a three-dollar sponge that had crossed the entire world in a shipping container only to land in my sink. The nomad inside me was waking up again, her grumble slowly turning into a roar.

An idea came down from the mountains with the morning mist and started to follow me around in my head: a tent in the mountains. Several months before, when Noah and I had been traveling across the United States, I'd had a chance to film with a female goatherd in Montana named Callie. Callie was a wild woman, the wildest I had ever met. She lived in a small canvas tent on a riverside overlooking the Rocky Mountains. Day in and day out, she herded her small tribe of goats, milked them, made cheese, and hiked into the wilderness. And while I had no intention of becoming a full-time goatherd, I was so moved by the simplicity and openness of Callie's life that, many months later, I still could not get her out of my head.

"I love that she lives in that little tent, so close to nature," I said to Noah after meeting her. "But one of her relationships broke down because her partner wanted to live in a real house and she wanted to live in a tent. She wanted to eat while sitting on the ground; he wanted to eat at a table. It's interesting, isn't it?"

"I can see why someone wouldn't want to eat while sitting on the ground," Noah responded. "Maybe her demands were a little unreasonable." I hadn't expected to hear this from him. My entire being related to Callie and her desire to live more simply, more freely, and I wanted him to feel it, too.

"I'm way past the stage of living uncomfortably," Noah added. "I'm happy to go on adventures, but I want to sleep in my own bed at night, not on the ground."

There was a lump of foreboding in my throat. I didn't think I was done with living a feral life, but I loved him so much that I swallowed it. After all, I knew there was nothing unreasonable about Noah's take on things. The vast majority of people in the world would prefer to sleep in a comfortable bed rather than on the ground, and would prefer to live in a house and not a tent. But the thing was, *we* were not supposed to be like the vast majority of people. I had allowed myself to fall in love with Noah because I believed we could live a feral life together: on the road, in a mountain cabin, or in a tent. Unlike everyone else. I believed he was just as wild as me, and that he craved the same wild things. To hear him reject these visions felt like a betrayal I hadn't seen coming.

All those months later, as the Italian cottage closed in on me a little more each day, I would have given my soul to move to the mountains and sleep on the ground, listening to the pitter-patter of rain bouncing off the canvas walls of my tent as I fell asleep, a little chilly, huddled inside a sleeping bag. I would have given anything to feel wild and free again, even if it meant being alone forever.

For me, by then so accustomed to spending time alone, moving to a cottage with a partner had been a very sudden and dramatic change. I was growing irritable and felt stifled in my own beautiful little life. The mountains that surrounded us didn't give me freedom, because I wasn't among them; they only hemmed me in and reminded me of where I wished I was. Every time I thought about traveling somewhere for a few weeks to film, the plans became tinged in my mind with that guilty feeling of leaving someone behind. I was dwelling once again in the world of frustration, half-feelings, and bittersweetness. And I thought I'd promised myself to leave those feelings in the past.

One afternoon, I suggested that Noah and I take a break. Maybe I just needed to recalibrate, have a little time alone. But the conversation spiraled. He didn't want a break. It was all or nothing—a state of mind I understood all too well. It was over almost as suddenly as it had begun. As I walked outside, the smell of wet earth was rising from the ground.

Leaving our cottage on that rainy day in December, I left all the furniture, everything we'd bought together, and I drove as far north as my body would allow before stopping for the night. I was headed for Poland.

chapter twenty-four

coming home

"What's wrong with me?" I asked the therapist sitting across the room from me. Behind her, floor-to-ceiling windows offered a view of Polish urban sprawl. The room was tastefully decorated in muted shades, comforting and unimposing. A couple of photos of something entirely forgettable (that I have now, predictably, forgotten) adorned the walls, enough to catch your eye if you needed the distraction, but not so bold as to steer you from your train of thought. The office was decorated precisely in the way one might decorate an office if one were a shrink hoping to ease clients into telling their darkest secrets: open to interpretation.

My nails were tapping against the china mug I cupped in my hands. My right knee was bouncing up and down. My whole body was jittering with nervous energy. It felt like all my hopes and dreams for the past couple of years had dissolved into thin air, leaving a gnawing feeling of failure in their place. I was desperate for answers, and I really hoped that this woman, who was not much older than me, had them.

Though I never did, at every session I was tempted to ask her about her other clients. I wanted to know how they navigated life and relationships and about the mistakes they'd made. I wanted to know what other "broken" people were struggling with, because this would help me gauge just how fucked-up *I* was in comparison. Was I just a little fucked-up, in need of a little tweak, or was I completely fucked-up and beyond repair? Where exactly was I on the fucked-up spectrum? Because I was growing slightly concerned that I might be somewhere off the chart.

Over the last few sessions, I'd told her my whole life history, everything I had done wrong, everything that had *gone* wrong, and about all the travel, all the solitude, and all the relationships. I'd analyzed my relationship with my mother and my father and the rest of my family. I'd given her a Freudian summary of the reasons I found comfort in the incessant movement of the nomadic life and why I had struggled in my previous relationships, digging deep into childhood wounds and traumas. I needed her to know that I was deeply aware of the mechanisms that put my psyche in motion. I was self-aware. I had spent enough time in solitude to figure myself out, or at least I thought I had.

She watched me intently as I spoke, making the occasional note, her poker face betraying nothing. Eventually, after telling her all of this, I asked the only question I really wanted to know the answer to: "What's wrong with me?"

She looked at me silently for a moment.

"What if I told you that there's nothing wrong with you?" she replied.

That was not what I'd expected to hear.

"Nothing? But I've failed so many times. I can't hold down a relationship. I can't stay in one place. Am I running from something? There must be something wrong with me," I insisted.

The relationship with Noah and its abrupt end had made me question everything that I thought I had learned about myself since leaving London—it seemed I still had the capacity to surprise myself, and, frankly, I felt awful about it all. The alternative, staying in that life of comfort and predictability, had not been an option if I was to remain happy and sane, and perhaps that wasn't so much of a surprise. But there was no doubt that the whole experience had shaken the very foundations that I had been building for myself all these years. I had started to wonder whether all those voices in the social media comments that doubted me, my motives, my chosen life path, might have a point. Maybe they were right and I had been wrong all along.

After I left the Italian cottage, and Noah in it, I'd raced to Poland to be closer to my family. Within a few days of arriving, I had found this therapist and signed up for the first counseling sessions of my life. I hoped that therapy would reset me, fix me. I didn't want to be different anymore; I didn't want to feel like a misfit, constantly trying to forge an invisible path that only I seemed to be walking. I just wanted to be like everyone else. After working out my unresolved issues, I presumed I would suddenly start to want all the things that everybody else wanted. If I healed my wounds, I would suddenly wake up and realize that all I'd ever wanted was a husband, a family, and a white picket fence. Wasn't that what all the well-adjusted people in the world wanted? Maybe that way, with some therapy, I would be able to get back together with Noah without feeling like I was giving up my freedom—the very thing that had saved me all those years ago. With therapy, maybe I could rewire myself into *wanting* a relationship.

She nodded slowly.

"I can see how it would feel that way. I'm sure that when you compare your life to the lives of people around you, living in a more conventional way, you could start to doubt yourself." She paused. "But when you're on your own, just you, single—how does that make you feel?"

"I feel good. Happy. Free." I scoured my mind for more adjectives. "I feel at peace when I'm alone."

That nod again.

"So why do you doubt yourself?" she continued. "Romantic love is a relatively new concept. And on a human level, we don't necessarily need romantic love to thrive and be happy. What we do need, I believe, is some kind of community. For most of human history, we lived in small groups, and that was what gave us purpose. I think you would really benefit from a community, but it sounds like you don't actually want a Prince Charming."

I listened.

"So what you're saying is that I don't *need* to be with anyone? It's not a prerequisite for human happiness?"

"Do you want to be in a romantic relationship?"

"No."

"Do you truly feel like you could be happy without a romantic partner in the future?"

"Yes."

"Well, there you have it." She gave a little smile.

It was becoming apparent that therapy wasn't a factory reset, because, despite the amount of time we spent on them, humans weren't mobile phones. According to the qualified professional sitting in front of me, I didn't need a reset. She was telling me that I was allowed not to want a relationship, that I didn't need to be fixed.

Over the years, I had already given myself permission to enjoy my solitude, to seek a wilder path, and to live my life on the feral side. But ultimately, even after I thought I had seen through the stereotype, I had needed someone else to shake me out of a concept that was deeply ingrained in my subconscious: the narrative that a woman without a man was a sad, lonely spinster, the idea that every "normal" woman should, if not need a man, want a man. The patriarchy ran that deep, even in my blood. I could see now why I had had a habit of falling into the arms of someone, of *wanting* to want a relationship, as I felt I was supposed to, only to wind up feeling trapped by it.

I had needed an external witness to give me permission to exist in the world as a woman without a man, to tell me that I did not need a "better half" to make me whole, to allow me to imagine that my story didn't need to end with a traditional romance. I had walked into her office for my first session expecting to be told by the end of it that I had failed at relationships because of a deep-rooted independence that I had acquired as a child, and that I would need years of therapy to untangle the mess. Instead, I was leaving her office feeling that I had permission to live as I pleased, in whatever way brought me happiness, and with that came an almost overpowering sense of relief. A little part of me, that had been mired in doubt, was now free.

Within a few days, I went all in on what felt like a radical idea: cutting men out of my life altogether. On my thirty-third birthday, at a time when most women were either raising children or starting to watch their biological clocks, I took a vow of celibacy. I wanted to galvanize this feeling of independence, of wholeness, that I now had. And from this conviction came the courage and self-reliance to do something I had been longing to do.

Since the day I'd imagined owning that forty-acre desert ranch a year and a half earlier, I had been waiting. Waiting for someone—waiting for a Noah—to validate it and make the leap with me, to give me the permission I felt I needed to make such a big and binding decision. To purchase land alone had always felt like too radical a step: What if I fell in love with someone who didn't want to live there with me? The specter of a hypothetical partner had hovered over my decision-making for so long, and, according to lore, the only women who moved into cottages in the forest alone were witches.

So be it.

I don't need to wait for anyone, I reassured myself that spring afternoon as I parked Odyssey in front of a notary's office. *If I keep waiting, I might end up waiting too long.*

In waiting for the perfect moment to take the leap, we overlook the possibility that the perfect moment may never come. It is the easiest thing in the world to talk yourself out of life-changing ideas. *This is too much, it's too radical, too soon. What if I regret it?*

Maybe you *will* regret it. Maybe *I* will regret it. But how many times can you stifle the impulse that urges you to go ahead? How many times can you put a pillow over the voice that promises there's something else out there for you? How many times can you deny that there may be another version of reality out there, where you are wilder, braver, and more alive than you've ever dreamt possible?

I had returned to the Carpathian Mountains in the south of Poland. I was back on the range where I had car-camped and come up with the plan for my Pan-American dream, where another dream had been right in front of me all along, but I just hadn't been ready to see it yet. I'd needed to road-trip, to burn out, to fall in love and leave that love again. I had needed to come to a point where I felt not only that I wanted to make plans for a future alone but that there was nothing "wrong" with doing that. So I was now back in the place that had enchanted me like no other.

The Carpathians do not have the dramatic splendor of their

better-known cousins, the Alps, but they have a mystery and a magic that hang like a fog over their meadows on a spring morning. And I was about to finalize the purchase of fifteen acres of wild Carpathian land. This was the last signature I required. As if I needed any more evidence that there were no missed opportunities and that everything happened in its own good time, I was not about to buy just any piece of land in the Carpathian Mountains, but the very stretch of meadow I had walked through over a year and a half ago with Kasia—a stretch that had not been for sale then. Through a series of fortuitous events, that meadow—now in the bloom of late spring—had ended up being sold as a number of smaller plots by several different owners. Kasia and Leszek had alerted me to the sale and helped me navigate village negotiations so that, within a few months, all I required was this last signature in order to own the entire meadow and a large stretch of forest around it. I still couldn't quite believe this was happening.

"And you're going to live there on your own, eh?" The question was a polite way of asking whether I was married. The seller of the land, alongside his wife, watched me intently once they were done counting the money. To pay for my new property, I'd been asked to bring an entire bag stuffed with cash: fresh banknotes packed into neat piles of ten. I was all too happy to part with the burden of a backpack filled with my life savings.

"Yes, that's the plan for now," I answered, eager for the deed to get signed. "Uh, but who knows, maybe that will change one day!" I couldn't help hastily adding, in case they found it suspicious that I seemed just a bit too happy to live alone on a mountaintop. After all, these were superstitious people with a well-founded fear of witches and other mythical beings.

The wife raised her eyebrows ever so slightly and said, "Well, good for you—I didn't get anything from this one." She looked at her husband sideways. Despite their having been married for over thirty years, none of the land was in her name, or even in their name as a couple. He was the rightful owner of all "their" land, including the land that "their" house stood on.

I felt a twinge of guilt. It seemed unjust that this was their arrangement. In fact, it seemed unjust that this had been the arrangement of so many married women for generations. To sit in that office, handing over the bulk of my own money that I had withdrawn from my own account to buy my own land, suddenly felt like a radical act. When I'd promised myself on the Kebanys' veranda in Socotra to radicalize myself into living more wildly, I could never have imagined that promise would eventually find me here, in this office, buying wild land to live on alone.

I said nothing. What was there to say? They were simple mountain people, raised on Catholic values in a tight-knit village community. A thirtysomething-year-old woman living on her own would be a suspicious "old maid" in their eyes. I was surprised that they had agreed to sell me their land, given that I was a complete newcomer to the area and so far out of their social circle. But I was paying a premium price, and my local friends Kasia and Leszek had vouched for me. Or perhaps I was being sold the land out of neighborly spite: maybe they preferred to sell to a stranger rather than to let another villager expand his grip.

"You know, the people who used to live on that land were quite eccentric, too," the man offered. I wondered whether he said "too" because he thought I was eccentric, or as a figure of speech. I had a feeling it was the former. "They lived in a wooden hut, just the two of them and some sheep and a cow. They were very superstitious people. Believed in ghosts and all kinds of spooky things."

"Did they have any kids?" I already knew the answer but wanted to hear him say it.

"No. No kids. No family. They were hermits. Very odd people."

Sounds like a good omen to me, I thought as I watched the man's hand penning his final signature on the last page of the deed.

"Well, all done." He sighed, putting the money away. We all smiled and shook hands. They left the office with a backpack full of cash. I left the office elated, with a single piece of paper that now made me a landowner.

An hour later, I was on my knees, my legs crumpling under the weight of a huge backpack and several other bags hanging off my arms and shoulders. Sweat was dripping down my forehead, my hands were caked in dirt, and I was climbing a fifty-degree incline en route to my new property. Since there was no road or trail, and the property was perched near the top of the mountain, I had to bushwhack my way to it through a neighbor's fields and then navigate my way through the woods. Vilk was making circles around me, waiting for an opportune moment to play his favorite game of "ambush." It was not *my* favorite, because it involved Vilk waiting in ambush until I got close enough and then pouncing on me with all his might. Having a large dog hurling himself at you playfully as you're trying to ascend a steep mountainside is not exactly the safest game to play. His last pounce had brought me to my knees, and there I was, dirt under my fingernails, scrapes along my ankles, sweat running down my back, the happiest I had been in months.

After some more bushwhacking and being ambushed, I finally arrived on the boundary of my property. The forest came to an abrupt halt, and the land opened up into a long, undulating meadow filled with the spring wildflowers of yellow *Arnica montana*, pink bistort, and the odd white flowers of mountain cranberries. In the middle stood the ruins of an old wooden cottage, a silent reminder of the lives once lived out here. The land was rugged and wild, the long flowering grasses mowed down by passing sheep a few times a year but untouched by human hands. It smelled sweet and crisp, of flowers, pine sap, and open sky. On all sides, framing the meadow, was a thick forest of beech trees dotted with pines and firs. As I made my way across the meadow, a gentle curve led me south, toward a wide opening. Turning the corner, I stopped dead in my tracks. In front of me, a massive panorama of tall, snowcapped peaks revealed itself in the distance. The High Tatras, one of the tallest and most dramatic mountain ranges in Europe, rose toward the sky, serrated and sharp, the long column of their backs stretching all the way across the horizon.

My meadow was still, save for the chirping of crickets in the grass and the song of warblers and whinchats in the trees. The long grass grazed my calves as I walked, and the soft rays of the afternoon sun warmed my skin. This was my land. The meadow, the forest, all of it. This wild and rugged piece of the earth was mine, according to a legal note. But as I stood there, having signed all the deeds and contracts, all sense of ownership and entitlement melted away. I was there not to own but to take care of this land. I took a deep breath, filling my lungs with the clear, floral air of this magical place. Looking around, I spoke out loud: "You are safe in my hands. I will not tame you. With me, you can be wild."

I was speaking to the land, to the trees, to the birds and the insects, the flowers and the springs. I was speaking to the spirits of this land and to all the souls that had once wandered it—and, on some level, I was speaking to myself. *I will keep the land wild, in the hope that it will keep me wild, too.*

And for the first time in my life, I knew what it felt like to be home.

chapter twenty-five

the witch in the forest

I raised the door of the canvas tent. It was another glimpse of morning on my property after a night sleeping under its skies, and I shrieked with joy. This view never got old. In the far distance, the High Tatra panorama caught the light of the rising sun, its jagged peaks resembling fiery torches. Closer to home, in my meadow, the grass glistened with morning dew. When I squinted, I could convince myself I was looking at a carpet of sapphires.

"Look, buddy!" I shouted to Vilk. "It's our home!" I stood up and grabbed his paws as he hopped up toward me. We did a happy little dance, and all the while I kept singing, "It's our home, we're home, look at our lovely home!"

Our first night on the land had been one of near silence; the only sounds in my meadow had been the ancient wind that whistled down from the watching mountains, accompanied by the chirping of crickets and the hooting calls of hunting Ural owls. Though I had my concerns about the large predators known to prowl these forests, Vilk's presence gave me all the peace of mind I needed: he was my wolf, after all, and he had grown substantially in a couple of years, from a twenty-pound ball of fluff into an imposing and alert ninety-pound dog. The sky had been so clear all night that I felt like I could almost hear the movement of the stars above me.

My new home was round and spacious: a white canvas bell tent, wide at the bottom and rising eight feet into the air in the middle, similar to a tepee. It was simple, and I'm sure that, to many, it would look like nothing more than a camping setup. At most, it might be viewed as a "glamp" (a "glamorous camp") to spend a few vacation days in. But when I looked at it, I saw a palace, a fairy tale; I saw a way to be at home *and* live wildly at the same time. I had doubted that satisfying both desires was even possible until now.

I thought back to the time Kasia had looked at me with her mysterious smile, telling me that "maybe someday" I would live here. I'd just returned from filming on Mount Kilimanjaro for National Geographic, and for the first time in my life, I had been excited to go home after traveling somewhere. After decades of roving, I not only *could* go home but I *wanted* to. This land held me and gave me the stability I had perhaps been searching for in relationships, but it never bound me to it or punished me for leaving it while I traveled. I was free to come and go as life demanded, or I desired. Every day it inspired me—with thoughts of everything I could do on this land, and everything I would not do so as to ensure that its wild and natural beauty remained protected, that it remained a realm largely beyond the human.

With their ancient, undulating forests and isolated villages, the Carpathians are said to be inhabited by timeless spirits and witches. Given that this mountain range is much less developed than Europe's better-known Alps and Dolomites, you can see how mystical beings might view it as a good hiding spot. Similar to the *molfars*—magical people with the ability to dissolve clouds, summon thunder, and speak to animals—on the Ukrainian stretch of the mountains, the Polish side is said to be home to all manner of supernatural beings, from the trickster spirits known as *biesy* to the *południce*—female spirits that threaten field workers at midday—and the *topielec*—water spirits born out of the souls of drowned humans—as well as to myriad sprites, witches, and fairies.

I didn't need to believe in the local lore of otherworldly beings to know this place was sacred, but I was starting to see how these beliefs had originated. Magic crackled in the air here, and I was bewitched. I wanted to share this place—its beauty and the joy it had already given me—with everyone. Thinking of the wife in the notary office, I wanted to show women everywhere that they could become landowners in their own right if they wanted to. They needn't wait for someone to make their dream come true either—and perhaps there were other women out there who, like I had, felt like they needed permission to live this wildly, alone. So I continued filming videos of my setup, sharing this new journey I was on of building a little nest, of which I was so proud and which I felt safe to fly from and back to again.

My tent stood in the center of the long meadow I'd first walked through on the way to somewhere else, with the opening facing the view of the snowcapped High Tatras. Kasia and Leszek had just helped me to build a simple wooden deck that the tent could stand on. I wanted to keep my promise and avoid making changes to the natural layout of the land wherever possible—so instead of flattening it, we simply worked with its shape, erecting the temporary wooden structure on top of a few concrete blocks.

Now that the tent was up, I was beginning to decorate it: a tatami mat that served as my bed, a couple of wicker baskets for storage, a low wooden table to work at, and a couple of floor cushions to recline on. The kitchen was a camping gas stove and a plastic storage box, inside which I kept my food, cup, knife, and spoon. The lid served as a cutting board and a prep surface. After a few weeks, I got a significant upgrade in the form of a baby-size woodstove, which stood on the deck outside, and warmed my hands and heated my water. While there was no bathroom, the forest was spacious enough, with plenty of soft topsoil. I took a near-perverse pleasure in dropping my shorts and peeing wherever I pleased: under a tree, by the bushes, in the middle of the meadow. It was my land and I would water it wherever I pleased. It helped that I had no visible neighbors.

Out there, my fresh water flowed not from a temperature-regulated tap, but from a mountain spring. My power came not from the inexhaustible grid, but from solar panels. I could not park my car conveniently in a driveway nearby—in order to reach my tent, I had to hike up the mountain with my own two feet, often carrying a heavy backpack and groceries. I thought back to all the things that had struck me as indulgent and overly comfortable when I was living in the Italian cottage, and I was relieved to be free from them.

The days moved slowly in the meadow, and I slowed to their rhythm. I lay on the grass and felt myself sink into it, become a part of it. I was barefoot, hairy, and makeup-free and was feeling more at home within myself than I ever had. With all the lore of strange beings in the area, I imagined that one day, the locals would tell folktales about me, the strange witch who had once inhabited this meadow, her bushy-haired spirit still roaming these forests and playing tricks on visitors. Meanwhile, and despite the fact that I am, by and large, a reasonable person who believes in science, I grew convinced that my land was indeed inhabited by sprites and fairies. They hung out by an old beech tree in the highest part of the meadow, as fairies are apparently wont to do. Feeling it was important not to simply dismiss ancient local customs, I brought them honey, jam, ribbons, and flowers as gifts, not unlike what I had seen people do at the Buddhist shrines in Nepal. After all, I was the newcomer here, and I wanted to appease the spirits of the land and put to rest any misgivings they might have about me. But first, it seemed they wanted me to pass a test, an initiation of sorts. I lost a studded ring somewhere in the grass. It was a pretty, shiny thing, exactly the kind of trinket I had been told fairies were partial to. Knowing that there was only one sensible, rational thing to do, I told them off for stealing my stuff.

"Guys, I know I'm new here, and I know that you've been here for a really long time, without much company." I paused, wondering whether one should be firm or lighthearted when speaking to fairies. *Do I set strict boundaries? Or do I turn this into a joke?* "But you can't just go around taking my stuff. Look, I brought you all these goodies already. If you return my ring, I'll bring you something else in exchange. I promise." I stood by the old beech tree and watched out for any sprite-like motion in the trees. There was none. But I could sense the forest listening all the same.

The next morning, I found the ring. Not in the grass where I had lost it, but at the bottom of my backpack. "Thank you," I said out loud as I put the ring back on. "I really appreciate it." In exchange, I brought them a suncatcher made from colorful crystals: I hung it up on the fairies' beech tree, where it glistened cheerfully and even more spectacularly than my ring.

Whether these spirits were real or not was moot to me. I knew why I spoke out loud, why I gave voice to these feelings, and it wasn't *really* to talk to fairies. My conversations with the land continued as a way of nurturing my relationship to it. Speaking my good intentions out loud, giving voice to how protective I felt of this beautiful place, was a way of turning something very abstract into a tangible relationship. Every morning, as I stepped out onto the dewy grass barefoot, I said thank you to my home.

"This is your home. This is where your roots are." My grandmother's words drifted in and out of mind as I sat on the cool grass, warming my hands in front of a small campfire. Vilk was chewing on a bone nearby, observing the boundaries of the land with one eye, and the moon was out, turning the mountain peaks silver. My grandmother had been right. I'd never thought I would end up finding my place in the country of my birth. For so many years, I'd chosen to estrange myself from it, swearing that to move back to my motherland would be to take a step back. I had left Poland all those years ago as a child, and from there, I'd kept moving up in the world: I'd earned a fancy degree; I'd had fancy jobs and a fancy husband. All those things had carried me further and further away from my roots as a girl from a small eastern European town.

It had taken a dark night of the soul and seven years of roaming around the world to come back here, to a place that felt like home, and to feel at peace here. But as I thought back to that girl who, several years prior, had left London on a flight east, hoping to find herself, I realized that she had been looking for the wrong thing. I don't think you ever truly find yourself. You are not a destination to be found, but a living, breathing, ever-changing being. You may find pieces of yourself along the way: little scraps of experience that lead you toward a life more authentic to who you are at your very core. Indeed, maybe the point is not at all to find yourself. Maybe the point is to make your life a journey so interesting that you never want to stop seeking.

"I barely look in the mirror anymore," I wrote in my journal. "Sometimes I'll go two days without looking at my own reflection, to the point where I forget that I even have a face." In a world that imposed your own reflection on you, in bathrooms, elevators, shops, cars, and glass buildings, it was rare to go even a few hours without confronting your own face. I was still recording videos on my camera, but I never checked whether I had dirt on my face or a bit of food in my teeth. I just pressed "record" and only went back to the footage several days later. It was a liberating experience to be able to dedicate my eyes to the pursuit of natural beauty, and not my own reflection.

I did still need to wash from time to time, though. So I hauled a metal tub up to the property on my own back. That afternoon, as I made my way from the road, up the usual steep hills all the way to my tent, a storm was brewing, and I got caught in the thunder and lightning. I was aware that dragging a huge tin tub during a storm made me a more likely target for a lightning strike, but I was spared that experience. The next day, I set the tub down next to the tent and filled it with water from a small spring nearby. Cup by cup, I filled up a metal bucket and then poured the water into the tub, a two-minute walk away. When I finally threw off my clothes and climbed into the tub, it might have been cramped, and the water might have been frigid, but it was crystal-clear mountain water straight from the earth, and the tub I bathed in came with a mountain view that transfixed me, transforming as it did in the mercurial light. *Without a doubt, the most luxurious bathtub in the world*, I thought to myself as I sat inside it, legs bent, my body cooling in the water on a warm summer day.

Being in a remote location, without immediate neighbors—which allowed me to bathe wherever I pleased but also meant that I had no one I could call if I needed help—I had put up trail cameras in a few spots around the property. I'd initially put them up for when I wasn't around, so that I could see who—if anyone—was walking across my land. But of late, I was feeling that I needed a sense of security while I was there, as I'd discovered that people on the internet had been talking about where my land was. Some had even emailed me with the exact location, saying, "Hey, you might want to look into this because I was able to find your property really easily on Google Maps." I felt I had made it clear that this place was sacred to me and was not to be intruded upon, even in a digital capacity—I shared only as much of it with the world as I wanted to and as I felt comfortable with; the rest of it was mine. I had earned this hard-won peace. This news had destabilized my sense of security somewhat, but I was sure that these trail cameras could rectify that. What I hadn't considered was that they might also offer some unexpected gifts.

When I got around to checking them, most of the recordings just showed Vilk and me passing through, or the occasional feral village cat out on an exploratory saunter, but one video showed an adult deer strolling down the footpath. He was a tall and muscular stag with an impressive set of antlers. When I clicked on the next video, I couldn't believe my eyes. It was a wolf. She was slim, with long legs and brown-gray fur, smaller than I would have expected. What she lacked in size she more than made up for in her presence. She walked right in front of the trail camera and paused for a moment, as if she wanted me to see her. I wondered where she had slept that night, and where she was headed—had she passed by the tent on her rounds? There was no fear in me when I saw her, only excitement. What a blessing to know that forest animals felt this land was wild enough for them to pass through.

As I sat there watching these magnificent creatures move through the land I called home, I wondered whether any of this would have been possible had I stayed with Noah. I knew he wouldn't have willingly moved into a tent in the mountains with no access to power, running water, or roads. If we had stayed together, we would have likely bought land somewhere and built a beautiful wooden house, furnished with all the beautiful things. We might even have become homesteaders. It would have been one of our many possible scenarios for a gorgeous life. But a part of me knew that, despite all the good things that could have happened for us, I needed something more radical than that. So in that moment, the question that felt more apt was: Did I want Noah here? Did I want *anyone* here? I imagined what it would be like to share this little slice of land with another human, and I was somewhat relieved to know that there *could* be space, one day. It wasn't out of the question. But not now. Because now, I wanted the space to go feral, I wanted to run in the forest barefoot, I wanted to not care whether I smelled good or bad to another human being. I wanted to just *be* here. No half-feelings, no missing halves.

That witches lived deep in the forest, all alone, with only their wolves for company, made all the sense in the world to me now—it was a damn good life. But it hadn't yet occurred to me that a witch's dark, wrathful reputation might be one she cultivated for her own benefit.

"There you are! I've been looking for you," he said as he marched toward me down my meadow, the long stalks of grass yielding to his heavy boots. My sacred, magical meadow. He was slim, but there was conviction in his presence; he moved fast and without hesitation. Vilk's hackles stood up on his back and he let out a low growl.

I hadn't been expecting anyone. Taken aback, I sped through my mental Rolodex. Was it the local shepherd? Or maybe the villager who'd wanted to help me with a fence? No, he looked nothing like either of them. Within a moment, he was close enough that I could see his face clearly. "I've finally found you," he said with a self-satisfied smile.

Now I recognized this man. I'd seen him earlier at the village shop. He'd introduced himself as a fan of my channel, which had been nothing out of the ordinary. We'd exchanged the usual polite chitchat about my films and my travels, and had gone our separate ways. I hadn't thought anything of the meeting, and the only things that had struck me as unusual were his piercing gaze and his intense eye contact.

What was he doing here, on my land? Alarm bells were going off in my head. I hadn't invited him here. I hadn't even told him where I lived. To reach my property, he would have had to make the same trek that I did: up the mountain, through private fields and woods, without a visible footpath. To reach my land, he would have had to know exactly where he was going. And as he had made clear with his own admission that he'd been looking for me, this was no coincidence.

"Right. Good evening," I said, aware that the sky was darkening and that my closest neighbors were not within earshot.

"It took me some time to get here." He kept approaching.

Not knowing what his intentions were, I needed to set a clear boundary as soon as possible. "I'm sorry, but you do realize that this is private property?" I said, calling Vilk over. I had known before I'd even met Vilk that one day he would be the line that a threat would decide not to cross. Now I knew this man was a threat.

"Well, yes," he said, glancing at Vilk, whose hackles were still up. "But I was just taking a walk." A walk? Off the mountain trails? Straight to my tent? A frozen breath of anxiety moved under my skin. Everything about his being there felt off. He shouldn't have been here. I looked down at Vilk, who returned my gaze. I didn't have to say a word: I knew he was ready to protect us and our home if need be, and I found the shred of confidence I needed in my dog's eyes.

"This is private land and you shouldn't be here. Please leave. I'm busy. I have to go," I said, and immediately turned toward my tent and walked off, picking up an axe that lay next to my fire. Vilk followed behind. I continued purposefully across the meadow until I got to the tent, and as I ducked inside, I did not look back, despite fear screaming at me to check whether the man was still there.

I had made a vow to avoid men, and somehow, in what felt like some twisted cosmic joke, all the worst men seemed to be turning up. Since I'd first arrived back in Poland from Italy, I also had been receiving unhinged emails from another male fan. Typically, the best tack with these kinds of parasocial approaches was to ignore them and the obsession would fizzle out, and that was exactly what I had done. I had not replied to a single one of his emails, in which he repeatedly stated that he believed we were destined to be together.

While I had been away filming on Mount Kilimanjaro, Kasia and Leszek had gotten in touch to warn me that this other man had come to the village to seek me out. Upon discovering that I wasn't there, through my carefully curated Instagram stories that never showed my live location but did show what country I was in, he found out where I was in the world. He then flew to Tanzania, published a "search manifesto" on his Instagram page explaining how he would seek me out, and painstakingly pieced together my exact location by lying to the local guides, professing to be my fiancé coming to surprise me. Eventually, he found me, with a bouquet of red roses in hand, a marriage proposal written out, and a honeymoon suite booked for that very night. I had never imagined anyone would take things this far—the leap from the virtual world to the real world was a deranged leap for a fan to take, and a very scary leap for a public person to experience. A man I had never met, or talked to, or exchanged a single emoji with, was, essentially, trying to hunt me down. Per his emails, he believed that we had a soul connection and that I would instantly fall in love with him. But my film crew, upon seeing him, confronted him and—in no uncertain terms—asked him to leave. Instead of agreeing to the engagement he'd hoped for, I filed a police report and got a restraining order against him.

"We deal with a lot of stalkers," the lawyer I hired told me matter-of-factly. "Most cases end with a restraining order. But you never really know what these people are plotting next. What are the gun laws like in Poland?"

I had laughed at that extreme suggestion and shaken the whole experience off as a fluke, an unlikely incident that would not happen again, because from then on, I decided that I needed to be even more careful about what I posted and when I posted it. I needed to draw things out longer. I decided that I was allowed not to post locations and that I was allowed to wait for weeks, if not months, to post content if I needed to—I was entitled to that. Previously, I'd always felt that I owed it to my followers to post as soon as I possibly could, but I now realized that that could not be at the cost of my own personal safety. What mattered was not whether people thought that I was posting fast enough, but that what I was posting was of value, and that I was posting from a place of safety.

With new safety protocols in place, I was determined not to allow parasocial relationships to shake my precious newfound sense of belonging to this land. I'd thought lightning wasn't supposed to strike the same place twice—it hadn't even struck me when I was carrying a tin bath. But now, within a few short weeks of that experience, just as I was settling into my home, feeling like it was mine, like I was free to finally stop moving and be still for a while, a second man stepped into my sacred space uninvited and unannounced. As I sat inside my tent, stroking Vilk as he continued to growl, holding the axe so firmly that my palms began to sweat, waiting for this man to leave my property, I knew I would also now have to leave this place. Even as I heard him walking off, I knew I would have to leave. Even after I checked the trail cameras to ensure that he had left, I knew I would have to leave. That peace of mind I had so desperately longed for was so fragile, and, after having been years in the making, had been so easily destroyed in a single moment.

I couldn't be sure that this man wasn't waiting somewhere out in the forest, getting drunk, planning to reappear when I went to sleep, or some other day or night when I least expected it. Within the tent, from this moment on, I knew I would no longer feel free, but would feel threatened; on the land, I would no longer feel safe, but vulnerable. And I hated these men for making me feel that way.

As I waited until the coast was clear, on my own land, I couldn't help but think back on my encounters with men over the years. I thought of Seif and every man who had felt like he was entitled to me—to women in general. I thought of every man who had made me feel vulnerable or afraid in every single country I had ever traveled to, even in my very home, and I couldn't help, in that moment and its aftermath, feeling a deep anger toward them. These men had trespassed into my world precisely because they knew there was not another man here, because I had chosen to be alone.

In the ensuing days and weeks, friends suggested that I fight fire with fire: "Find yourself a big, burly man and pretend he's your new boyfriend! Nobody will bother you again." I did get to the point of asking a male friend if he would do that for me, and he readily agreed. But in the end, I decided against it. I didn't want to hide behind a pretend boyfriend just to ensure my own safety—that was not a world I wanted to live in. I wanted to live in a world where I could feel safe living alone wherever I chose to. That was what I would always fight for.

Instead, I chose to ramp up Vilk's personal protection training.

I got myself a gun permit. And I showed everyone on social media that I had one.

In time, if anything, this experience would make me cherish the many good men I had in my life—who would do anything to make me feel safe—all the more dearly. I knew that almost all the men who watched my videos did it out of a desire to support and encourage me, and the best among them with a willingness to learn from a woman.

This land was meant to be a place I could always come back to when the world got too heavy, or when the adventure became too long, too tiring. This land was meant to be my safe haven and a place just for me and Vilk to belong. But I had lost all of that now. Within a couple of hours of the strange man's appearance, I was walking through the forest in complete darkness, down the mountain, toward my truck, where I could lock the doors, and drive away if need be.

So I left. I left my fairyland, my sacred meadow, my witch's hideout. As I stumbled over the forest's roots in the dark, making my way toward safety, I prayed that if I ran into something out there, it would be another wolf and not another man.

chapter twenty-six

the finish line

The floor of snow was caving in under the weight of my body. Every time my foot hit the ground, I sank a couple of inches, descending until the snow compacted and crunched under my weight. Instead of helping me stay on top of the soft snow, the snowshoes I was wearing were sucked beneath the white surface, too. The arctic sky of northern Sweden danced above me in shades of fading neon as the now-familiar northern lights painted streaks across the still-sleeping bed of stars. Everything around me, including the clouds I exhaled, seemed to creak with cold.

I was pulling a fully loaded pulk—an arctic expedition sled, this one weighing nearly fifty pounds—behind me, filled to the brim with everything I needed to survive ten days in the arctic wilderness alone, where temperatures were known to vary from a balmy 23 degrees Fahrenheit to a punishing minus 4 degrees. The snow pulled me down as the pulk pulled me back, as I was doing my very best to go forward.

After the intrusion on my land in the autumn, I'd needed a way to recalibrate myself. I'd searched for *something*, a challenge unlike any other, something that might push me to the brink of the realization I had been desperately searching for: what my next steps should be. I wanted something extreme that would force the opening of a new chapter in my life.

I'd thought that buying the land would put an end to the uncertainty that had been as constant as the North Star ever since I'd left my old life in London. The land was meant to be the central point of my roving compass rose—my roots—during the periods when I was unsure of what to do next; I would always have something to do on that land, just by being there. It was supposed to be the nest at the end of my every migration. It was supposed to be my shelter, my home, a space to dream in and be wild in. But that had been snatched away by men who had left me feeling uncertain and unsafe. In the place where I felt most secure, my personal safety had been called into question. I did not know how I would resolve this dissonance in the long term.

Several months had passed, during which time I'd kept myself so busy that I didn't have time to think about what was next. I had been preparing to premiere my own show with National Geographic, and the postproduction schedule was intense, keeping me tied to my laptop for hours every day. I'd also been filming for my own YouTube channel, getting ready for an expedition-style challenge that would consist of a ten-day, 320-mile footrace in the Arctic Circle in northern Sweden in the middle of winter.

In recent years, I'd been making trail running and hiking a big part of my life. It was something I did to clear my mind, connect with nature, and get stronger. I did it for my own satisfaction at first, but then ended up competing in several ultramarathons, ranging in distance between forty and 155 miles. My specialty became trail running in the mountains, and there was something that kept drawing me back for more—ever in search of something more extreme.

That was how I ended up here: dragging myself through the soft snow, one foot plunged beneath the frozen surface at a time. I was over two hundred miles into a grueling, freezing, dangerous race.

At this stage in my life, perhaps I should have been light-years ahead of that past version of myself who had struggled so much she had almost given up on her hike toward the Everest Base Camp. But as I strained to lift my feet from the weighted blanket of the snow, I had a flashback to that Eva from seven years ago, who'd felt like her ankles were fettered by invisible weights, and who'd crumpled by the side of the trail, her face in her hands, thinking she could not make it.

Can I make it?

I had been trudging along the long trail for almost a week now, making slow progress through the Arctic as I raced, snail-like, toward the finish line. But, like a mercurial demon, the snow would not let me pass without taking whatever it could from me.

It was a crisp winter morning. The sun had been beating down on the snowpack since dawn, warming it and making it soft and fluffy—the perfect kind of snow to play in, but the worst kind of snow to attempt a 320-mile trek in. Even without this added challenge, I had already been straining under the weight of the distance, the cold, and the exhaustion. Over the past few days, I had spent an average of sixteen hours each day marching through the frigid forests of spruce and pine and across the frozen lakes of northern Sweden, completely alone. And if I hoped to make it to the finish line before the hard ten-day cutoff, I needed to keep moving as much as humanly possible every single day, which meant there was very little time for sleeping, for my body to rest and recover from the extreme labor of each and every day. The sleep deprivation and the effort of burning through more than seven thousand calories daily for days on end had left me feeling like an empty shell. I had nothing left inside—you could have tapped me and the sound would have rung out across the land. I was so exhausted that I started dozing off while walking, my brain drifting off for a sweet few seconds of rest before jolting itself awake again. A couple of days before, I'd knelt by the side of my sled and let my brain switch off. It had taken me a moment to realize how dangerous it was to take an impromptu nap by the side of a frozen trail at minus 4 degrees with nobody else around. Missing Vilk, who was staying with an acquaintance while I was out on the trail, I had been hallucinating and seeing dogs in the forest where there were none. Upon seeing a small poodle in the trees at night, I grew furious that anyone could leave a small puppy unattended in the arctic darkness. But when I walked past it, I realized it was just a small bush. Whenever I was not seeing things that weren't there, or dozing off against my better judgment, I spent my energy bargaining with myself to keep from quitting the race.

After so many days moving through the freezing cold, my body was drained and my mind crumbling like a cliff edge, falling into a deep, dark sea of nothingness.

"I hate this. I hate this. I hate this," I repeated to myself out loud after yet another hour spent crossing a vast frozen bog that would not end.

I did not want to be there anymore.

I'd set myself this challenge because I secretly hoped that by spending so many days in the wilderness, away from screens and to-do lists, simply putting one foot in front of the other, I would be granted the mental space to figure out my more metaphysical next steps.

Prior to the intrusion of two men on my land, I'd had a plan for the future: I wanted to experiment with a rewilding theme, which would have me spending the winter in my tent there. This would also allow me to spend less time on the road and more time grounded, connected. I had finally come to appreciate how desperately I had been craving that sense of belonging after nearly a decade of wandering. But given that I no longer felt safe on my land, this had ceased to be an option. How ironic that to travel the world alone felt safer than to stay in my own home.

In deciding to do a self-sufficient race, I'd hoped that the extreme environment and the even more extreme effort would yield answers that were not forthcoming in everyday life, that I would experience a slow and intangible process of transformation, and the person I would become at the end of it would have the answers I longed for. Should I go back to traveling overland, even though it had burned me out before? Should I focus on making documentaries rather than YouTube videos? Should I find an alternative home elsewhere?

I was aware that to be at this kind of crossroads was a huge privilege. But that still didn't make it any easier to pick a direction. And now my plan seemed to be backfiring. Instead of the full mental clarity I had been hoping for, I descended into a void. The bog beneath my feet might have been frozen solid with ice, but it felt like it was seeping up my aching legs and into my mind.

"What the fuck am I even doing here?!" I screamed into the void. The response was a deafening silence of unmoving glacial air—air so still that it was like a vacuum that immediately swallowed up the echo of my voice.

I was out in the freezing Arctic, far from my sacred land, and without Vilk by my side. The sleep deprivation and exhaustion rendered me so mentally fragile that I sobbed every time I stopped moving. I burst into tears every time my headphone jack disconnected from my phone due to the cold. Every time I switched on my camera to record anything, every time I opened my mouth to speak, every time I stumbled, and every time anything—no matter how minor—shook me out of the stupor of just slogging ahead, I sobbed. As soon as I made it past the halfway point of the race, exhaustion hit me so hard that I fell into an emotional black hole.

This was not what I wanted. This was not bringing me any joy.

I cast the remnants of my mind back to the times when Vilk and I had torn down the trails of the Carpathians, narrowly avoiding sharp turns, jumping over tree roots, and racing across mountain pastures, my bodily experience elevated to a quasi-spiritual one by every pine-covered switchback. I thought about the calm, warm summer nights spent in front a campfire by the side of my canvas tent. I let my mind wander off to the long grass that caressed my ankles, the easy birdsong coming from the trees, and the sweet smell of summer's wildflowers in my meadow. *That's it.* I could feel those summer days soaring within me like a sun, and as they became more vivid with each recollection, I felt a ray of defiance. My mind flashed white.

A searing pain shot up my leg. My foot had landed awkwardly in my snowshoe. I looked around. Fuck. I was still in the Arctic. The pain exploded like fire, raging up and down my freezing shin.

"Just put one foot in front of the other," I coaxed myself. "One foot in front of the other."

I did keep putting one foot in front of the other, and it sounded straightforward enough: one more step, then another, then another. But after a week of covering between thirty and forty miles every day, in the freezing cold, while pulling a fully loaded sled, every single step required a mammoth mental effort. The physical pain I had been experiencing in all its manifestations was becoming something I was no longer sure I could continue to overcome, despite the painkillers. I still had one hundred miles to go—another two hundred thousand steps. The plastic straps of the snowshoes dug into my waterproof trainers, causing them to rub against my feet. I could feel new blisters forming where the old ones had just popped, every step a livid sting. And the only thing that was now steering my attention away from the blisters was this agonizing pain that had started shooting up my right shin, returning every second step as soon as my right foot landed on the ground. Over the past few days, I had befriended all kinds of pain: the dull ache in my back, the raw soreness in my thighs, the sharp crick in my neck, and the stiff discomfort of the soles of my feet. All of this, though unpleasant, had been just about bearable. But the shin splints were a different beast. Every time my foot fell at a slightly awkward angle, it was as if a thick needle stabbed inside my bone. Sometimes, when the painkillers wore off, the pain grew so intense that I had to pause and gasp for air, shocked that an unbroken bone could hurt so much.

Quitting would have solved all these issues. I could have simply pressed the emergency button on my SOS device, and at some point, someone would have picked me up and shuttled me off to a nice warm room, and I could be done with it. I so wanted to be done with it.

"Fuck that, and fuck this, and fuck me for choosing to be here," I had started muttering to myself out loud. Every second word that came out of my mouth cursed something or other—usually myself, for signing up to do the race in the first place.

I continued to put one foot in front of the other until, on the eighth night, I arrived at a small wooden cabin just on the edge of latitude 66.5, the point where the Arctic Circle begins its official spread to the north. The cabin was a small, ancient structure, a shabby thing, but to me it might as well have been a palace. It was gearing up to be the coldest night so far, with the temperature predicted to drop to around minus 13 degrees Fahrenheit. Arriving at this cabin meant that I wouldn't have to spend another night sleeping in my tent outside.

I unhooked myself from my sled harness, grabbed my dehydrated food pouch and sleeping kit from the pulk, and wrestled open the heavy wooden door. Inside, the cabin was completely dark: no lights, no candles. I looked around, the light of my head torch sweeping across the cramped room. There were a few old chairs, a couple of bunk beds to sleep on, a cupboard that looked like it would fall apart if I touched it, a table, and . . . a wood-burning stove. If I'd had the energy I would have screamed with joy. I dropped my belongings on the bunk bed and got to work building a fire. Some trail angels had left enough firewood in the cabin to last an entire week. Though I only had a few hours here before I needed to head off again, the wood was bone-dry and I knew that at least I had one warm night ahead of me. I wondered if it would be enough to get me through.

I worked quickly, finding reserves of energy I hadn't known I had, and got to chopping up a couple of logs into smaller pieces. I tore the dry bark off them, shredding it into thinner strips and rolling these into little curls. Inside the stove, I built a small tepee-shaped structure out of the small pieces of wood, then threw in the bark. My lighter had been inside my jacket pocket for the entirety of the race, pressed up against my chest, where it was warmest, in case I ever needed to make an emergency fire. I was not sure if a crisis of faith in my ability to continue could be classified as a trail emergency, but I lit up the bark, and within a few minutes, the world seemed like a much warmer, more welcoming place. The frozen darkness that I had been walking through, that had felt so all-consuming out there, melted away as I felt the cabin stove warm up. I held my icy hands out in front of the rising flames, and the image of warming my hands on an autumn night in front of the baby stove on my land overwhelmed reality. For a few seconds, it was all I could see.

The room, silent in the arctic night except for the exquisite crackling of the fire, slowly warmed up enough for me to take off my shoes, which were soaked from the long day of trudging through soft snow. Then I pulled off my sodden socks, hanging everything on a chair next to the stove in the hope that it would dry off before I had to set off again in a few hours. To have dry, warm socks to continue the trudge in was all I could have asked for in the world at that moment. I sat down and examined the state of my feet in front of the fire. After marinating inside a pair of wet shoes for sixteen hours, my feet were a mess. The colony of blisters I'd acquired just a couple of days prior had all burst spontaneously and become a damp mass of white calluses. I peeled skin from my feet like it was filo pastry. The big toenail on my right foot was bruised purple and hanging in what looked like a futile attempt to remain attached to my foot—the nail had already been ripped off on one side. *A pedicurist would not go within a hundred miles of this foot,* I thought as I inspected my toes for any signs of serious trouble.

Seven years earlier, with my perfect pedicure, I would have probably gagged at the sight of my toenail about to fall off. But somewhere along the way, somehow, my tolerance for pain and discomfort had expanded. So many years of full-time travel, with all the chaos, adventure, and unpredictability that this entailed, had taught me to look past the small inconveniences and focus on the bigger journey at hand, to witness the moment of potential defeat, and to walk through it, beyond it, and out the other side. Through the prism of years spent wandering, everything had become wondrous to me. A hot shower would never again be taken for granted. No meal would be expected, but all meals would be appreciated.

A little stove, crusted red with rust, somewhere deep in the Arctic, would be worth more to me than all the diamonds in the world.

The fire crackled, comforting and easing my every sense, and I threw in another couple of logs. I wolfed down my dehydrated meal of vegetarian chili and wriggled into my sleeping bag. I lay there, hoping for sleep to find me immediately, but my mind, though drained, was unable to calm down. It raced through the events of the day and then ahead to the next sixty miles on the trail, the distance I still needed to cross if I wanted to reach the finish line. Did I want to reach the finish line, though? I was exhausted, sleep-deprived, and in pain. Every cell in my body was begging me, in fitful screams, to quit the race and be done with the discomfort.

"I have come all this way," I said to myself steadily, hanging on to my last shreds of strength. "I can't give up now." That spark of defiance I'd felt before the lightning pain of my shin began smoldering again. "In five hours, I *will* get out of this sleeping bag, I *will* pack my things, and I *will* head out again. This may be one of the hardest things I've ever done, but I *will not* let it conquer me."

I will not let it conquer me.

"The miles no longer impress me. Whether there's one hundred, two hundred, or six hundred of them, they leave me indifferent, because I must cross that distance anyway," my grandfather had written. "I'm not afraid of distances anymore."

Neither was I.

The mental clarity I had so longed for—and had so lacked for the entire duration of the race until this moment in the cabin—finally burst through the night like an aurora, lighting up my mind. I let myself drift back to my happy place once more, with its rolling hills and its green grass. My sanctuary. My escape. My interpretation of that desert island paradise I had fantasized about all my life. And then it struck me: By leaving my land behind, by abandoning it and abandoning my dream, I was letting strangers define how I lived my life, the life I had worked so hard to create. A wave of anger rose again.

How had it come to this? I wondered, looking at the wooden roof of the cabin and remembering staring peacefully at the ceiling of my white bell tent, night after perfect night. *How am I letting these men I do not know choose my direction for me, when my heart's compass points to home?*

Freedom is never granted; it is always fought for and earned. I had become adept at forever seeking freedom in new places, new landscapes, new people. But if I wanted to keep my land and my home, I could see now that I would need to stay and fight, regardless of intruders, stalkers, and strangers. I would need to show the land, show myself, that this one beautiful thing was truly mine.

If I wanted wildness, I first needed to claim my space. If I wanted my freedom, I had to do as I'd told myself to do at the very beginning of this new life: I had to deprive myself of the luxury of fear. I had to stand up for my freedom. If I wanted this wild and free life, I needed to resist the naysayers, the intruders, and whoever else might stand in the way of this dream.

It had taken the hardest bodily endurance test I ever wanted to experience, but as I clawed my way through it, mile by mile, step by step, I clawed my way to the answer I had been seeking. I clawed my way back to the land. Now I knew, in my tired and heavy bones, what I would do next.

My mind felt as clear as the air as I approached the finish line of the race two days later, after ten days spent covering 320 miles. And there was my wolf, jumping out of a friend's car, just five miles from the finish line. I gasped and my heart lifted high above this frozen land, higher even than the white, cold sun at the sight of him. For once, I was not hallucinating dogs: Vilk really was right in front of me, standing in the snow several feet away, jumping with unbridled excitement at our reunion. I was no longer heaving myself through the snow. I bounced up and down with him. His happy face blurred as my eyes filled with tears, and I realized I was crying with joy for the first time in over three hundred miles. It had all been worth it, just for this. With Vilk back at my side, shadowing my every step, all the suffering and darkness of the preceding miles lifted as if by magic, leaving a pure image in its midst: Vilk and me running through the Carpathians on a warm summer day, on our way home. I was going home.

epilogue

We shall not cease from exploration
And the end of all our exploring
Will be to arrive where we started
And know the place for the first time.
T. S. Eliot, "Little Gidding"

Since I started traveling full-time, I've come to suspect that the idea of "finding yourself" is pure fiction. Sure, it is a convenient story, and something we would all like to believe in. After all, it feels reassuring to think that the anxiety, chaos, and doubt that one experiences aren't going to stick around forever, that somewhere out there, there is a singular version of you that you can aspire to, who knows what she wants, and knows her purpose in life, and is content and happy. Because the "found" version of you doesn't question life. *She* has already discovered all the answers.

But I've searched everywhere, on all the continents, in almost a hundred countries, on mountaintops, in forests, and across frozen swamps, in rushing rivers and arctic wildernesses, in the depths of the taiga and along roads that lead to the ends of the earth. Perhaps you could say that, through all my travels, I've failed, for I never did find myself. In this sense, I'm still that girl with a giant purple backpack who stood in front of Heathrow Airport, hoping that the open road would give her the answers she couldn't find in London. She was seeking something. Today, I still seek. On the surface, not much has changed.

But even though I've failed to find myself, I have come to understand a few things along the way. And those things—rather than a desire for clear-cut answers—guide me today.

In Pakistan, I learned firsthand that challenging your own beliefs can lead you down unexpected, life-changing paths. True bravery isn't about being a daredevil—it's about treading through life with the courage to ask questions, stumble, and pick yourself up again.

Mongolia gave me my love of solitude and a guiding principle I still live by: that the real meaning of life is to simply know the experience of being alive, connected to the world and connected to yourself. Or, as one of my favorite thinkers, Joseph Campbell, put it, to live "so that we actually feel the rapture of being alive."

In Socotra, my wild self began to awaken, and once she did, she could no longer be tamed. Once I reached the United States, I was ready to start living by my own rules, however feral and incomprehensible they might have appeared to outsiders (and to me, at first). And now, after reading this book, you have hopefully gleaned an understanding of why scrubbing your dirty dishes with a pinecone can be a very fulfilling thing to do.

And then there is home, that little plot of land in the Carpathians. My home continues to teach me that freedom can be found in places where you least expect it. On a tatami mat, under a ceiling of stars, in a tin tub filled with ice-cold mountain water, among the blades of grass in a meadow.

In a world this generous and rich, I think that to find myself would be to squander an opportunity to keep growing as a human being. Yes, I no longer aspire to find myself. At this juncture, I'm happy to keep seeking. That sounds a lot more fun.

As the sun sets over the Carpathians, I sit cross-legged on the edge of my deck. Behind me, the little solar fairy lights switch on, illuminating the white walls of my canvas tent. They turn a warm hue of yellow, cozy, like home. The daily concert of warm summer evenings begins, as the grasshoppers and crickets start talking to each other in a language I cannot understand. I scan the long grass in front of me and spot a couple of fireflies spinning in the air like the sparks of a fire.

I have no idea if this will be my home forever, but it feels like home now. This much I know.

Ten years ago, I would have never thought myself capable of living out here and spending days without power, running water, or a working toilet. It took a very long journey and a whole lot of soul-searching to find this wild little life, and to allow myself the joy of having it all to myself.

Vilk stretches out behind me and lets out a long, deep sigh, as if to remind me that we're in this together. He is right. I am not alone.

At the end of it all, the sum of my travels has shown me that there is not one single way to live out the short time we get on this earth. We are all travelers as we bushwhack our own paths through the dense foliage. Everyone has a way.

My way is a wilder way. Wilder than anything I ever thought possible.

And if you decide to set off on such a journey—whatever it means to you—let me caution you: it won't be easy. The hard thing about pursuing your own path is that there is no blueprint for it. Nobody can tell you what it looks like or how to get there.

Your path is yours only, and nobody else's. You will need to sketch out the map *and* the way, both. You will need to decide which way to turn and how fast or slow to go. You will need to figure out what to do when the map ends.

I reach out my hand and hold Vilk's big, warm paw. I take a deep breath. The meadow still smells crisp and sweet, like freedom. Far in the distance, the High Tatras slowly melt into the night. As I look up at the ceiling of stars above me, I remember my grandfather's words:

"I simply get into my vehicle and I drive so far and for so long, in absolute peace, until I finally reach the destination that I have set for myself. I also don't let the discomforts bother me, be it a hard seat, heat, dust, or the lack of water. All of this, in its own way, is beautiful and wonderful."

acknowledgments

This book was brewing inside me for many years, and yet with every passing month, I somehow managed to convince myself that I wasn't ready to write it. In all honesty, it would not have materialized without the help of many wonderful people. Thank you to:

Jade Angeles Fitton, for being the best editor I could have hoped for: you lifted me up, helped me become a better writer, and taught me to follow my heart as an author. This book wouldn't have happened without you. Thank you, Jade.

Zennor Compton, my editor at Century, Penguin Random House (UK), for reaching out to me with the proposal to write a book. Without your initiative and your belief in my story, I might not have written this book for another decade. Thank you for always reminding me to write from the heart.

Hannah Braaten, my editor at Gallery Books, Simon & Schuster (US), for your spot-on editorial guidance and for believing in this memoir from the start. You really made me feel that this would be a powerful book.

Jennifer Gates and Laura Nolan, my agents at Aevitas Creative, who believed in the true potential of this memoir, and who helped me navigate a new and unknown realm: the world of publishing.

Somaya, Jackie, Monet, and Rachel for your thoughtful notes and feedback, which gave me the confidence that this book might matter to some people after all.

Erica and Aslat Huuva, for renting me your beautiful home in the heart of Sápmi in the Arctic Circle, which became my writing sanctuary in the winter of 2025.

My mom, Sylwia (pronounced with a *v*), who never judged me and always supported me.

My dad, Rafał, for coming around and cheering me on.

My grandparents: Jola, for instilling a love of books and learning in me from a very young age; Irena, for making me feel like I always had a place to come back to; Krystian, for teaching me how to be a better person; and Leszek, for being my inspiration, my North Star, my guardian angel.

My uncle Andrzej and his wife, Ula, for always believing in me and for being on my side.

My dear friends Kasia and Leszek, for guiding me home.

Vilk, for being my best friend. (I realize you have no idea that I even wrote this book, but that's fine.)

Rea Kariž, my video editor: thank you for being such an integral part of the YouTube channel over the course of half a decade, and for lending your immense talents to the mission. Lola Martinez, my manager, for bringing me peace of mind even in the most turbulent of times, and for all the growth and opportunities that you have brought our way.

Dan Baird, for encouraging me to always aim higher.

My former partners, for all your love and lessons.

All the families and individuals who hosted me on my travels.

Everyone who helped me whenever Odyssey broke down and

needed fixing: Pepek, Zabol, Maciej, Moni, Ricardo, Rifat, Tobias, Brian, and many others.

Maxime, Ness, Pervaiz, Goher Nema, Sifat Shah and the whole Posh family, Bibi Nigor, Zayer, Buyna, Mendee, Sukhbataar, Hamid, Sadeq, Salem, Mohammed and the whole Kebany family, Rob, Matteo, Fede, Enni, Ginny, Callie, Alla and Garrett, Iza, Sheelagh, Mathilde and Nick, Nazima, and the countless other people I've met and befriended along the way: you turned my travels into a journey, and for that I will always be grateful.

I especially want to thank my community on YouTube, Instagram, and Facebook. Thank you for being open to receiving another human's life story. Thank you for every single time you turned a page of this book, watched a video, or wrote a message. None of this would have been possible without you.